Social Identities and Social Justice: Reconceiving Ethics and Politics in the Wake of Wokeism

William Franke

Social Identities and Social Justice: Reconceiving Ethics and Politics in the Wake of Wokeism

William Franke

Academica Press
Washington

Figure 1:Themis, goddess of justice, blindfolded. Freedesignfile.com

Library of Congress Cataloging-in-Publication Data

Names: Franke, William (author)

Title: Social identities and social justice : reconceiving ethics and politics in the wake of wokeism |

Franke, William.

Description: Washington : Academica Press, 2025. | Includes references.

Identifiers: LCCN 2025937172 | ISBN 9781680533811 (hardcover) | 9781680533538 (paperback) | 9781680533828 (e-book)

Contents

"These captive men are the hidden price for a hidden lie: the righteous must be able to locate the damned." James Baldwin[1]

"For we wrestle not against flesh and blood, but against principalities, against powers, against the rulers of the darkness of this world, against spiritual wickedness in high places." Saint Paul, Ephesians 6:12[2]

---

[1] James Baldwin, *If Beale Street Could Talk* (New York: Dial, 1972), 192.
[2] Bible citations are from The Authorized King James Version modified in light of the Greek New Testament.

List of Illustrations

1.
Prologue and Acknowledgments

I was spurred to take on this project by a couple of invitations to give addresses on the topic of wokeism. The book began as a paper written in preparation for a keynote address titled: "Unsaying Wokeism, or the Role of Self-Critique in Judging Others" at an international conference on "Tracking Global Wokeism" at the Global Studies Center, Gulf University of Science and Technology (GUST), Mubarak Al-Abdullah, Kuwait, February 8, 2023.[3] For including me in this project giving me the incentive to engage in issues new to my research agenda, I thank the Center's director Professor Thorsten Botz-Bornstein and his supporting staff at GUST, along with the other participants.

I subsequently adapted my argument for presentation as a plenary address in a symposium on René Girard and the Bible: "Girard, Lecteur de l'Écriture" in Paris, France, at the Collège des Bernardins, December 15, 2023. It was delivered in French as: "Kénose et wokisme: une alternative à l'instrumentalisation de la justice sociale" ["Kenosis and Wokeism: An Alternative to the Weaponizing of Social Justice"].[4] I thank Professor Félix Resch of the Faculté Notre-Dame, Collège des Bernardins, for this opportunity.

A further occasion was offered me by Giorgio Sandrini, Professor Emeritus of Neurological Science of the University of Pavia. With his research group "Neurofilosofia," Sandrini continues to break new ground through programs and publications hybridizing neurology and philosophy.

---

[3] Apophatic Ethics as an Alternative to Identity Politics or How to Avoid Wokeism - Global Studies Center. Fragments of chapters 4, 7, 8, 12, 13, 23, 48 appear in preliminary versions as "Unsaying Wokeism, or the Role of Self-Critique in Judging Others," in *Tracking Global Wokeism*, ed. Thorsten Botz-Bornstein (Amsterdam: Brill, 2025), pp. 107-26.

[4] William Franke, Conférence sur le Wokisme à Paris - YouTube.

At his invitation, I lectured in Italian on "Politiche identitarie e giustizia sociale: Come rifondare l'etica e la politica dopo la rivoluzione woke?" ["Identity Politics and Social Justice: Some Equivocations. How to Refound Ethics and Politics after the Woke Revolution"] at the Collegio Cairoli, Pavia, on May 2, 2024.[5] I am grateful also to Professor Sandrini's collaborators, professors Walter Minella and Andrea Loffi, for making this event exceptionally rewarding.

Quite a voluminous literature on wokeism has accumulated over the time during which I have been engaged on this topic, not to mention the broader subject of social justice, and my views have evolved along with it, gleaning insights from authors on both sides of the controversy. Most significantly, however, I have found that the challenges posed by wokeism have forced me to rethink the very foundations of ethics in the imperative to recognize others and count their interests at least equally with one's own. Wokeism aims at this ideal and derives its force of persuasion from the irrecusable validity of such a principle. At the same time, the woke phenomenon makes manifest how, paradoxically, such a commitment to recognition of alterity is susceptible of inversion, of devolving into blind self-assertion of force driven by mob psychology and its suppression of others whose views differ from one's own.

We are left perplexed at how a movement so clearly right in principle can have led to such ugly forms of disrespect of others—to shouting down speakers with whom one disagrees ideologically on college campuses and other forms of intolerance, censorship, and incivility. Wokeism confronts us with many scarcely ponderable dilemmas and ironies that arise when we undertake to realize the demands of social justice in specific applications in our pluralistic and perhaps irreparably fractured world today.

My ongoing engagements with this topic included, most recently, a series of seminars invited by Professor Montserrat Herrero at the Institute for Culture and Society (Instituto Cultura y Sociedad) of the University of Navarra in Spain.[6] These seminars on social justice and wokeism began on January 21, 2025, the day after the inauguration of Donald Trump as

---

[5] Franke, Come rifondare l'etica e la politica dopo la rivoluzione woke? (youtube.com)
[6] Seminarios Filosofia Navarra 2024-2025 – William Franke

47th US president and his inaugural speech signaling a 180-degree turnabout in American politics. I had been treating wokeism as an inexorably advancing revolution, but all of a sudden, as I began these lectures, and as this manuscript was about to go to press, we entered into a counter-revolutionary phase. We were now going to see things from a dizzyingly different perspective. In crucial respects, wokeism will be on the defensive rather than the all-conquering force it had become in the years leading up to this precipitous turning point. This type of reversal is typical of revolutions and counterrevolutions.

The woke ideology had reigned supreme, since, say, 2009, when Barack Obama became president, but most intensively during the Biden-Harris administration (2020-2024), over the last two years of which my reflections have been elaborated. Their sense and purport vary as the context into which they are read shifts. However, the analyses remain intact whichever side has the upper hand. They position themselves on neither side of the embittered debates around wokeist politics. They address, instead, the polarization of politics into mutually deaf factions. This tragic incomprehension is likely to worsen, not to end or attenuate, due to the diametrical about-turn of politics from Biden to Trump. My message becomes thereby only the more pertinent and urgent.

What is unique about my approach is viewing the question from an "apophatic" perspective (*apo*—away from; *phasis*—speech) that strives to look from beyond the perimeters of discourse with its ineluctable divisions and fractiousness. I derive these ultra-discursive optics from traditions that have developed since antiquity under the sign of "Negative Theology." I have previously reconstructed the history of such thinking in the margins of the mainstream Logos tradition of philosophy. My counter-history of thought, focusing on "what cannot be said," moves from Greek Neoplatonism and biblical anti-idolatry prophetism, traverses medieval mysticism, baroque paradox, Romantic overreaching, modernist modes of aesthetic silence, and other expressions of ineffability, down to postmodern deconstructive discourses on irreducible difference.[7] On this

---

[7] *On What Cannot Be Said: Apophatic Discourses in Philosophy, Religion, Literature, and the Arts*, 2 vols., edited with Theoretical and Critical Essays by William Franke

basis, I have developed an "apophatic" philosophy for our times.[8] I have extended this work into an intercultural philosophy.[9] And I have applied this philosophy to burning questions of the present such as postmodern identity politics, culture wars over the curriculum and the canon of literary classics, media studies, cognitive sciences in their challenge to the humanities, and the place of religious knowledge in contemporary epistemology and critical theory.[10]

Apophatic thinking, as I practice it, starts always from what resists being rendered in discursive form and therefore obliges us to a self-reflective suspension of our own fixed assumptions and closed systems of interpretation in a moment of openness to others and even to the irreducibly Other. The real in itself remains mysteriously other to whatever presumable knowledge our formulations in human language and concepts are capable of furnishing. This real, which remains ungraspable beyond all our construals and codings of it, can be revealed only partially and provisionally and only through respectful consideration of the multiplicity of interpretations, which are often contradictory. Such an exercise in reflection alone enables us to decide which views are responsible—which means responsive to all concerned and also right for us in our given circumstances. In my current work, I continue to draw from this same source spring of philosophical and spiritual insight to address urgent issues that we are forced to face, including environmental apocalypse, pandemics, and war.[11] Information on the engagements mentioned above can be found at: https://my.vanderbilt.edu/williamfranke/. In the present work, I extend my reflection to social justice and identity as one of the crucial issues

(Notre Dame, Indiana: University of Notre Dame Press, 2007). Vol. I: Classic Formulations; Vol. II: Modern and Contemporary Transformations.

[8] *A Philosophy of the Unsayable* (Notre Dame: University of Notre Dame Press, 2014).
[9] *Apophatic Paths from Europe to China: Regions Without Borders* (Albany: State University of New York Press, 2018).
[10] *On the Universality of What Is Not: The Apophatic Turn in Critical Thinking* (Notre Dame: University of Notre Dame Press, 2020).
[11] See my *Pandemics and Apocalypse in World Literature: The Hope for Planetary Salvation* (New York: Routledge, 2025). On war, see my "Not War, nor Peace. Are War and Peace Mutually Exclusive Alternatives?" *War: Thinking the Unthinkable,* Special Issue of *Continental Thought and Theory: A Journal of Intellectual Freedom* 4/1 (2023): 25-35, eds. Cindy Zeiher and Mike Grimshaw.

bearing most tellingly on the coherence of modern society and the future possibilities for human community and collective survival in today's world.

Today we are confronted with an amorphous phenomenon christened "wokeism" that reveals deep schisms in our collective life in modern democratic societies and has called forth analysis as a type of scapegoating. While it is tempting to treat a certain identity group as the great offender, the guilty transgressor, the sole party responsible for everything culpable and heinous in history, theories of scapegoating such as René Girard's invite us to de-essentialize these accusations and see that the same mechanism can and will function for other, eventually all other, identity groups. At the moment, identifying the white heterosexual male as the culprit enables other identity groups to be represented as innocent. An operative scenario (admittedly a ridiculous caricature) in some woke culture reads: just dethrone the Western white heteronormative male, and then all God's children—female, black and brown, yellow and red, gay, queer, and trans—will be restored to peace and amity in the Garden of Eden. Girard's work wakes us up to the fact that it is not the essential evil of any one identity group—male, white, Western, or heteronormative— but the social role of the scapegoat that is essential. The scapegoat's supposed guilt is instrumental to the mutual reconciliation of the other groups and of individuals rivaling one another for power in competitive societies and in accordance with the dictates of mimetic desire.

The current empowerment of women and minorities is certainly long overdue. It is just and in the interest of all. However, an equitable and sustainable basis for it can be found not in current identitarian ideologies but rather in an apophatic ethics. One concrete form of such ethics is the biblical paradigm of *kenosis* or "self-emptying." This model entails the Christic gesture which, for Girard, was the definitive act of self-sacrifice that put an end to the need for repetition of the scapegoating mechanism, which always necessarily misunderstands itself. Any model based on rivalry for advantages between competing identity groups always needs to find other scapegoats: next will be black men or straight women who have not expressly genuflected to the going social justice agenda. Each identity group is destined to serve as scapegoat in their turn. Such, at least, is the analysis of wokeism elaborated in detail by Joshua Mitchell in *American Awakening* (2020). This analysis can take on more depth and penetration in the light of Girard's theories. The tragic seriousness of the scapegoat's role of being put to death as sacrificial victim can be brought forth in all its pathos by our contemporary social struggles and the recriminations engendered by and around wokeism. The victim is sacrificed supposedly for its sins but in reality because of the cumulative "guilt," the reciprocal violent aggression, generated among all groups in a competitive world generally.

Wokeism is absolutely compelling to the extent that it insists on the imperative of freedom and justice for all without exclusions. However, it typically takes this truth over in ways that make it serve as a means of consolidating power for those who hold the levers of control within the movement and who make themselves its priests or executors. One establishes and secures one's own power by oppressing rivals who could contest it. And this is what happens when wokeism becomes established and indeed dominant: it can tend to dictate to all what is to be considered right and wrong and what is acceptable to say and even to think. Paradoxically, today, in numerous spheres and sectors, woke cultural politics, conceived in the name and interest of the dominated, are exercising the type of domination and censorship that they were supposed to contest and that all too constantly characterize repressive regimes.[12]

This book, in extending my apophatic philosophy, shows how the unflinchingly critical spirit of the West, despite its ostensible historical dominations (white, male, heteronormative), has directly led to the revindications of presumably oppressed minorities. As taken up by woke ideologues, these recriminations alleging discrimination are turned into a litany of victimization deploring the subjection and exploitation of all groups socially identified as different from the group constituted by the supposedly dominant markers. Making the white cisgendered Occidental male guilty of all evil serves to render innocent all other groups that can be demarcated as diverse from this purported oppressor. However, while

---

[12] Bari Weiss, We Got Here Because of Cowardice. We Get Out With Courage – Commentary Magazine presents telling examples of such repressive measures currently operating in society. Accessed 5-21-2024.

this crude emotional logic (like its inversion) is pervasively operative throughout our society, it aggravates rather than relieves conflict. It feeds resentment and impedes the emergence of a consensual basis for civic community.

A more promising path to true power for just and fruitful shared living can only be that of self-emptying (*kenosis*) rather than the diminishing of others—self-critique rather than vilifying others. This Christic (but also Buddhist, or Indigenous, or you name it . . .) motif of kenosis conceives empowerment as consisting of freeing oneself from selfish drives and motives. Through the apophatic examination and kenotic approach proposed here, we are challenged to reframe the issue not as one of determining who has more power and privilege, to the end of accusing dominant groups of immorality or of crime or injustice and demanding on moral grounds that their power and wealth be taken away and given to others who have less and presumably deserve a larger share. Instead, the crucial issue is how each individual and social group can be enabled and motivated to give their all to the common good and contribute to the joint project of building an inclusive society. Not beating others in a competition for more privilege but developing one's own ability to contribute to the good of all to a maximum degree is the goal that has always fostered the highest human worth and that can still promote the greatest human flourishing. Taking this approach does not mean ignoring the imperative of radical redistribution of resources but rather enabling it to come about as a natural and necessary result of free activity rather than trying to coerce it by moralistic demands sure to engender diehard resistance.

This approach alone, of course, is not sufficient, but it is necessary working in tandem with other, more conflictual approaches based on contestation and confrontation. Such a combination of approaches is necessary if any are to succeed at all because only so will the demands for equity be seen as *just* and not just as assertions of resentment or exertions of superior force. Hardly anyone self-identifies anymore as "woke," yet its constitutive tendencies, in various guises and degrees, are still all-pervasive and need constantly to be confronted.

My aim here is neither to attack nor to defend wokeism but to separate out what is most valuable, indeed indispensable, from what is potentially lethal, in the so-called "social justice" movements. I attempt to model how we can put an end to the cycles of retaliation that characterize our histories by self-critical recognition of the limitedness of our own judgment and by assuming responsibility for our part in the wrongs of the world. May this effort serve as an open invitation for correction by others. Most welcome is correction by other critically thinking and creatively open-minded persons such as are so necessary to our survival and salvation—beyond all monolithic constructions of identity.

As to its structure, the book unfolds as a continuous series of ethical-political reflections. They relate to and recall one another backwards and forwards in myriad, unchartable ways. The sections are organized into Parts around selected overarching and titled themes on which each sequence of sections converges. The model is not analytic so much as symphonic in producing an ensemble of resonating and harmonized considerations that together compose a distinctive ethical and political vision. This vision consists in a constellation of reflections that are glimpsed in the process of being eclipsed, blended out by the rising light of day into which each distinct point disappears. Articulated discourses and their divisive formulas are transcended by the luminous unknowing of hearts infinitely open to one another, from which alone ultimately salutary ethical and political relations can emerge.

Part I.

From Revolution to Religion

2.

The Woke Revolution—Its Founding of Social Power on Victimhood

We are witnessing today a cultural and social revolution whose shorthand name is "woke." This term, which resonates with "awake," was originally coined by black Americans who became acutely aware of racial discrimination. They used it to signal their politically and socially *awakened* consciousness. A deeper historical genealogy of the woke movement might be traced from the 18th century European Enlightenment, which culminates in Revolution, signally in 1789-99 in France. Today we are repeating this historical cycle moving from Enlightenment to Revolution. But, specifically in our own era, we are witnessing the revolution of the *victims*.[13] Proponents of the woke cause demand rights for the oppressed. Political and social power are exercised or claimed in the name of our civilization's victims and casualties.

This revolution has been remarkably, almost miraculously, successful. For society today, nothing counts as more sacred than the victim. Defending or taking up the cause of victims justifies everything, every use or abuse of power. The same logic is used even by the Russian and Chinese leaders, and the North Korean and Iranian regimes, in their bids for power. Their political and cultural agendas aim to liberate the world considered as the victim of the West, both historically and currently. However, the ideology of victimhood, validated by the woke movement, originates first from inside Western society, as a revolution or movement of contestation within its bosom, before threatening and attacking it from the outside.

---

[13] Bruce Bawer, *The Victims' Revolution: The Rise of Identity Studies and the Closing of the Liberal Mind* (New York: HarperCollins, 2012).

Why does this mentality recruit such fervent supporters and have such a seductive effect on so many? Many join, or at least sympathize, with this moral revolution so as to feel good about themselves, to ward off the onus of guilt in a world that seems to be unbearably unjust. Especially privileged young people find relief in declaring their alignment with what are recognizably woke causes. Identifying as anti-racist, feminist, pro-LGBTQIA, etc., is the way to portray oneself as moral and socially acceptable in many mainstream milieus today. Such public self-profiling is now appropriately called "virtue signaling." Adhering to some form of wokeism can be understood as an attempt to exonerate oneself of blame in a world that is felt to be shamefully unfair and immoral. Professing politically correct allegiances serves as balsam for wounds of a sorely hurting conscience. At least, this explains a certain surface of this widespread sociological phenomenon.

More subliminally, identifying a guilty and responsible party not only alleviates moral anguish, effecting a kind of emotional catharsis; it also seems to promise a solution for fixing what is wrong with society. The culprit, according to wokeist discourses, is identified in the Western white male as subjugator, dominator, and exploiter. From the Crusades in the Middle Ages and Imperialism and Colonization in the modern period to contemporary Capitalism, this identity—concretely, the heterosexual white man, who is ruthless, greedy, destructive, and predatory—is to blame for almost all the world's woes. And so we have the scapegoat needed as foundation for the grand narrative that re-envisions all of world history from a revolutionary, woke perspective. Such scapegoating is potentially a more sinister aspect of the woke revolution.

Wokeness is founded on an ethical-political sensibility that I believe is certainly correct and morally right. It appeals to noble principles of equity and equal dignity of all. But how is this ethical appeal being played out today and institutionalized? It results in condemnations or pardons according to *social identities*. The path to power in a culture steeped in wokeness lies in declaring oneself to be a victim of the dominant group or, better yet, in simply *identifying* with apparently oppressed minorities in publicly declared, outspoken solidarity.

Various sorts of abstract self-identification are producing effects of intolerance, belligerence, and incivility. In the name of such identities, nominally liberal societies prove perfectly capable of producing phenomena of coercion or intimidation against their own ideals of free speech and expression. These values are in crisis among us. Strident debates on pertinent issues confront us with deep dilemmas. Student protests and their repression issue in unacceptable violence and appalling disrespect. How can we not condemn hateful, inflammatory, anti-Semitic, or otherwise racist speech? Can an open society tolerate intolerance? But how can we dictate to citizens what they must say and think to be politically correct?

To attempt to approach the nerve of this issue, I begin by telling a story. There is a basis for it in fact, but I have lost track of the account I heard or read. Therefore, I propose it simply as an invention. I work a lot with fictions, *poiesis*—the prophetic poetry of Dante and the Bible or the classics, Homer and Virgil, as well as the revelatory work of moderns: Shakespeare, Milton, Goethe, Joyce, Woolf, Morrison. For Aristotle, the truth of poetry is universal and higher than that of history. History only says what happened while poetry says what *must* or *should* happen. The possible is higher than the actual or factual—it has a higher degree of necessity.

So here is the story. The New York police commissioner was scheduled to give a public lecture on a college campus. It was to take place shortly after the tragic death of George Floyd that had fueled the "Black Lives Matter" (BLM) movement and sparked off conflagrations on a national scale. Demonstrations and riots were raging across the country; many protestors were demanding that the police be defunded. Some cities had cut police funds: there were calls for this type of action almost everywhere. The Commissioner wanted to explain why that was not a good idea. He wanted to show how in the previous year in New York City, the police had reduced the violent deaths of young black males by 75% through intense action, a harsh "crackdown" on gang violence. He meant to suggest that if you truly believe that black lives matter, then the best policy is not defunding the police, as was being called for in the wave of protests that portrayed the police as the enemy of people of color and demanded that the police should be eliminated, or at least greatly limited, in the interest of protecting these victims.

The Commissioner was unable to deliver his speech. He was booed and shouted down from the podium with interruptions and harassment and was removed from the campus. Unfortunately, this type of scenario is not a pure fiction: it has occurred repeatedly, particularly in our universities, especially in the United States, but also in France and elsewhere. These incidents belong to what we can recognize as the George Floyd effect. Floyd's horrendous murder became a motive and an alibi for lawlessness and violence. It became a symbol of black victimization by the police— which exists and is reprehensible. But this event triggered a reaction that, in turn, incited to violence, delirium, and a dangerous spiral of racial tensions.

The Floyd incident was elevated by woke political agendas to an unprecedented level of prominence as an emblem of all-pervasive racism. Floyd's killing was taken as the epitome of the racism of an entire society. Yet, the policeman, Derek Chauvin, who killed Floyd, had no history of racism. In the trial, there was no evidence that he was racist or despised people of color. Nothing on this issue was raised by the prosecution, and it could hardly have remained unnoticed and unexamined if it had existed. Chauvin's act was not a racist crime, but it was taken as a symbol of precisely that by those who wanted to signal their condemnation of racism—and also perhaps incentivize angry mobs intent on looting and vandalism. Portland and Seattle, among other cities, still bear the scars.

This is an illustration of how the media and political networks that are largely beholden to certain ideologies and entrenched camps seize upon certain facts that trigger powerful emotions to create a movement that all too easily loses its sense of reality and suppresses respect for truth. Emotional reaction can be motivated by the passion for an ideal that is very good in itself but is metamorphosed into a myth and exploited to incite further violence and to nourish resentment and anger. In highly tense and fraught situations, especially today, propaganda on all sides proliferates at alarming rates unchecked, given the unprecedented technological means of its dissemination in contemporary culture.

There are, of course, innumerable instances of such strategic abuse and distortion also on the other end of the political spectrum. Violently destructive mob behavior is at least as likely to erupt in the anti-woke camp. Ignited by the stabbing to death of three young girls at a Taylor Swift-themed public dance event in Southport, England in July 2024, widespread civic unrest and devastating riots rampaged through the UK. The flames were fanned by misinformation spread on the internet concerning the immigrant origins of the nineteen-year-old killer by militant groups opposing immigration and inclined to violence, both verbal and physical, against immigrants. In the overwrought nervousness of our current cultural climate, any incident can be weaponized for ideological warfare. Truth is the first victim.

The name George Floyd commemorates a horrific, inexcusable incident, but to take it as representative of all American society and of the history of the West as a whole—as the true revelation of the quintessence of this civilization, as was often the case in the heat and fury of the protest and revolt—is a grotesque mythification. Like almost any other revolutionary or political movement, the woke revolution is susceptible of perpetrating such distortions. Meanwhile, it is forgotten that Western civilization has done more than perhaps any other to combat and curb racism—which exists in virtually all civilizations, historically and currently. Slavery was abolished first by the British Empire (1807, 1834) and then in the USA at the cost of a harrowing Civil War (1861-65).[14]

The Floyd event became an organizing symbol, like the storming of the Bastille that sparked the French Revolution. It also raised a rallying cry for much peaceful protest and popular revolt. People of all races and ages came together in harmoniously affirming their common commitment to an anti-racist ideal. This was an uplifting, edifying sight to behold. Nonetheless, the Floyd incident was also used to justify and motivate the cultural revolution that is fostered and fomented by a new woke clergy— a certain "clerical" class of professors and administrators and politicians and "influencers" of all kinds in the media and on social networks. There

---

[14] Oxford University historian Nigel Biggar credits the British Empire for worldwide abolition of slavery in *Colonialism: A Moral Reckoning* (London: HarperCollins, 2023).

can be no precise definition of who or what is "woke," yet this apparently new and revolutionary sensibility translates into political action, legislation, and cultural reform. The demands for decolonization, antiracism, anti-sexism, gay and trans rights, etc., have in fact swept through institutions and policymaking at all levels and become tacit, difficult-to-resist litmus tests by which we judge and are judged.

A lot of the push-back against wokeism is frankly counter-revolutionary and reactionary. "Woke" is now used most often as a term of abuse. The Floyd incident turns up regularly as evidence on exhibit in anti-woke narratives denouncing revolutionary excess and atrocity.[15] The conflict has become unproductive and even crippling for our society. My concern is with how we can get out of this impasse.

My point in mentioning the late, regretted Mr. Floyd is not to defend police racism, which is a terribly serious problem. It is soul-shattering especially in its extension to the prison system.[16] But making people believe that police everywhere attack blacks gratuitously because they are black, and with impunity, is a false fabrication instrumentalized by interested, power-mongering parties to discredit and destroy an entire civilization.[17] Derek Chauvin was condemned to life imprisonment. His act was not condoned or excused or adjudged legitimate or normative or held up as an example to be emulated by other police officers.

Just a few years earlier, in 2016 in Texas, there was another incident that was strikingly similar. A man 32 years old was throttled by the aggressive action of the police. Like Floyd, the man was in fragile health and was dependent on drugs. Pressed to the ground during his arrest, the man was heard saying "You are killing me, I need medication"—much like Floyd's famous "I can't breathe." He was "neutralized" for about 14 minutes by a police officer holding him down with pressure on his back.

---

[15] See, for example, Sarah Downey's thesis that politically correct witch-hunting is killing freedom of expression: This politically-correct witch-hunt is killing free speech (substack.com).

[16] 13TH | FULL FEATURE | Netflix (youtube.com). Accessed 5-26-2024.

[17] Journalist Douglas Murray, in *The War on the West: How to Prevail in the Age of Unreason* (London: HarperCollins, 2022), argues this case, pushing back against the typical woke narratives, also in numerous podcasts and internet interviews. See, for instance, Douglas Murray on the George Floyd protests, rioting & COVID hypocrisy - BQ #18 - YouTube.

When removed from the spot, he was dead. His name is not known to a wide public, nor is this incident generally remembered. He was called Tony Timpa. He was white. Of the five policemen involved in the arrest, three returned to active duty and two are now honorably retired.

George Floyd is not an isolated case. There is much discrimination in police action and everywhere in society. But it is not only or always deliberately against blacks, women, gays, etc. Violence is endemic to human societies. To treat violence in terms of social identities compounds rather than resolves it because social identities as such are neither victims nor perpetrators. They are abstractions, and although these characteristics count and are real in numberless specific contexts, to base particular judgments on them is to cede to prejudice. It involves invidious generalizing and an abstract mode of reasoning that is bound to commit injustice against individuals and also against groups. We erect stereotyped images that serve to funnel the passions of mobs into various types of action, including war, setting specific groups over against others.

Inimical groups can be identified in terms of race or ethnicity or sexual orientation, but also in terms of nationality. The latter type of label is typically used by war propaganda for the purpose of fomenting hatred between peoples or nations or states. This results in demonizing Germans or Japanese or Russians or Chinese or Americans or Spaniards (*Leyenda Negra*). To form a harmonious human community, we need, instead, not to fixate on such identities, much less on categories such as Jews or homosexuals or women, and especially not on such labels as markers of power differentials, because they divide us by an oppositional logic rather than uniting various groups in ways that enable them to celebrate true human diversity.

3.

Nietzschean Insight into the Will to Power in Christianity—and its Woke Extension

Why did the Black Lives Matter movement interpret the George Floyd incident in this archetypal way—and with the support of a large part of society, including a wide consensus among white people, perhaps especially the young, but not only? The movement included many people of all ages and diverse political persuasions. Presumably, one reason is an acute and widespread ethical sense that traverses all identity groups. Positive jubilation in agreeing on some basic moral principles with people across socio-economic and ethnic divides was exhilarating and certainly an important motive. But there was more to it. Why the need to denounce racism in such public and demonstrative ways, with all the parades and protests in the streets? And why the frenzy to tear down the statues of white men who were heroes of history (Washington, Jefferson, Churchill, Victor Hugo, etc.)? Why the proliferating paroxysms of "cancel culture"? They occur not just to defend the vulnerable and reject something ethically reprehensible and odious. As symbolic gestures, such demonstrations are as likely to provoke as to prevent violence.

Of course, real moral compunction is being made manifest in this movement, and this is a crucial basis for building necessary social consensus and cohesion. But there is also a manifest desire to overthrow the power of the dominant—and then also to dominate. This perennial dynamic and dialectic of power is revealed symptomatically by the phenomenon of wokeism in our society. In theory, wokeism serves to free everyone from an overbearing dominator—the hetero-normative white male. But, like other theoretically liberationist movements, it becomes, according to the analysis of sociologists (see Part II), something else, something approaching a totalitarianism, a seizing of power that represses any possibility of opposition, or even just of critical questioning.

Wokeism begins with virtue signaling and with gestures of self-exculpation. But it discloses and becomes more. Wokeism in its infiltration and takeover of institutions throughout society manifests a will to power (*Wille zur Macht*), to invoke Nietzsche's terms. I believe that Nietzsche's interpretation of Judeo-Christian morality as a devious strategy on the part of priests to exercise power by siding with the weak masses sheds light on the phenomenon we now call "woke." The weak and vulnerable, or those who define themselves as victims—and especially those who only align themselves with victims, posing as their defenders—too often demand rights as a means of overthrowing those who are otherwise stronger or richer or more influential. Those who seem to be on top are likely to be resented by those who see themselves as in an inferior position. Yet determined parties building on this resentment can deviously scheme to seize power and establish their own dominion.

For Nietzsche, the absolute respect for the Other inscribed within Judeo-Christian ethics is anathema: it is false, decadent, and nihilistic. It represents the denaturation of the instinct of the healthy animal that fights for survival according to the law of the jungle. Such is the imperative of life. Nietzsche analyzes the genealogy of morality in its descent from Judeo-Christianity as a denial of life, as suppression of the vital drive for self-preservation and struggle for mastery. The "slave morality" of Christianity preaches self-denial and self-humbling and guilt: it turns the species against its own vital instincts. This is nihilism, according to Nietzsche's analysis in *On the Genealogy of Morality*. It infects an entire society and culture. Even "healthy" individuals are seduced by this ideology.

I think that Nietzsche prophetically foresaw and denounced something of what wokeism embodies. However, unlike Nietzsche, I do not want to give up the ethics of unconditional respect for others and defending the weak. I believe in the sacredness of the victim as revealed in the Bible, especially the Gospels, as well as in much profane anthropology, as René Girard demonstrates. Yet woke morality, like the Christian morality from which it derives, becomes another means of seizing power to dominate others, another manifestation of the will to power. We see this usurpation of power by exploiting the "social justice" agenda achieved, often in surreptitious ways, by the woke revolution. In the name of social justice, wokeism, in certain of its more uncompromising forms, produces power brokers dictating who is entitled to what. Woke ideologues are rearranging things to their own advantage—and woe betide anyone who dissents or disagrees. "Social justice," like the morality of good and evil (*Gut und Böse*) for Nietzsche, becomes a mask for the attempt to dominate through more subtle means, moral means, branding the strong as evil (*Böse*) and valorizing the losers, or the "socially disadvantaged," as if they were losers or disadvantaged because they are more moral, less aggressive, therefore "good," in Nietzsche's apt and penetrating analysis.

I do not accept Nietzsche's idea that in order to promote the development of the species we must not protect and preserve the weak. The Nazis embraced precisely this idea at the core of their program of eugenics. On the contrary, I see the ideal of the Judeo-Christian religion, in which all are equal in dignity before God, as among the highest attainments by which humanity surpasses itself in an exemplary fashion. This is the exact opposite of the ideal of the Nietzschean *superman* (*Übermensch*). Yet the idea that taking the side of the masses considered as victims can be used as a means to take possession of power is true of woke influencers in our time, even as it is true of the figure of the Christian priest in Nietzsche's analysis. Such a maneuver, characteristic of the caste of ascetic and moralizing priests, is practiced against the "warrior" class— those who excel in effective power through real performance rather than by a moralizing discourse that condemns effectual strength and power. Nietzsche's clairvoyant analysis reveals all too well an aspect of the current situation in our woke-saturated democratic society. Woke elites, with their moralizing narrative, can function like Nietzsche's ascetic priests. They teach in effect, if not in express intent, that subaltern groups or classes are good and that true virtue lies not in skills and performance but in belonging to morally innocent groups—different from the white man, condemned for his racial suprematism and his imposition of oppressive patriarchy.

Our society has become self-critical of domination by force in a way never before seen in history, and this is a great achievement. But this acute sensitivity in our times is being used as a weapon against the Western civilization that first produced it. Criticism of the dominant power is too often used by wokes as a means of attack on certain general categories of human beings deemed to be dominant, or even on Western civilization as such, condemned on account of its history of colonialism, slavery, economic exploitation, social subjugation, and the rest. We are constantly confronted with the insinuation that there has never been a civilization as oppressive as the West, as proved by the unparalleled global dominance it achieved in the modern era. Such "criticism" has turned into an accusation and an attack and is used to *vie* for power, *not* to counter and to renounce it.

Wokeism has evolved in our society into a formidable engine for garnering and redeploying power. It gives traction to strategies of self-promotion whereby one gains advancement not strictly for one's own merits and achievements but for one's belonging to designated groups. It rewards hypocrisy in aligning oneself with these underdogs and thereby styling oneself as politically virtuous. To be seen as a good person, commendable and frequentable, today, in many social contexts, you are expected to embrace a whole host of minority causes—anti-racism, feminism, gay rights, trans rights, etc. This new ethos is made official in institutional forms, as well as operating diffusely in countless more amorphous ways.

Nearly all university positions in the USA today require adherence to a "diversity statement." To be hired, you must underwrite a policy that gives preferential treatment to women and minorities. You must often explain how you personally will commit to implementing such policies. Employees and even student bodies are obliged to undergo training in DEI (Diversity, Equality, Inclusion). Ethically, it is right to grant priority to the disadvantaged, but the culture of wokeism uses this ethical principle as an instrument of control to demand confessions of faith and professions of loyalty. Dissenters are silenced or banished. Not effective skills and ability but adherence to the reigning authorities and the ideology they decree becomes decisive for promotion.

Explicit adherence to the principles of diversity, equity, and inclusion is often mandatory not only for employees of American universities but also for personnel of government agencies and even of private businesses. "Political correctness" has entered the laws and has been applied in explicit and binding regulations, as well as in subtler, softer, persuasive but pervasive forms of power. The underlying principles are ethically valid, theoretically based on respect for others and for everyone, but their woke applications are susceptible of being turned into grotesque parodies of power politics. A formally imposed virtue ethics is bound to generate hypocrisy. We are required to ape certain formal rites or to fulfill prescribed exercises and protocols, bowing down to a reigning orthodoxy. Wokeism can slip from its role as defense of the victims to a certain imposition of power that becomes all-encompassing and is often felt to be oppressive. Critics and sociologists warn that we are sliding towards a totalitarianism, where it will no longer be possible to express an honest opinion that does not consist of parroting the party line.

Already a certain conformity to institutional views and statements is being required so as not to be fired from one's job or excluded from "good" society. A famous example is Jordan Peterson, the Canadian psychology professor who refused to let the Canadian law dictate the pronouns that he was obliged to use with his students. He lost his professorship and his license to practice psychiatry. However, he became one of the most famous public intellectuals of our time by airing his grievances.

Another prominent public intellectual, Susanne Schröter, formerly director of the Institute for Ethnology at the University of Frankfurt, was similarly slandered and persecuted for thinking independently of the reigning woke ideology. She delivers a detailed account of how her scholarly integrity and scientific accuracy were attacked but finally vindicated. Extrapolating far beyond her own case, she analyzes how wokeist politics has threatened the objectivity and freedom of research at the university.[18] A highly vernacular and sometimes shrill testimony from the world of journalism is delivered with panache by Julie Burchill.[19]

---

[18] Susanne Schröter, *Der neue Kulturkampf: Wie eine woke Linke Wissenschaft, Kultur und Gesellschaft bedroht* (Freiburg: Herder, 2024), especially Chapter 2.
[19] Julie Burchill, *Welcome to the Woke Trials: How #Identity Killed Progressive Politics* (Washington: Academica Press, 2021).

Schröter's research documents how "antiracism" has been built up through the universities into a "profitable business" ("einträglichen Geschäftsmodell," 106). This is part of a wide-ranging take-over for their kind of politics by those she designates as the "woke Left."

> In recent years, the woke Left has succeeded in establishing a hegemonic discourse in large sectors of the sciences, the media, and cultural and educational domains. A giant market of opportunities has arisen enabling graduates trained in postcolonialism to find well-paid positions and professional careers. This allows them to extend their network into further fields. They support and affirm one another and form a united front against critics, who are silenced through baseless allegations. A minority thereby dominates the majority of the population.

> In den vergangenen Jahren ist es der woken Linken gelungen, in großen Bereichen der Wissenschaft, der Medien und des Kultur- und Bildungsbereichs die Diskurshoheit zu erlangen. Ein riesiger Markt der Möglichkeiten ist entstanden, in dem postkolonial geschulte Universitätsabsolventen gut bezahlte Anstellungen finden und berufliche Karrieren verfolgen können. Diese erlauben es ihnen, ihre Netzwerke in wichtigen Sektoren weiter auszubauen. Man unterstützt und bestätigt sich und geht gemeinsam gegen Kritiker vor, die mit haltlosen Vorwürfen mundtot gemacht werden. Eine Minderheit dominiert dadurch die Mehrheit der Bevölkerung. (105)

Of course, this anti-woke narrative too can be exaggerated and has been subjected to incisive, perspicacious critique. Notably, Tony McKenna analyzes its motives and brings out its excesses.[20] Adrian Daub similarly emphasizes the "disproportion" of reactions especially in European media to American phenomena of political correctness that are not actually new.[21] On the left and on the right alike, becoming embroiled in the struggle for power as the first aim, rather than putting truth and objectivity first, leads to distortion and abuse. At stake, as always, is how power works and how it undermines impartiality and corrupts even basic

---

[20] Tony McKenna, *Has Political Correctness Gone Mad? Interrogating a Right-wing Conspiracy Theory* (London: Bloomsbury Academic, 2024).
[21] Adrian Daub, *The Cancel Culture Panic: How an American Obsession Went Global* (Stanford: Stanford University Press, 2024).

intellectual honesty.

It is noble, as well as persuasive, to favor individuals presumed to be disadvantaged and considered victims of social discrimination. Such action can be well-intentioned, but there is often also another, unconscious, darker reason for it. To achieve a more in-depth analysis of how power is exercised in the institutions that have been transformed by heavy-handed application of "woke" criteria such as diversity and inclusion, I will return in due course to the scapegoat mechanism as it is astutely theorized by René Girard (1923-2015). I apply Girard's theories to identity politics, which came fully into vogue a little after his time. A certain social identity, usually male, white, cisgender, is held to be responsible for patriarchy and white suprematism. This identity is guilty of all the evils, from colonialism to capitalism, for which Western civilization is routinely flogged. We witness a paroxysmic rejection of this entire culture seen as the culprit and as needing to be exorcised. I extend a Girardian analysis of scapegoating to our current situation with the help especially of contemporary French and German sociologists.

However, all this in due course (Part II). I want first to adumbrate my larger project of a thoroughgoing re-foundation of ethics and politics in the wake of wokeism (to be completed in Parts V-VI). This purpose, too, has to be approached rather indirectly because the re-foundation in question is more of an anti- or a non-foundation than something that can simply be defined and stated as such. It is more of the order of an aspiration to be inculcated by assiduous means of education, through contemplating social history and imaginative literature. Such cultivation stimulates the work of individual consciences to appropriate principles in ways that prove to be irreducibly personal and impossible to predict or dictate. This is the invaluable work that education in the humanities has fostered for millennia.[22]

---

[22] My own approach, as distilled into numerous works such as *The Revelation of Imagination: From Homer and the Bible through Virgil and Augustine to Dante* (Evanston: Northwestern University Press, 2015), has centered on the reading of so-called Great Books. My further works in this vein include *Secular Scriptures: Modern Theological Poetics in the Wake of Dante* (Columbus: Ohio State University Press: 2016) and *Don Quixote's Impossible Quest for the Absolute in Literature: Fiction, Reflection, and Negative Theology* (New York: Routledge, 2024).

4.

General Stakes and Styles of Wokeism

I wish to avoid judging wokeism as such because like any broad, amorphous cultural phenomenon it arises from all sorts of diverse and contradictory motives and works in myriad different directions all at once, often contrary to the intention of the agents involved. However, certain dominant tendencies associated with this banner term can be identified and evaluated, and we are called upon morally and pragmatically to take positions and engage in actions vis-à-vis the destiny-laden developments marching under this ensign in our highly fraught social and cultural milieus. Still, from what position and in the name of whom do we make such evaluations and judgments?

There may be a claim, and a legitimate one with universal validity, to be made in the name of Justice, but any judgment is also inevitably a formulation in language that belongs to a specific time and place and is inflected by certain social groups within the greater whole of humanity, not to mention of the universe at large, with its innumerable other species—those commonly recognized as animals but also other entities such as mountains, forests, and rivers. The latter are now being recognized legally as persons in response to Indigenous (Māori) reclamations in New Zealand.[23]

If there is a reproach to be made against wokeism in general, it can only be that it is not woke enough, not aware enough of its own biases and of the others to whom it may be unjust by not being fully awake itself, not fully aware and accepting of others. Full recognition may possibly require acknowledgment even of some great Other in a more metaphysical or

---

[23]   https://www.lemonde.fr/planete/article/2017/03/20/la-nouvelle-zelande-dote-un-fleuve-d-une-personnalite-juridique_5097268_3244.html

religious sense. At least we need to recognize the often religious sensibilities for some sort of transcendent otherness that hold sway among so many other peoples and cultures—"other" to a typically secularized, modern, Western consciousness, in any case. The exigencies of justice toward others, including eventually also other species, can always be pushed harder and farther.

If wokeism is inspired essentially by this awareness of others and of the injustice that follows from their non-recognition, from the overlooking or downgrading of minorities and marginalized groups, we can only greet it with enthusiastic affirmation. There is something unmistakably right in the demand for justice for all regardless of class, race, gender, or whatever other descriptor of social identity. This claim in the name of basic human fairness can hardly be denied on moral or ethical grounds. However, a lot depends on the *style* in which it is propounded and pronounced. Indeed, style can make all the difference as an indicator of the purport and propensities of this movement or, more broadly, culture.

Is the manner of self-assertion championed by wokeism fair to all regardless of social determinations and characteristics, or is woke ideology (in some of its cruder versions) being used as a weapon to vilify certain classes and categories judged by partial perspectives and prejudice and passion to be the guilty parties in history and society? In practice, certain groups may be made to serve as scapegoats for the sake of enabling those wielding woke ideology to posture as avenging angels charged with the mission of rectifying the injustices of history. We must ask: What exactly in society is foregrounded, and what parts of history are focused on or blended out in arriving at the judgments advocated under auspices that are now recognized (for lack of a better term) as "woke"? These judgments may seem self-evident to some, but certainly not to all. We can all too easily slip across the line from generally recognized claims of justice to controversial positions embedded in partisan politics and ideologies.

"Wokeism" is a vague and loaded term. Critics will surely demand more concrete and precise designations. The term serves, however, to address some elusive yet pervasive and perennial tendencies in human affairs and does so in ways capturing the specificity of our historical moment. It can furnish conceptual keys that unlock hidden dimensions of power relations which escape purely empirical analysis and plain propositional statement. It can afford peripheral awareness of certain subtly ineffable and paradoxical aspects of social power. Rational calculation and explicitness alone are never enough to fully comprehend human complexity.

Wokeism, of course, comes in many different forms and not all of them are vulnerable to the same objections. But in its more virulent versions, wokeism distinguishes—in effect, if not in intent—between innocent and guilty groups. People are divided, as in a caste system, into clean and unclean identities.[24] Unclean are those born into "privilege." The most unclean identities include especially white, male, heterosexual, Western, monotheistic, Christian. In contrast, those are clean who belong to identity groups that have a recognized history of oppression—namely, women, blacks, gays, lesbians, transgender persons, indigenous peoples, the handicapped, the obese, etc. The latter are accorded a legitimacy that is denied to the former, inverting the bias of the dominant society of the past according to revisionist woke history. In this history, "white privilege" figures as a sort of Original Sin.

Those with clean identities can look to the state for patronage. At universities, departments and chairs of feminist, black, and indigenous studies are established, and human-rights commissions are newly instituted at various levels of government. "Diversity" bureaucracies proliferate. Compensations for medical interventions, special gender-affirming care and well-being clinics, as well as restoration of property are earmarked for certain identity groups. The corporate world, too, has embraced wokeism as a means of polishing the reputations of companies and for purposes of marketing products tailored to the lifestyles and tastes of specific classes of consumers.[25] "Activism" becomes a slogan crucial to the agenda of corporations seeking the most economic ways of

---

[24] Joshua Mitchell, *American Awakening: Identity Politics and Other Afflictions of our Time* (New York: Encounter Books, 2020).
[25] Robin DiAngelo, author of *White Fragility: Why It's So Hard for White People to Talk About Racism* (Boston: Beacon Press, 2018), has been an important promoter of this trend in the corporate world.

sanitizing their public images with a minimum of investment in actual change.[26]

James Patterson comments, "Wokeness is the opiate of the elites. None of the patronage directly benefits struggling communities; it simply moves funds from state institutions, global corporations, and universities to diversity, equity, and inclusion consultants. These consultants, in turn, serve as moral and spiritual alibis, helping to rehabilitate institutions' public image whenever issues of prejudice emerge."[27] This attack is typical of the backlash that the term "woke" now typically provokes. Whatever its validity, this remark accurately points to wokeism's inextricable entanglement in the politics of image-making. Of course, reciprocally, woke bashing, now quite a common reflex, tends to elicit opposition and even slander in kind. Tony McKenna (*Has Political Correctness Gone Mad?*) effectively demonstrates how right-wing politics exaggerates certain dangers and distorts the allegedly leftist motives of woke causes including antiracism, transgenderism, #MeToo, and cancel culture.

The battle for justice concerns us all, but it may not so easily be boiled down to the righteous on one side and the reprobate on the other—certainly not when such discriminations are made in terms of blanket, abstract identities such as black or white, male or female, straight or gay or trans. Such polarizations animated by propagandistic phantasms often seem to dominate debate in our currently envenomed cultural climate in society in general and especially at the university. This is why I feel challenged by the phenomenon of wokeism and even provoked by certain forms and instances of its manifestation to tease out the following, sometimes tormented reflections on a complex phenomenon raising sensitive—not to say inflammatory—social and political issues. There are some genuine conundrums riddling our ethical lives to be faced here. They are entangled also with some epistemological paradoxes concerning universal identities and real individuals that need to be carefully unraveled.

---

[26] Vivek Ramaswamy, *Woke, Inc.: Inside Corporate America's Social Justice Scam* (New York: Hachette Books, 2021). Carl Rhodes, *Woke Capitalism: How Corporate Morality Is Sabotaging Democracy* (Bristol: Bristol University Press, 2022).
[27] James M. Patterson, Wokeness and the New Religious Establishment | National Affairs. Accessed 5-27-2024.

In the end, our metaphysical visions and assumptions about reality are called into play and into question.

The cause of social justice, under whose insignia wokeism advances on parade, cannot but be wholeheartedly endorsed. This movement expresses an ethical orientation and imperative such as have been worked out philosophically with particular acuity and poignancy by Emmanuel Levinas in his understanding of ethics as founded on infinite obligation to the other. The core of ethics can be most simply expressed by the common civility of bowing to others and letting them pass before oneself: "After you, sir" ("après-vous-Monsieur").[28] Or shall we say today, "Après vous, Madame" or even "After her/him/they," updating Levinas's gendering of this deferential gesture? In any case, the principle of putting the Other first is highlighted as the heart of ethics.

Levinas's basic ethical maxim is a critical principle laying down an imperative for individuals and communities. However, Levinas's ethics of infinite obligation to the other is refractory to general linguistic formulation. Such an ethics belongs to the originating principle of discourse that is inevitably betrayed by actual discourse. For Levinas, the Said ("le *Dit*") always and inescapably falsifies the Saying ("le *Dire*").[29] Every fixed formulation in language betrays its own free forming in mind or spirit. The "face" of the Other ("le visage de l'Autre") "speaks" necessarily without and from beyond words. When wokeism becomes an ism, not to mention a discourse and an ideology, is it still capable of acting to raise awareness of the injustice done to others? Or is it liable to become itself another invidious form of blaming and shaming, or at least of demeaning and disparaging, certain designated identities as belonging to stigmatized or disgraced groups—even when this stigma attaches to groups that historically have been accounted privileged? Does it then treat these categories as being essentially less moral and less deserving of

---

[28] Levinas offers this banal, single-phrase formulation of his ethical principle in *Autrement qu'être ou au-delà de l'essence* (The Hague: Martinus Nijhoff, 1974), 150. The work is translated by Alphonso Lingis as *Otherwise than Being and Beyond Essence* (Dordrecht: Kluwer, 1991).

[29] I read Levinas in this "apophatic" key pivoting on what language cannot say in *On What Cannot Be Said: Apophatic Discourses in Philosophy, Religion, Literature, and the Arts* (Notre Dame: University of Notre Dame Press, 2007), vol. 2, 406-10.

common respect and of a common share in the benefits of human community? Can wokeism, in certain of its expressions, foster another type of identity formation based on prejudice? Can it be used for bludgeoning an enemy or rival identified by certain labels in the social battle for prestige and power? If this happens, the sacred mission of historical movements for social justice in the name of civil rights—in whose lineage wokeism, at its best, stands—has been egregiously betrayed.

Today, wokeism becomes something with a definite meaning and content mostly in the imagination of those who oppose it. The term is generally not used by those taken to represent its positions militating for racial, gender, or class justice. "Wokeism" is largely a phantasm created by passions of fear and loathing on the part of those who feel themselves under attack by it or who see it as a threat to traditional culture and society.[30] Both those identified as representing wokeism and its detractors tend to enter into a kind of rhetorical inflation based on abstractions bloated with emotion.

Social identities, whether racial or sexual, or national or religious, are not first-degree facts: they are rather complicated constructions of symbols made possible by the linguistic capacities of abstraction and generalization. "Wokeism," too, is obviously an abstraction, an amalgam serving as a vector for emotions of righteous indignation. The outcry of so-called wokes against the injustice of society and of a whole civilization as racist and sexist and imperialist is matched—with an ironic kind of symmetry— by the decrying of wokeism as itself generic and degenerate and a totalitarian movement. Both contrary modes of accusation, although impassioned, ring somewhat hollow when taken to the level of exactly who is supposed to be guilty of what. Of course, we cannot simply avoid abstractions in language and discourse. But with the awareness that "wokeism" is a highly constructed and loaded term, we can interrogate the possible attitudes and arguments that are dressed up in this outfit. The notion of wokeism certainly raises crucial questions. It focuses burning, even if elusive, issues of great public purport. At stake is the ethical sense of society and the conscience of the human community.

---

[30] Albert Ogien, *Émancipations. Luttes minoritaires, luttes universelles* (Paris: Textuel, 2023).

A crucial question is: Are the currents we call wokeism using social descriptors regarding class, race, and gender, for purposes of even-handed inclusion in the interests of progress toward a peaceful and harmonious society, or are they deepening division and separation between those presumed to be guilty and those pronounced unconditionally innocent by a moralizing narrative esteeming certain identities as good and to be fostered, while others are treated as bad or to be discredited and put to shame? Such discriminations tend to be based on a sweeping narrative of historical guilt and victimhood. One can find oneself valorized or stigmatized for one's social identities quite apart from one's own acts and commitments. This way of evaluating, then, reproduces the evil at the core of racism.[31] Those most apt to be identified as wokes, at least in one extreme posture, alas, embrace their gospel of social progress as absolute truth as much as Hegel ever did, but without his acute sense of the truth as always dialectical, as interpenetrated by its opposite in a comprehensive, organic whole.

The breakthroughs for ethical insight championed by wokeism highlight in some ways—but in others conceal—human beings' mutual implication in one another's glorious achievements and appalling failures. Revindication for certain racial, religious, national, or gender identities and their agendas can turn these critical insights into myths that create fixed moral valences for generic categories of human beings. These identities can then be instrumentalized for garnering social power and exercising a kind of political or social tyranny. Such campaigns for empowerment can be carried out with the sophisticated and seemingly objective instruments of "scientific" knowing. Yet knowledge that is penetratingly analytical is also by its nature sectorial and partial: it brings into focus specific areas but only by separating them from others and

---

[31] Columbia University linguist John McWhorter, *Woke Racism: How a New Religion Has Betrayed Black America* (New York: Portfolio/Penguin, 2021) contends that antiracism in woke discourse has become racist and that it inadvertently damages particularly blacks. A similar point is made by Thomas Chatterton Williams in his articles in *The Atlantic*, notably "Saving Classics from Identity Politics," https://www.theatlantic.com/ideas/archive/2022/01/ideas-vs-identity-liberal-arts-montas-padilla/621241/, to be developed in his forthcoming book *Nothing Was the Same: The Pandemic Summer of George Floyd and the Shift in Western Consciousness* (New York: Knopf, 2025).

blending out what surrounds them. "Scientific" analysis needs to be supplemented by more holistic approaches to knowing and understanding that can accommodate complexity and contradiction as woven into the very fabric of our world and the relations that make it up.[32]

The underlying and ongoing ethical, social, political, and revolutionary movement that demands equal recognition for minorities and for all subaltern groups is actually integral to the deep self-critique that has characterized and distinguished Western democratic culture across centuries and millennia. This moral basis of wokeism is a leaven of truth that demands constant purging of our all-too-human tendency to exempt and shield ourselves from guilt, projecting it onto others from whom typically we wall ourselves off. A necessary and salutary shaking up of complacencies through a critical questioning of systematically biased histories of race, class, and gender is currently underway driven by wokeism. Revisionary, woke-inspired histories have exposed the unconscionable horrors of slavery and colonialism with previously unimaginable vividness, with pathos and power to convert hearts and transform humanity.[33] But this project of deeply searching criticism is also sorely at risk of being coopted into another institutionalized establishment that dissociates humans and obscures their complex connectedness, separating them into the guilty and the innocent based on their social identities.

---

[32] "Involved Knowing: On the Poetic Epistemology of the Humanities" in Franke (2015), 3-28.

[33] Poignant and readily available examples of such material include Never to Be Forgotten. The History of Colonialism - YouTube and BBC Documentary: The History of Racism - YouTube. The way the US prison system has been used to perpetrate racism is chillingly revealed by the documentary 13TH | FULL FEATURE | Netflix (youtube.com).

5.

From Invidious Cultural Politics to Spiritually Inspired Community

Owning up to the outrages of history is a necessary and a salutary premise preliminary to reconciliation, to righting wrongs, and to reestablishing the bases for social justice and cooperation. In a traditionally Judeo-Christian and biblical vocabulary, this step in the process of atonement (literally at-one-ment) comprises acts such as acknowledging guilt, confessing sins, asking for forgiveness, and performing concrete actions of penance and reparation. This culture and its concepts often find themselves under attack in outspokenly woke milieus. Judeo-Christian culture is often stereotyped in spite of (but also, perhaps, covertly because of) its semitic origins, as white, male, patriarchal, and Western, all of which designators, in sum, connote "colonialist," "imperialist," and generally also "capitalist." Still, the contributions of this civilization to laying out the premises of justice that figure decisively in the social justice discourse of the cultural elite of the American academy today are equally unmistakable. Have not the principles of international law and human rights and social justice been developed eminently in modern Western democracies, in this reputedly white, male, heteronormative-dominated society? Is not this very intellectual tradition being resourced by woke culture and its spokespersons in order to claim restitutions and rectifications?

The dynamics of power bring into prominence certain groups who form elites along lines generally calqued on criteria such as race, class, and gender. Individuals in certain groups identify with one another and work together on the basis of common understanding among the like-minded. This is not per se evil. That white men gained ostensible preeminence in certain cultures across the globe is due to historical conditions that demanded specific capabilities. However, in primordial heroic and subsistence societies, any position of supremacy is more about the shouldering of responsibilities than about laying claim to privileges. Material and social conditions have changed, and the requisite natural fitness and competences have shifted so that other groups are now called on to assume primary responsibility in new domains.

At the university, in my experience, particularly in the humanities, in English and the liberal arts, but also in divinity and law, in business and education schools, women and non-whites and, most recently, nonbinaries or non-heteronormative individuals have increasingly taken over leadership roles as deans and department chairs and directors of programs and research centers. They are perhaps best equipped to most effectively guide current transitions. New identity groups are dominating the scene, and I think it in every one's interest to cooperate pacifically and enthusiastically rather than to resist the revolutionary sea changes now underway. Yet we should not illude ourselves that this upheaval is more than another very partial correction of certain corrosive biases. This revolution, like most others, is rife with its own distortions, paradoxes, and contradictions.

Militant wokeism has made a crusade out of replacing some groups by others, or at least of compensatory favoritism. This action goes beyond simply facilitating natural shifts recognized as advantageous for all alike. The standard woke rhetoric speaks of "equality," "inclusion," and "diversity" in the interests of "social justice." But the designated scenario is still based on individuals competing for privilege. In effect, such a situation arises only in an affluent and individualistic society sick and suffering from its own material "success." It is a situation far removed from the organic communities under pressures of the struggle for survival, where different roles were fulfilled by those best adapted to fulfill them in serving the necessities of the community at large. Wokeism is a phenomenon produced by a highly individualistic phase of the modern Western model of democratic society originating from Greco-Roman and Judeo-Christian civilizations with their largely patriarchal traditions, which wokeism so stridently contests.

Wokeism's outspoken moralism emerges as the visible, self-profiling face of a decadent, self-indulgent phase of this civilization. A sort of systemic hypocrisy understandably prompts contempt from around the world in more traditional cultures for woke-saturated society in the "progressive" West. Decadent democracy becomes vulnerable to being criticized by the likes of Vladmir Putin. Unfortunately, this sometimes-sinister perspective is not all wrong. It resonates with the acute analysis of well over a century ago by Friedrich Nietzsche of moralistic decadence as registering a denaturing of healthy animal instinct, as well as with Oswald Spengler's theory of the decline of the West (*Der Untergang des Abendlands*, 1923).

Nietzsche diagnosed our sanctimonious moralizing, our genuflection to the "other," as denaturing the primal instinct of self-preservation—the first imperative for existing at all. Such a "Christian" morality is based on denial of our vital impulses. It relies, instead, on championing and safeguarding weakness over against strength. It turns natural order on its head and asserts an unnatural basis for what is right. Physical force, as a natural good or power, "virtue" in a literal sense, is condemned by a moral judgment as evil—at least in certain of its uses, for example, to dominate others who are weaker. In Nietzsche's view, such moralizing denatures and sickens us and causes our culture to plummet into nihilism. It makes us ashamed of our own strength and teaches us to feel guilty about our natural power and its inherent prerogatives.[34]

Typically woke ideology decries any form of domination whatever as injustice. It does so in the name of an ethics posited as above argument. Those who disagree with woke positions and policies can be shouted down or sanctioned or lose their licenses to practice their professions. Some of the more extreme, unself-critical forms of wokeism provide a sobering illustration of how the noblest ethical ideals can be perverted and turned into camouflaged instruments of assertion of the will-to-power in the mode of revenge such as were unmasked by Nietzsche in his analysis of the genealogy of morality. To convincingly answer Nietzsche's challenge in

---

[34] Nietzsche elaborates this argument concentratedly in *Zur Genealogie der Moral: Eine Streitschrift* (1887), trans. Walter Kaufman as *On the Genealogy of Morality: A Polemic* (New York: Vintage, 1967).

our contemporary context, we need to return to the more remote roots of the current social justice ideology.

Justice in Judeo-Christian traditions and in the Western democratic cultures built on them was never meant to be the exclusive province of any specific gender, race, or class. The whole point and purpose of Western conceptions of justice was their general validity for all. Granted, God was gendered for the most part as male, and human rights were first declared as the "Rights of Man." Still, the revolution of the Christian religion was to make the highest and most essential truth a truth of the heart rather than of intellect and formal learning. Truth therewith became a matter equally accessible to women and children and slaves. Apprehension of ultimate truth was no longer reserved for the intellectual elite in the schools of Plato's Academy or Aristotle's Lyceum. Truth was rather hidden from these elites and their leaders because of their pride in the "flesh." This word—*sarx* (σάρξ) in New Testament Greek—means birthright and social standing in the world. The highest truth was revealed, instead, to children and to women and the downtrodden through the purity of heart that comes with freedom from overweening pride in one's own person or in one's high social status. The latter are burdens constantly needing to be upheld and therewith forms of enslavement. Even contemporary, self-declared atheist philosophers including Alain Badiou, Slovej Žižek, and Giorgio Agamben effectively bring out this progressive purport of Christianity as ushering in a world-historical social revolution.[35]

Saints of all colors and continents, male and female, have beaconed *exempla* of renunciation of privilege for the sake of justice especially on behalf of the poor. Maybe we now have to include "trans" saints as well, although the Globe Theatre's production making Saint Joan of Arc a non-binary has been felt by J. K. Rowling to be an unacceptable erasure of Joan

---

[35] Alain Badiou, *Saint Paul: La fondation de l'universalisme* (Paris: Presses Universitaires de France, 1997), trans. Ray Brassier as *Saint Paul: The Foundation of Universalism* (Stanford, CA: Stanford University Press, 2003); Giorgio Agamben, *Il tempo che resta: Un commento alla lettera ai Romani* (Turin: Bollati Boringhieri, 2000), trans. Patricia Dailey as *The Time That Remains: A Commentary on the Letter to the Romans* (Stanford, CA: Stanford University Press, 2005); Slavoj Žižek, *The Fragile Absolute—or, Why Is the Christian Legacy Worth Fighting For?* (London: Verso, 2000).

as a woman.[36] The canonical saints have often treated life itself not as a right to be revindicated but as a privilege—one that they have been willing to renounce or relinquish. Christian saints have followed Jesus's precept and example of laying down one's life for one's friends (John 15: 13)— and loving one's enemies (Matthew 5: 43-45). They ought not to be erased by a cancel culture movement because their religion happens not to be in vogue among those now claiming to minister a sweeping rectification of historical injustice. The same recognition should certainly be accorded to Muslims or Buddhists or atheists or any other religious or non-religious social group.

Historically, legitimation of the slave revolt in ancient Rome came out of the revolutionary word of the Gospel. Christianity was excoriated influentially as "slave morality" by Nietzsche. It grated against and riled his aristocratic sensibilities.[37] However, for the same reason, modern Marxist and atheistic philosophers such as Žižek and Agamben, writing in the wake of Badiou and his *Saint Paul: The Foundation of Universalism* (1997), have found the principles of Christianity to be sources for overturning oppressive power hierarchies and even for exalting the power of powerlessness. Such is the spiritual message of the Christian Gospel, which is rooted in the ethics of the Hebrew Bible and especially in its prophetic critique of social injustice. Wokeism, to my mind, confirms and

---

[36] J. K. Rowling's objection to the Globe Theatre's presentation of Joan of Arc as nonbinary is that it erases women and all that they have achieved. Gender non-conforming women are not considered women in the perspective of this production. The play de-womanizes Joan. Wokeism's pretension to rewrite history in this instance falsifies it because heroines identifying as women are obliterated by an alien political agenda. Binary logic can certainly be a cause of conflict and in some ways we might all like to transcend it. However, this appropriation of Saint Joan of Arc targets more than just the bad effects of binary reasoning and obliterates symbolic formations in which people as groups are earnestly invested. Binary logic is necessary for any symbolic formation whatsoever, even while creating exclusionary categories and deploying potentially invidious distinctions. We cannot sanitize symbolic representation by fiat. Instead, our categories need to be applied in fair and flexible ways. This will not occur free of criticism and debate—and this takes discussion and requires humility and sensitivity to others on all sides rather than self-righteousness. Interestingly engaging these issues is Douglas Murray praises JK Rowling's 'leadership' as she takes a stand on gender issues (youtube.com). Accessed 4-15-2024.
[37] Friedrich Nietzsche, *Jenseits von Gut und Böse* (*Beyond Good and Evil*), section 260. Projekt Gutenberg.

continues to ride on the coattails of this Christian morality, which consists of demanding respect even—and especially—for the weak and defenseless, "the orphan, the widow, and the stranger within your gates," in the language of the Hebrew prophets. Wokeism erases the deeper historical motives for this commitment yet holds the inalienable rights of all to be ethically self-evident truths that assert themselves without mediation as necessary and binding. Such a claim resonates as generally incontestable in democratic cultures.

We need not be surprised, then, by the irony that heroes and patron saints of wokeism, like James Baldwin, were totally steeped in Christian preaching and teaching. Church culture is absolutely integral to Baldwin's rhetoric of fiction and to his whole spiritual vision.[38] Baldwin's political engagement lends itself to interpretation as a negative political theology of specifically Christian derivation.[39] The central thrust of his work is to extend the prophetic critique of idolatry from biblical times to our own. Idolatry consists in identifying ultimate authority with worldly or racialized powers like whiteness or paternalism. It entails overlooking the transcendence by the human individual of all such generic identifying characteristics. Such transcendence alone, which is beyond any definable identity, makes the human being sacred. This negative truth of the non-identity of the holy (whether in us or in God) with any definable characteristics can only be known critically. Such critical knowing for Baldwin was "freedom," as announced by Christ in his saying: "Ye shall know the truth and the truth shall set you free" (John 8: 32).[40] This is why I believe that any appropriation of Baldwin for a cult of wokeness pivoting on positive assertion of identities ironically misprisions his message and reverses the deeper meaning of his work.

Certain forms of wokeism tend to condemn whole cultures and especially "Western"—which means primarily Judeo-Christian plus

---

[38] Eddie S. Glaude, Jr., *Begin Again: James Baldwin's America and its Urgent Lessons for Our Own* (New York: Penguin Random House, 2021).

[39] Vincent Lloyd, "The Negative Political Theology of James Baldwin," in *A Political Companion to James Baldwin*, ed. Susan J. McWilliams (Lexington, KY: The University Press of Kentucky, 2017), 171–94.

[40] James Baldwin, *Collected Essays* (New York: Library of America, 1998), 432. Cf. 840 for reference to René Girard.

Greco-Roman—culture as principal cause of the injustice in the world. At the same time, they weaponize the very moral and judicial principles that this culture has produced and fostered. This culture's having created the very possibility of the critique being levied against it is suppressed or ignored. The idea is that if we can condemn and dethrone the parties responsible for history's ethical transgressions from colonialism and imperialism to capitalism, the rest of us will be free to spontaneously realize the natural order of justice on earth—like innocent, uncorrupted children of the Golden Age of human origins and original virtue and right. Those who can call out the sins and guilt of the culprits thereby style themselves as the righteous who are acting with clairvoyant vision and exceptional courage in the general interest to condemn and therewith clean up the immorality of the past.[41]

But you can never simply erase history and start over again from a position outside it. "Apocalypse" strains after a visionary perspective reaching beyond history. Yet, as concretely expressed, it can only offer another inner-historical perspective. Any version of history and human destiny is inevitably partial and perspectival when formulated in a particular language, with its specific cultural baggage. It is written by authors from a certain cultural and socioeconomic background. Indeed, "apocalypse" is another Judeo-Christian concept transmitted through *koiné* Greek, the "common" language of the Hellenistic world. Every human history has a history behind it to which responsible parties ought to own up. They must not simply assume that their version represents universal truth but must attempt to negotiate with their fellows a fair, consensual, or at least a mutually understandable, representation of the past.

The injustice wrought throughout history is patent. Yet the temptation of summing it all up in a few simple formulas claiming to know who is guilty and assigning blame or innocence and immunity based on identity labels is almost transparently illusory and will inevitably be used in self-serving ways. Every monolithic form of canceling historical wrong and

---

[41] Frank Furedi, *The War Against the Past: Why the West Must Fight for its History* (Cambridge: Polity, 2024) challenges complacent consensus that our past is evil. He calls for vigorous defense against the current onslaught.

supposedly undoing its effects is liable to produce injustices of its own rather than to work cleanly and purely as a restoration of pristine justice. The latter scenario of a return to the Garden of Eden through the purging of transgressors has too often been the naïve pretense of divisive, identity-based cultural politics such as those of wokeism. Unmistakable here, yet again, ironically, is the ineffaceable debt owed to Judeo-Christianity (specifically Genesis 3 recounting the Fall).

6.

Mutually Imitative Rivals for Power

The basic dynamic of social power as founded on rivalry and using superior force to triumph over one's presumable oppressors tends to be reproduced and reinforced rather than diffused or deconstructed by much of the protest and critique marshalled under the battle ensigns of wokeism. A typically (and crudely) woke identity politics is called radically into question by the more subtle and penetrating critiques produced within the cultural traditions that are being rejected and condemned. The biblical tradition, for instance, with its inveterate patriarchy and hierarchical authoritarianism supposedly in the image of a monotheistic God, often figures among the chief targets of wokeism. At least this tradition stands as an underlying source of the culture of domination that wokeism claims to be shaking off and correcting.

However, sources of the critique in the name of justice and equality can be traced to this same tradition. They lie in the social revolution brought about by Christianity, as Paul preached it, transcending binary social distinctions: "There is neither Jew nor Greek, there is neither slave nor free, there is neither male nor female; for you are all one in Christ Jesus" (Galatians 3: 28). The monotheistic God before whom all are equal, whether man or woman, Gentile or Jew, freeman or slave, is the model of the infinite value of each individual, which has been the primary source of egalitarian ideologies in messianic Marxism and in virtually every other social liberation movement. Such movements on behalf of the poor and powerless can be followed down to Latin American liberation theology, where this biblical provenance becomes transparent and is made explicit.[42]

---

[42] Gustavo Guttiérez, *Teología de la liberación* (1971).

Working essentially in and from this biblical tradition, René Girard clairvoyantly recognizes the primordial facts of rivalry among human beings as foundational for society. They are represented archetypally in jealousy between brothers from Cain and Abel to Esau and Jacob. [43] However, the resources for overcoming this tragic predicament are also found in the same biblical tradition. Christ's sacrifice is to refuse to have anything for himself over against others, his rivals. He breaks that cycle of competition by giving himself up for love of others. "Greater love hath no man than this, that a man lay down his life for his friends" (Gospel of John, 15: 13). The human predicament is determined by the mechanism of mimetic desire whereby all desire the same objects. All fatally become rivals because desire is fundamentally engendered by imitation of the model. Esau and Jacob compete for their father Isaac's blessing, Cain and Abel for their Creator's favor. The sacrifice of Christ, in contrast, models accepting what no one desires, namely, infamy, torture, and annihilation, for love of others and for the sake of breaking the cycle of rivalrous mimetic desire. It puts an end to the ongoing chain of production of victims and always renewed mimetic rivalries. The classical rivalry between Polyneices and Eteocles, Oedipus's sons, each a claimant to the royal succession in Thebes, remains simply tragic until it finds its resolution in the Christ event. This is, for Girard, simply anthropology rather than theology.

Wokeism unwittingly reinforces and participates in the ongoing struggle for the very same objects as are supposedly desired and monopolized by those it criticizes and condemns—namely, power and wealth, recognition and prestige, social legitimacy and privilege. To use Girard's terms, we could say that wokeism constitutes an accentuation and perpetuation of "appropriative mimesis": desire for identical objects by members of the same community, which destroys social cohesion. [44] Social

---

[43] Girard expounds his theory of mimetic desire throughout his voluminous work and very often in relation to the biblical sources that were so important to him, for instance, in *Je vois Satan tomber comme l'éclair* (Paris: Grasset, 1999), trans. James G. Wilson as *I See Satan Fall Like Lightning* (Maryknoll: Orbis Books, 2001).

[44] René Girard, with J.-M. Oughourlian and Guy Lefort, *Des choses cachées depuis le commencement du monde* (Paris: Grasset, 2001), 11-55, trans. Stephen Bann and Michael Metteer as *Things Hidden Since the Foundation of the World* (Stanford: Stanford University Press, 1987). See particularly Chapter 1: Le mechanisme victimaire: fondation du religieux.

life in its entirety, from primordial tribal cultures to present mass societies, is comprehended by Girard as determined by the violence engendered through mimetic desire. Human community is constituted, furthermore, by the modes of diverting, defusing, and controlling such violence. Religion, rites, taboos, moral interdictions, and especially the institution of sacrifice all demonstrate this existential necessity pertaining to every form of organized human life.

Wokeism, at its worst, can tend to take over and accentuate the aggressive, competitive aspects of Western culture, while missing or ignoring its more fundamentally critical and especially self-critical thrust, which forms the foundation for a culture of caring. Militant woke attitudes can tend to adopt and mimetically reproduce the crass rather than the refined aspects of the culture under attack. Wokeism maintains that, because of being aware or "woke" regarding the horrors of discrimination in history, it does not itself participate in the ongoing injustice of this history in contemporary society. Yet it foregrounds certain oppressions while ignoring or occulting others.

Again, crucial here are style and tone. Surely, wokes would say that they are advocating inclusion and diversity, not a politics of replacement of certain social groups or identities by others, but that is exactly what it has meant (however wrongly) to not a few white men, mostly working class, marching in the streets to the slogan "you will not replace us." This example is not a pretty spectacle, but we need to try and understand how these people (they, too, are persons) think and why they feel morally outraged and unfairly treated. Criminalizing them for their outlook will surely confirm their sense of being oppressed and discriminated against and therefore called on to react violently to defend themselves. They may feel that their very honor as men or as white or as human is under attack, calling for defense as if of something sacred.

Woke*ism* leverages what are undeniably just causes—against racial, gender, and class discrimination—but all too often for the elevation of oneself to a supposedly superior position of being morally enabled and entitled to judge and condemn others. The pushback from less privileged groups—for instance, of indigent or socially degraded and often despised white men against privileged academics—requires and deserves, in a first moment, understanding before being covered with opprobrium and reprobation.

Typically wokeist sentiment presses vehemently for condemnation of groups like the protestors in Charlottesville, Virginia chanting "You will not replace us" or the crowds assailing the US capital building, evidently in denial of the Trump 2020 electoral defeat. The violence is to be severely condemned, but still we need to understand the people involved and what provokes them. Even if they are to be treated as psychopaths or sociopaths beyond the pale of humanity, we need to find the path back to the human beings they once were and understand what went awry. Conceivably, they feel themselves to be marginalized and subjugated by what they perceive as a new superior caste of empowered professionals asserting their exclusive right to set the terms of what is right and wrong.

An arguably hysterical reaction has sometimes been piloted by woke-dominated media and publicity campaigns against what are characterized as attacks against the foundations of American democracy. Understanding of these revolts and their motives has perhaps been impeded by ideologically loaded rhetoric fomenting angry outrage. Unfortunately, this type of reaction is all too like the heinous violence and disrespect that it inveighs against. This mimetic reactivity, which degenerates into a warlike resolve to destroy one's putative enemy, occurs exemplarily also in the reaction to terrorist attacks. It became patent with the self-righteous, inflationary rhetoric, for example, of the operation labeled "Infinite Justice" by the Bush Administration in reaction to the 9/11, 2001 attacks on New York City's World Trade Center and the Pentagon. Common to such reactions is the complete lack of effort to try and understand the other side and their story of oppression. Alienated groups need to see evidence that their message has at least been heard rather than dismissed and despised before they are going to moderate rather than radicalize their protests.

Of course, this can all be said to be a crude misrepresentation of wokeist activism, which in reality advocates a politics of "diversity," not of "replacement." And this objection is valid, seen from the standpoint of many moderate, more reflective versions of wokeism and the social justice movement that we cannot but enthusiastically endorse. However, the unconscious logic and effectual workings of this ideology are liable to operate also at subliminal levels in the more primitive, unreflective ways adumbrated above.

7.

Toward Critical *Non-Identity*
—Wokeism and the University

My own perception of this topic is determined by my experience over several decades at a self-styled elite American university. This carefully controlled greenhouse culture of academia is the seedbed where wokeism germinated and first asserted itself. I have seen the curriculum dismantled to the mantras of "diversity" and "inclusion." I should say, to be more politically correct, "reformed" and "opened up" rather than dismantled. It is, indeed, refreshing to add James Baldwin and Toni Morrison and others to our great authors curriculum. However, an uncontrollable result of all the radical reshuffling and sometimes aggressive attack against the "canon" as male chauvinist, white supremacist, and Eurocentric has been a general dissolution of the humanities. Tearing down the prestige of the dead white men, Shakespeare and the rest, seeing in them nothing but their race and gender, has contributed to the crisis in which the humanities have undermined their own cultural credibility and have rendered themselves largely irrelevant in the public view.[45]

Critique of the canon needs to be understood, instead, as issuing from, and not against, these canonical authors, who have now become targets to be defamed and discarded if they are of the wrong race or gender. Ironically, these authors have been among the sharpest dissidents and critically creative spirits who have initiated deeply self-reflective questioning of our civilization. Figures like John Milton, William Blake,

---

[45] Heather MacDonald, *The Diversity Delusion: How Race and Gender Pandering Corrupt the University and Undermine Our Culture* (New York: St. Martin's Press, 2018) effectively deplores the university's catering to current race and gender shibboleths instead of correcting fallacious reasoning and critiquing delusive thinking.

Walt Whitman, and countless others stand out among our culture's greatest revolutionaries.

Politicized agendas pursued in the interests of inclusion and diversity have left in shambles the educational curricula that were in place when I entered the academic profession over three decades ago and began my career in college teaching at a liberal arts college within a leading research university. We have eliminated most programs in the humanities and denatured what remains to such an extent as to place the future of the Western humanities tradition in peril. This invaluable heritage is being compromised and canceled. At least this is my gut feeling; I wish that others would show me to be wrong.

I do not wish to remain attached to a past in lachrymose nostalgia or to condemn the social movements currently underway and changing the landscape of education, but a certain circumspection and critical regard is nevertheless called for. A self-critical perspective is necessary for keeping even the most well-meant and rigorously justified of liberation movements from turning into oppressors in their turn. We need to encourage open and internal debate rather than allowing imposition of a politically correct orthodoxy that tolerates no dissent. Despite its secular matrix in the university, wokeism has become much like a religion, replete with the typical attendant tendencies to dogmatism and intolerance.[46]

Wokeism, in certain of its more insidious manifestations, tends to require us all to take certain positions as obviously the only correct ones. Sometimes some forms of solidarity seem really to be spontaneous and appropriate. Ukrainians banding together to defend their country, at least as it was seen through most Western journalism, appeared to be a case in point. But often certain positions are defined as the only morally acceptable ones, and those who do not accept them are *ipso facto* subjected to revilement and disqualification. This can be a deleterious effect of overconfident wokeism. The temptation of thinking oneself to be

---

[46] Jean-François Braunstein, *La religion woke* (Paris: Gasset, 2022) details how this "religion" is "born in the universities" ("née dans les universitées"). See, further, Les dangers du wokisme - Jean-François Braunstein - Conférence - YouTube and "La religion Woke": Jean-François Braunstein est l'invité de Culture médias (youtube.com)

unequivocally in the right imperceptibly turns into a trap of self-righteousness.

What we need, ironically, is not less but more self-critical self-examination. This is ironic because Western culture has undermined itself precisely through its overzealous self-critique. But the critique has not been deep and honest, or lucid and true, enough to see past a superficially divisive logic that furnishes simple, binary solutions. We have wanted to identify guilty parties who can be purged rather than understand systemically the roots of evil in social violence and injustice.

Although it is difficult for us to think without defined concepts of finite entities, a first step to overcoming exclusionary violence and to thinking genuine inclusiveness is recognition of the *non-identical*, or thinking from the common ground that is not yet identified or articulated in anyone's lexicon and can be intimated only before all definitions by whatever groups or individuals. This I take to be the key to transcending divisive identities and delusions of total control. The *non-identical* is what self-reflection reveals when we look self-critically into the abyss of the self—or even into any collective identity. The self gapes open as a great Void without any identity all its own. It is constituted, instead, by relations, by having infinite possibilities of relation.[47] The same holds for collective selves or group identities. They are defined *relationally*.

A crucial question facing our world, especially in the present critical climate is: How are we going to stop fighting with one another? Republicans against Democrats, Russia against the West, China against Taiwan and the United States, wokes against rednecks—or, in other words, supposedly forward-looking progressives against diehard conservatives or even violent reactionaries? The healthy competition between rivals built into the model of democratic self-government has been degraded and turned into a deadly duel to discredit, subdue, and even destroy one's

---

[47] I demonstrate this for the modern subject emergent in Hamlet, Don Quixote, and especially Dante of the *Vita Nuova* in *Dante's* Vita Nuova *and the New Testament: Hermeneutics and the Poetics of Revelation* (Cambridge, UK: Cambridge University Press, 2021), 61-63. My videorecorded lectures on the subject include: William Franke, "Dante's New Life, or How Phenomenological Reduction Enables Theological Revelation" and Revolution in Poetic Language: Dante's Use of the Vernacular as Vehicle for Theological Revelation.

opponent. The political adversary becomes one's inadmissible nemesis and is condemned to be done in and done away with. The fact that each side needs the other as a corrective to its own inevitable biases and oversights has been completely forgotten. Debate too often turns into venomous vituperation without any genuine attempt to sympathetically understand what might be right, or at least sincere, in the position of the other side.

8.

Transcending Divisive Identities and Delusions of Total Control: The Role of Religion

Wokeism turns out to be more about who is right than about what is right: it shifts the debate in a way that focuses on who one is rather than on the content of one's ideas or even the tenor of one's acts. Its seminal and enabling insight is that we do all speak and act from certain concrete socioeconomic positions with their specific histories. This awareness has been fostered by various strands of Critical Theory, especially since the Frankfurt School in the 1960s. Core wokeist ideology denies transcendent values and reduces us to class, gender, race, and other material grounds of our values and thinking. Paradoxically, the *who* in question here consists only in *what* categories one is subsumed under and erases *who* one is as an individual person and free agent or subject.

In the cultural climate in which wokeism arises and which it nurtures, we have become so conscious of these classifying descriptors that divide us—and so wary and even disdainful of anything claiming to be "universal"—that we are speaking always only from within entrenched camps and exclusionary categories. Yet truly universal is only our being, each of us, a unique person. In this respect, indeed, we are all one and equal—but not in our socially constructed races and genders and classes. These constructions can be declared to be juridically equal, and should be, but more concretely we are constituted differently and incommensurably in the case of each individual. Generic categories play out as qualitative differences that count significantly, and sometimes immensely, only in actual appropriation and performance of each individual's *singularity* manifesting its own unique fingerprint and inimitable aura.

Acknowledging our different socio-economic, religious, national, ethnic, racial, and gender backgrounds is thus necessary and appropriate for appreciating who a given individual is, but classification by these descriptors has become dominant and decisive in our current woke-saturated culture. This is so to such a degree as to impede us from looking past such differences to a common sense of humanity in which we all share. That this common humanity, like any universal, is only potential and nothing positively present or definable or fixed, and ultimately a non-identity, accounts for its being generally overlooked and ignored, shunted aside by more officiously visible identities.

Consciousness of such divisively defined identities becomes a motive for exclusionary and invidious valuations and behaviors and thus becomes tyrannical in its turn. Although identity-inflected claims and judgments are based on very relative determinations through artificially constructed definitions, such identities become the ground for binding moral imperatives and even come to operate as absolutes in a sense that calls to be analyzed as religious. Wherever one recognizes absolutes esteemed to be binding also for others universally, one has entered upon the terrain of religion.

Religions sometimes assert a will to total control of individuals and societies in the name of sacred principles that no one has a right to question, much less violate. The sacred is, in its very conception, altogether above human prerogatives and power and beyond questioning. In woke discourses, such a sacred function is generally attributed to the exigency of equality for all. Of course, this is a principle deeply ingrained already in the Judeo-Christian religion. This reference to a Christian heritage, incidentally, exposes the unacknowledged and, for woke ideologues, often inconvenient biblical provenance of woke ideology. All are declared equal before God. God's messianic action promises to be the great social leveler. As prophesied, picturesquely, for example, by Isaiah (and echoed famously by the Reverand Martin Luther King): "every valley shall be exalted, and every mountain and hill shall be made low" (40: 4). Saint Paul emphasizes the direct relation of each individual to God as overriding all social inequalities and as placing all—including Gentiles and Jews, women and men, slaves and free (Galatians 3: 28)—on a fundamentally equal footing before divine judgment (2 Corinthians 5: 15-17).

The transcendent authority of God relativizes all socially sanctioned authority and makes all subject to judgment by one transcendent but indefinable power. Crucial is that this power remain in principle out of reach for any human agent. To *identify* it with any human group or innerworldly instance is idolatry. An anti-idolatry imperative holds also for Islamic monotheism exemplarily and is even accentuated in principle by the lack of formal hierarchy in the Islamic *ummah*. It is God's being above and beyond all finite, definable, human identities that alone can preserve religion from perversion. When God is no longer transcendent, the sacred becomes available for instrumentalization by political power and by the worldly ambition of vying and conniving human agents. Religions, almost universally, reveal this transcendent and revolutionary power, but in translating it into forms of worldly power they pervert and betray it.

The American negro spirituals, in contrast, are based on a sense of transcendence in the face of the constant threat of death. Nonetheless, death is never triumphant over life. The spirituals imagine death as the site of an imminent and immanent immortality in which slaves are already free.[48]

> Oh Freedom! Oh Freedom!
> Oh Freedom, I love thee!
> And before I'll be a slave,
> I'll be buried in my grave,
> And go home to my Lord and be free.[49]

Religion proves to be an indispensable dimension of any absolute moral principle since such a principle claims to be universally binding. Religion is operative, whether it is recognized or not, in wokeism,

---

[48] Howard Thurman, "The Negro Spiritual Speaks of Life and Death," in *"Deep River" and "The Negro Spiritual Speaks of Life and Death"* (Richmond, IN: Friends United Press, 1975), 13.
[49] Corey D. B. Walker, "The Race for Theology: Toward a Critical Political Theology of Freedom," in *Race and Political Theology*, ed. Vincent W. Lloyd (Stanford: Stanford University Press, 2012), 146-49.

specifically in its claiming a kind of absolute and binding authority for its moral exigencies (etymologically, religion is "re-binding," *re-ligare*). Concretely and socially, recognition of the transcendence of God or the Absolute expresses itself most palpably as an absolute respect for the alterity of other persons.

The declared aims of fostering equal opportunity for disadvantaged groups are irreproachable. They issue an irrecusable moral call and imperative to us all. We cannot be content simply to do nothing to defend and promote justice with the excuse that it is divine will (if not incontrovertible chance) that alone rules the world. If divinity works in the world, it does so through human acts of justice and mercy. In Christian teaching, humans are called on to act as the body of Christ. Yet, in taking up our part of responsibility, we need to be aware also of the limits of our authority and capability. We do not control all the outcomes of our actions and do not lay down the overarching rules governing the world.[50] We play only a part and have to scrupulously examine our role to ensure that it serves the general good.

Wokeism, as a governing paradigm, assumes a general overview that seems to enable definitive judgments assigning guilt and innocence. Its social justice agenda is a gigantic meta-narrative that has its immediate effects and purposes in *profiling* those who resort to it and assert their power through it more than in actual righting of wrongs and ameliorating of oppressions. Wokeism, in the age of mediatic self-image confection, is often more a means of self-promotion and self-aggrandizement than of lifting up the downtrodden. It works with morally saturated identity categories that in many cases turn into pure presumption of guilt or innocence based on individuals' falling on the fair or the foul side of color, gender, and class lines. Of course, its more reflective and insightful adherents would certainly wish to distance themselves from any such amalgamating paradigm.

Wokeism is arguing for an indisputably just cause on behalf of marginalized groups, but oftentimes it is doing so in such a way as to be

---

[50] Hartmut Rosa, *Unverfügbarkeit* (Frankfurt a.M.: Suhrkamp, 2018), trans. James Wagner as *The Uncontrollability of the World* (New York: Polity, 2020) calls attention to the capital importance of our relation to the world as what we cannot control.

more about the posturing of the individuals making the claim than about those on behalf of whom it is made. The point and purpose can become that of profiling woke leaders themselves as righteous and casting blame on others, particularly their political opponents, as immoral—so as to buttress and shore up the woke brigade's own hold on power. Viewed from this angle, wokeism can be understood fundamentally as a style of discourse, as a manner of presenting oneself by projecting a certain kind of self-image. This has always been the case, of course, with whatever force, party, or movement in its bid for power in competitive political systems. What has changed are the technical means available for doing so, especially with the explosion of social media and the exponential increase in possibilities of inauthentic and fraudulent self-representation and manipulative consensus-building.[51]

As woke, we wish to think and style ourselves as moral by virtue of promoting minorities and the underprivileged and disadvantaged. More authentic than this self-styling, however, is genuine love of all cultures and individuals for what and who they are and for the beauty they can produce for others and put into play in the world. Our moralizations are about us and our own self-esteem. They are ways of profiling ourselves and are inherently self-interested. In contrast, to be sincerely enraptured by the attractions of black art or queer culture or indigenous songs to the earth enables a giving and receiving from above or from the Other and is no longer just about us and about who possesses how much. Such attention to the Other takes us beyond ourselves and promotes the infinite openness to one another in which alone our social salvation can be worked out and made real. At this point, the aesthetic register opens into the religious.

---

[51] See, for example, Jordan Peterson's war against woke (youtube.com)

9.

Language:
Between Total Control and Indeterminacy

The cause and claims of equality and fairness make some appeal to most anyone and belong in some form to the express aims of almost any constituency. The whole spectrum of political persuasions from neo-Nazi movements to leftist terrorist cells generally speak the language of demanding liberation from unjust oppressions. Still, these claims can be couched in terms that are epidermically objectionable to many, if not to virtually all. In fact, any terms whatever are bound to be found offensive by some. Only by avoiding (or at least looking past) terms altogether and aspiring to an ineffable source of all beyond articulation in language can we hope to find a common cause that all can embrace.

As with so many difficult political issues, everything depends on the partitioning across delicate membranes that are set up between what is said and what is left unsaid. Certain facts may be evident to all, and from a variety of perspectives, but when they are formulated in one language or another, they come to be framed in an identifiable discourse tainted with a specific culture and ideology: they then become controversial, if not downright offensive, to certain constituencies with their own prejudices and *partis pris*. The very same facts or circumstances can be made to change color and metamorphose almost into their opposites simply by being taken up consciously and voiced, as opposed to being left alone lying in silence, where different parties will interpret them in their own different ways. The art of diplomacy, as key to conciliatory politics, can consist principally in knowing what *not* to say, or what to leave unsaid. Different parties to disputed themes are left a margin of freedom to construe common terms in somewhat divergent manners that are acceptable to them, even though at this further level of implication, were it to be made explicit, the various parties to the accord would no longer be able to agree.

This approach means renouncing complete control over the process and acknowledging a space of free play, a margin of freedom in reaction to new developments in which the parties must remain responsive to one another and to situations that reveal themselves progressively. Not everything in interactive human relations can be made clear or be subjected to explicit constraint, especially not all at once. This creates an opportunity to exercise deference and self-restraint and to practice gestures of recognition of the other and of their rights and diverse interests.

Woke attitudes all too often project an illusion of total control and of knowing what is right, as if we could impose it by fiat—and as if we knew full well what everyone deserves. The presumption is that only the perverse will of reactionaries attached to their privileges prevents us from instituting what is uncontroversially right for all. All efforts to take control of society based on such presumption and dogma run into dilemmas. The others involved feel shamed into silence by this assertion of a superior moral power that interferes with the openness of working together flexibly and respectfully with one another to jointly resolve problems for all concerned.

Someone is presumed responsible and to blame for however things are. We always have to find a culpable party: nothing is accepted simply as being the way it is. Every fact and given situation is thus moralized, and our judgments—our preferences and prejudices—come to determine our relation to everything whatsoever. There is nothing we meet in the world that is not subject to our judgment. We are then totally surrounded by what we judge as right or wrong, and we can no longer encounter the world or life as it is in reality. Such encounter requires an ability to transcend ourselves and the frame we place on the world. I do not mean to imply that we can ever encounter absolute reality as a plain fact but rather that we must allow for a reality beyond the facts that we perceive and construe. This obliges us to work constructively with others to relate to what is other and even absolute—in a sense that we can never fully determine.

Granted, a part of human responsibility may be discerned in every situation as confronted by human beings, but by wanting to make some identifiable party totally responsible for it, we lose sight of the limits of human knowledge and control. We operate with the fiction that necessarily someone identifiable is guilty and to be held accountable for any fact or circumstance that is not to our liking or advantage. We take the high moral stance that being from poorer countries or dryer regions entitles one to compensations from others who are not subject to the specific privations that are being highlighted in a certain social justice discourse.

This logic almost inevitably slides even further into the conviction that whoever does not suffer what I suffer is guilty of my suffering. This perspective has become progressively plausible and perhaps even inescapable in our increasingly globalized and interconnected world. Lost, however, is the vision and awareness of all that cannot be globalized and technologized—lost is what is simply real or "absolute." We enclose ourselves in a purely human world of our own making, and it is doomed to implode for lack of any external support.[52] It becomes a human hell of endless mutual recriminations and revindications for lack of grace and relation to a Giver of all, who alone can be absolutely unstinting because alone above all our party politics.

The very fact of anything existing at all is nothing if not purely gratuitous—a Gift with no specifiable or identifiable Giver, what some call "grace." Of course, all manner of interpretations then become possible in terms of one's own faith or worldview. Ultimately, justice may not be a human virtue, nor a human possibility at all. This could be inferred even from the penetrating examinations of justice in Plato's *Republic* and in Aristotle's *Nicomachean Ethics*.[53] In Christian revelation, justice is gratuitous and unmeasured. It is founded on the beatitudes as pronounced by Jesus at the beginning of the Sermon on the Mount (Matthew 5: 1-12). Jesus remarks, furthermore, that the heavenly Father "maketh his sun to rise on the evil and on the good, and sendeth rain on the just and on the

---

[52] I lay out this problem in "Amphibolies of the Postmodern: Hyper-Secularity or the Return of the Religious?" in *Sacred and the Everyday: Comparative Approaches to Literature, Religious and Sacred*, ed. Stephen Morgan (Macau: University of Saint Joseph Academic Press, 2021), 9-33.

[53] I develop such an interpretation in "Plato's Apophatic Legacy," *Archives of the History of Philosophy* 69 (2024), special issue for Professor Seweryn Blandzi, ed. Dariusz Piętka.

unjust" (5: 45). Without mercy, in the Bible, there is no justice that is not rather a condemnation of all. Justice cannot be totally appropriated by humans without becoming idolatrous and even demonic. Humans' own highest good lies beyond their own grasp.[54]

---

[54] Saitya Brata Das, in *Political Theology of Life* (Eugene, Oregon: Pickwick, 2023), demonstrates this through an eschatological framing of human life based on the philosophical theologies of Eckhart, Schelling, and Kierkegaard.

10.

Ethics Degraded to Entitlements and the Discourse of Victimhood

I have embraced the Levinasian ethics of "the Other first" as a principle indicating something that is absolutely right about wokeist ideology. This position, however, might be seen as a luxury that can be afforded only if one is in a position of being generally respected by others and does not have to fight for the right to exist. Unsurprisingly, then, all today like to position themselves as victims and as barely "visible" at all. This posturing alone affords leverage in the revindication of rights and priority.[55] The Enlightenment emphasis on meritocracy is to a considerable degree being replaced now by a notion of entitlement based on wrongs of the past and a program to change the balance of power and wealth between various social groups. Historically disadvantaged groups are now being championed as deserving compensations as their moral due.[56]

We cannot refuse the imperatives of morality, but I think that we can and must think them more profoundly than in terms of socially assigned identities. Morality, conceived more nobly, is about the imperative incumbent on each individual to give their best to all others. It should be focused on how much you can give rather than on what you are entitled to receive from others as compensation for wrongs of the past. In matters of

---

[55] Pascal Bruckner, *La tyrannie de la pénitence: Essai sur le masochisme occidental* (Paris: Grasset, 2006) is one of many powerful statements of the tyrannical power of victimhood today. Girard expounds "the sacralization of the victim" in *Je vois Satan tomber du ciel*, chapter 13: Le soucie moderne des victimes, 249-61.

[56] Christopher Caldwell, *The Age of Entitlement: America Since the Sixties* (New York: Simon & Schuster, 2020) shows that since the Civil Rights Act of 1964 the US Constitution of 1788 has been progressively undermined by curtailment of rights such as free speech and meritocratic selection in hiring or college admissions seen as potentially disadvantaging minorities.

morality, we can judge only ourselves, not others. As Saint Paul put it, "For what man knows the things of a man except the spirit of the man which is in him?" (1 Corinthians 2: 11). Kant's moral philosophy (informed by Protestant Christianity) stresses that free determination of the will is crucial to moral action. And such moral determination can only be the action of a self-reflective rational agent. Moral agents have to be self-critical before they can be critical of others.

Jesus in the Gospels, implored by the crowd to condemn the woman taken in adultery, replied, "Let him who is without sin cast the first stone" (John 8: 7). When all her accusers had left one by one, "convicted by their conscience," he then said to the woman, "Has no one condemned you? . . . Neither do I condemn you. Go, and sin no more" (8: 10-11). Jesus's challenge places self-critique before any kind of judgment that criticizes others. As he says in the Sermon on the Mount: "And why beholdest thou the mote that is in thy brother's eye, but considerest not the beam that is in thine own eye?" (Matthew 7: 3) Human affairs are notoriously complicated. The accusatory tone whitewashing some generic categories while tarring others with blame is not conducive to fostering community and reconciling differences so as to enable us to face together our common problems and tensions. Needed here, instead, is a critical reflection on wokeism's ideology and its own place in history.

Beyond and above the perspective pivoting on the individual looms a relational understanding in the context of an organic community. This broader view makes claims of certain parties against others look different because individuals are not conceived of separately in terms of individual rights. Instead, all individuals are seen as serving together for a common end and purpose beyond themselves and as supporting one another, according to their different functions, in this collective endeavor. Individual rights are no longer the measure of progress, and gaining political power is not the goal. When these goals become ends in themselves, they are perversions that supposedly subaltern peoples might prefer to renounce rather than revindicate in the form of entitlements that have been denied them as victims. Our individualistic modern Western democracies stand to be corrected, in this regard, by the example of traditional communities such as indigenous tribes. For this purpose, it is crucial that the latter be seen not primarily through the optics of victimhood.

Anishinaabe author Gerald Vizenor has effectively criticized "victimry" as the worst fate that a group identifying as victims can bring on its members. They thereby render themselves impotent rather than concretely engaging in the challenges of self-improvement and self-empowerment.[57] We must question whether the typically woke definitions of groups profiling them as victims are socially necessary and constructive or, rather, deleterious. However, the problem, considered apophatically, is even more radical. Being defined in any way, whether by others or by oneself, is already to be a victim in some sense of a divisive language and the tyranny of its terms. Any generic definition of a group is liable to box it in unjustly. Roland Barthes famously remarked in his 1977 inaugural lecture at the Collège de France that every classification is oppressive ("toute classification est oppressive") and that language is "quite simply fascist" ("tout simplement fasciste").[58]

Authentic self-expression requires creating one's own terms rather than being promoted through anyone else's system of rights and entitlements. American Indians tend to be acutely aware of this and have proved remarkably resistant, typically eschewing most forms of assimilation. And yet claims to authenticity and to being purely autochthonous are also notoriously suspect of ignoring the intrinsically relational nature of any construction of identity. Authentic identity is always deeper than any of its definitions. Gerald Vizenor, for one, is very receptive to and influenced by French post-structuralist thought on this issue. He hilariously debunks the idea of the "authentic Indian" with his figure of the "post-Indian."[59]

The violence wrought simply by definitions and essentializing concepts has been brought to a forum in Indigenous debate around the

---

[57] Gerald Vizenor, *Hiroshima Bugi: Atomu 57* (Lincoln: University of Nebraska Press, 2003), 36, 64.

[58] The lecture can be heard online at: https://www.roland-barthes.org/lecon.html. Accessed 7-23-2023. Quoted statement: 5:52-58. It is a magnificent demonstration of the scattered and practically unopposable nature of power in language.

[59] Vizenor, *Fugitive Poses: Native American Indian Scenes of Absence and Presence* (Lincoln: University of Nebraska Press, 1998).

issue of "authenticity." The various contributions to a collective volume on *Native Authenticity* already make certain complicated dilemmas plain: "The issue of authenticity or 'Indian-ness' generates a controversial debate in studies of indigenous American literatures. The articulation of Native identity through the prism of Euro-American attempts to confine 'Indian' groups to essentialized spaces is resisted by some Native writers, while others recognize a need for essentialist categories as a key strategy in the struggle for social justice and a perpetually renewed sense of Native sovereignty."[60] Recognition of the ethical dilemmas inherent in any language, including that of the self-designated victim, must precede any decision pretending to be the universally right or correct way to speak.

It may be that the pressures to articulate and "voice" one's own being are themselves condemned to inevitable inauthenticity. This type of debate itself creates a certain tension between a Western format and a native-style powwow. I find it necessary and crucial that we listen to what is *not* being said and *cannot* be said, especially in delicate situations, in order to respect and appreciate what any of us authentically says and is. Only strategies of *not* saying can make manifest what could then be recognized as a more authentic mode of expression. Here we touch on what I consider to be a "religious," or at least a negative theological, "apophatic" dimension. Of course, religions can be noisily rhetorical, as well as silently mystical. Still, the core metaphysical truths that they affirm can be known or verified only in an act of personal witness in the silence that follows speech or preaching.

---

[60] Deborah L. Madsen, ed., *Native Authenticity: Transnational Perspectives on Native American Literary Studies* (New York: SUNY Press, 2010), back cover.

11.

Progressive History Catalyzed
by Elites, or Organic Community?

Wokes consider themselves—and generally prefer to call themselves—"progressives." An indispensable basis for wokeism is a progressive view of history. Wokes—or progressives—identify with various liberationist movements as marking progress in history. Progressive ideals, in their view, are worth fighting for and require vigilant and sometimes even forceful measures. At a certain point, however, genuine and sustainable progress in our multicultural world can come about only if we can dismantle the vicious and deadly war of opposing parties and identities. Discourse designated as "woke" has had a tendency to aggravate ideological divisions and stiffen resistance rather than to allay anger and diffuse resentment.

Almost all in the West generally share the view applauding and congratulating democratic societies for abolition of slavery and for securing women's rights. However, to exalt ourselves and our modern, secularized society as unequivocally just and enlightened over against all allegedly racist and sexist societies past and present is more to repeat than to overcome racism and sexism. It can be questioned, and can hardly help being doubted, whether modern and now postmodern, globalized society is making the world more just and happy. At least we can differentiate in what respects some people have certainly gained some benefits and recognize others in which many people surely have lost, perhaps even more fundamentally, in basic worth and dignity. Much depends on whether we evaluate the lot of individuals in isolation or in collectivities.[61]

In a non-consensual, radically multicultural society, it is very difficult to define what progress is. To assume that one's own vision of the progress of history is valid for all suppresses or fails to respect others who have a different vision. Indigenous peoples, notably, do not necessarily view "progress" as a value at all. Mastery over nature and its resources and gains in human comfort and individual freedom and all the other modern values that have made for "progress" may not be among their goals. Innumerable other cleavages, furthermore, open up within modern society itself as to what is genuine progress. In any case, it is almost impossible not to apply, at least unconsciously, one's own standards instead of those proper to the persons being evaluated in their own different contexts. They may have a different feel for everything.

Abortion rights, for instance, are considered necessary to progress by wokes—and perhaps by most, if not all, liberal-minded citizens. Yet there is also a powerful backlash against this sentiment. Is it just a few crazy fanatics, some of whom happen to sit on the Supreme Court of the USA, or is there some wider base, some silent counter-consensus that accounts for such an upheaval in the law concerning abortion as the US Supreme Court's 2022 overturning of Roe v. Wade in its consideration of abortion as a constitutional right? Of course, the critique and controversy does not generally deal with the court's precise ruling that the right to abortion is not guaranteed by the 1789 US constitution and was a matter for states to decide. Instead, the wokes' sense of outrage comes from their own conviction that abortion should be a constitutional right of women. This reaction evinces a tendency to believe that one's own moral sense should determine the law for all and that anyone with a different view is benighted.

Are such deep ideological differences from what wokes proclaim as universal right and truth just irrational violence against the bodies of women? The anti-abortionist camp, too, speaks, at least at times, from a

---

[61] On collective identity and narratively generated competing normativities, see Klaus Eder, "Europe as a Narrative Network: Taking the Social Embeddedness of Identity Constructions Seriously," in S. Lucarelli, F. Cerutti, and V. A. Schmidt (eds), *Debating Political Identity and Legitimacy in the European Union: Interdisciplinary Views* (London: Routledge, 2011), 38–54.

deeply moral sense that every human life has a right to be protected and preserved. To absolutize and sacralize one's own cherished value— whether it is "human life," as if that were not already prejudicial to other forms of life, or "my body, my choice," as if we did not all belong to embodied human communities where what we do with our bodies has consequences for others—is to fail to recognize the other as always already having rights, or at least ethical claims, on us. Others and their claims on us penetrate within us and are constitutive of our moral existence and even of our individual physical being. Our very freedom of choice is entirely dependent on others and their respective freedoms. Although I would never wish to obligate any woman to carry to term an unwanted pregnancy, such a decision can certainly affect other lives. They include the unborn and deserve to be taken into consideration, too, by the individual directly involved and responsible for making such choices.

To a considerable extent, the ideological divisiveness or fractiousness that we experience on this issue is explicable as a luxury that only a rich and powerful society can afford. When all have to work together in order to survive, society necessarily becomes more consensual. However, when some can profile themselves over against others as infallible moral umpires and champions of all the right causes, we move into a different logic from that of an organic society.

The liberal—and woke—agenda is based on rights of individuals being absolutized, yet every individual's rights can, in truth, be justified only relative to everyone else's. Wokeism tends to be the product of a desperately individualistic (neo-liberal) society and leverages the sacrosanct status of individual rights as a weapon to attack complex, functional relations of domination and submission that are the texture of traditional society—not to mention of nature itself, with its countless intricate hierarchies and pecking orders such as hold sway throughout the animal kingdom. I say "functional" as opposed to ideological because such a conception entails composing an organic body, or functional whole, rather than constructing rights based on certain artificially defined identities of individuals. Even plant life consists largely in struggle among various species for survival and for domination.

We can react with knee-jerk immediacy to any kind of "domination" as oppressive and ethically intolerable. But there are usually intricate and complex reasons for forms of hierarchy or chains of command that enduringly establish themselves. These reasons, at least originally, have to do with who is most capable of assuming what type of responsibility. The blanket refusal of all forms of "domination" is ideological: it is based on an ideal of free and equal community rather than on pragmatic considerations. It entails an emotional reaction expressing a distaste for certain words and concepts while ignoring the underlying realities and the exigencies that give rise to them. The complex relations of domination and submission that run all through the animal kingdom and organic nature itself are rooted in something real. The generic ideological protest against "domination" is animated all too often by its own sense of self-righteousness alone. The important distinction is between disinterested, universally beneficent exercise of control and selfish, unprincipled exploitation of others for one's own advantage.

The basic problem with wokeism as an "ism" is that it makes certain social identities good and others bad, reversing what were presumably valorized as positive and negative identities in a previous dispensation of society. Nietzsche argues in *On the Genealogy of Morals* that Christianity made the slaves and their own weakness and misery "good" while it made the strength and superior excellence of aristocrats "bad." Christianity praised being meek and loving one's enemies and preached dependence on God. Being humble and yielding even to one's enemies rather than summoning superior strength to prevail against them was hypocritically exalted as virtue. Christianity simply reversed the values that had thitherto prevailed, just as wokeism now does with the hitherto supposedly valorized identities of white, male, heterosexual, making these bad in favor of black, female, and the LGBTQIA cocktail. Nietzsche deplored that what is naturally strong and dominant should be undermined and maligned on hypocritically moral grounds by those too weak to dominate otherwise. To consider certain races or sexes as naturally weaker now seems laughable. However, some natural differences may still be relevant.

As current history rather alarmingly demonstrates, it is possible to erode and reverse any value system by persuasion and politics and manipulation of the means of communication that are generally available to nearly all. The question is who is doing it and why? To the extent that it is the action of a narrowly self-interested elite to take or keep control of power, others, those who are being disempowered and contained, will surely be spurred to resist. Historically, the "Great Awokenings" of the 1920s, 1960s, and 1980s, have been much more about refurbishing images and assuaging consciences of the elites than about fundamental social change. They have actually served to consolidate the power and privilege of elites, and the same is true of the present woke movement dating from about 2011.[62]

Any movement like wokeism tends to need an elite to take the lead in developing an outlook and approach that subsequently might be embraced by many, if not most, throughout society. But an elite also readily becomes an end unto itself, a means of cultivating and consolidating its own power rather than a catalyst for liberating creative and perhaps revolutionary energy across society and its classes. Historically, progressive movements have certainly needed elites, even while being eventually and almost inevitably betrayed by them. This tendency toward formation of elites, notably at the university, applies manifestly to the phenomenon of wokeism and can be observed operating in the perennial dialectic of revolution and counter-revolution. The paradox of revolution as its own self-undoing is demonstrable in both the American and the French revolutions. While clearing away old forms of oppression, they placed new elites in power, and these new ruling classes engendered new structures of control and exploitation.

Apophasis and kenosis indicate an alternative path. They demonstrate that a superior use of power lies in renunciation of power as a means of lording it over others. The power of self-sacrifice and love is foregrounded instead. Especially mystic religions, those of Sufis or Vedantists or Kabbalistic or Christian contemplatives, have furnished classical texts and life-forms along these lines converging on the overcoming of self in self-giving and service to others. However, this is not generally the spirit

---

[62] This instrumentalization of the language of social justice is painstakingly documented by Musa al-Gharbi, *We Have Never Been Woke: The Cultural Contradictions of a New Elite* (Princeton: Princeton University Press, 2024).

animating the woke movement, with its aggressively political revindications, although wokeism, too, evinces ambiguously religious tendencies.

12.

The New Religion of Wokeism

Numerous voices can now be heard likening wokeism to a religion. Sometimes described as a new form of civil religion (a notion going back to the final chapter of Jean-Jacques Rousseau's *Social Contract*, 1762), wokeism makes value claims that are absolute and thus lend themselves to being understood theologically. One commentator writes aptly of a "deification of group identity."[63] Wokeism is making claims to absolute truth in the name of equality and justice. In effect, wokeism divinizes the values that it defends, but it also makes them socially concrete and specific, unlike the God of the mystics, who always transcends any finite determinations in human language. Certain identities over against others are valorized by wokeism, and these judgments may even take on a sacred aura. It becomes our moral duty to defend certain identifiable groups (women, blacks, homosexuals, queers, etc.)—as if all groups equally and all humanity had not the same claim to be heard and respected.

It is all too common today to take up a truth that resonates with a certain group as if it were an absolute truth for all. Women generally (though there are exceptions) can all agree about women being oppressed. They have experienced, at the very least, discomfort in being women in certain situations. However, men too can focus on situations in which they have felt that their gender puts them under pressure or at a disadvantage. One's preconception on such matters entirely biases one's perceptions; it pre-programs what one is attentive to and what passes unnoticed. The world is full of contrariness for whoever you are. We select what to pay attention to based on the narratives that are operating in our minds and that

---

[63] James M. Patterson, Wokeness and the New Religious Establishment | National Affairs. Accessed 8-27-2023.

enable us to perceive a behavior or phenomenon because we expect it and see the world in terms of it. We should not confuse these perceptions with universal truth.

There are, of course, countless terrible insults against women as women being unfurled all the time. But does that mean that we cannot perceive that men too are constantly insulted, often *as* men? Woke and particularly feminist discourse itself can be very insulting toward men. Whether that counts or is rather excused and justified as only a defensive countering of the violence that the other sex has initiated depends on presuppositions and prejudices. As in any war, each party holds the other to be solely responsible for the conflict. At some point, another more reflective view, one that embraces the perspectives of both belligerents, has to be found or forged in order to avoid mutual total destruction. Group grievances can be transcended into a dimension demanding universal liberation and take on a religious sort of truth.

The expression "woke"—as is politically appropriate to its revindications in terms of race—comes from an originally Afro-American usage connoting awareness of systemic racial discrimination and prejudice. However, in current usage, which is not necessarily mindful of this origin, being "woke" counts, at least nominally, as akin to being "enlightened" or "illuminated." I would go so far as to discern in the background here the tradition of the eighteenth-century "illuminate" ("*illuminés*"), the rationalist "philosophes" of the French *Lumières* as well as the modern thinkers and prophets of the German *Aufklärung*. Modern American democracy, along with German Idealism and the French revolution and republic, were all forged in the afterglow and aftermath of this broad social movement of a presumably progressive modernity. History, despite all its setbacks, was viewed as a gradual process of liberation for all peoples and individuals.

In wokeism, as continuous with the secular Enlightenment tradition, religion tends to be viewed as one of the chains of the past from which progressives liberate themselves. Yet there is another aspect of religions in history whereby they have nurtured and matured the communitarian values needed for constructing organic societies. This is the case with Levinas's ethical philosophy, which has its roots in Jewish community, as can be seen in his Talmudic reflections written in a different voice from his strictly philosophical works.[64]

Of course, the woke idea is that these supposedly disadvantaged groups should share equally in the privileges already accorded automatically to others, but its effectual working is to sacralize certain groups and desacralize or even damn others. Without respect for the holiness of what I have called the non-identical, wokeism tends to engage, instead, in a politics riveted to supposedly hard-edged categorial identity markers and commits to favoring certain identities over others. Certain identities acquire an aura of sanctity while others result in their members being treated virtually as untouchables.

Certain bloggers are openly hostile to the new religion of wokeism, which is seen as sweeping through the world like a tidal wave: "This religion masquerades under the guise of compassion and justice, but underneath is an evil ideology that is incompatible with western values and incongruent with the Christian worldview. ... If left unchecked, this new religion could lead to a complete unravelling of western culture."[65]

Numerous commentators (including Möller, McWhorter, Levet, O'Sullivan, Burchill, Braunstein, Buckner, and more) emphasize how wokeism becomes a religion and reproduces some of the most repressive features of religion as a dogmatic orthodoxy demanding conformity of conscience, as well as of outward action and symbolic gestures of allegiance. Some discern atavistic throwbacks to forms of tribalism characterized by warring between clans and family dynasties as the basis for militant group identities.

Stripped to essentials, in its actual working, and not in what it purports or aims to do, the procedure of wokeism is to point to historical wrongs done by a certain group, generally Western, white, heterosexual males (who do not form a group at all except through the abstractions of social identities), and to judge that group as morally unfit to have a leadership role in society. The solution is to substitute other, innocent groups in their

---

[64] Levinas, *L'au-delà du verset. Lectures et discours Talmudiques* (Paris: Minuit, 1982), trans. Gary Mole as *Beyond the Verse: Talmudic Readings and Lectures* (London: The Athlone Press, 1994).
[65] Max Funk, Wokeism – The New Religion of The West - Converge Media. Accessed 1-22-2023.

stead, or at least to "diversify" leadership roles. The criminal justice system works somewhat this way, by eliminating guilty parties through incarceration if not death sentences, on the assumption that others are good, law-abiding citizens.

But to condemn a whole gender or race for any crime committed by some of its members is a travesty; it approximates crude racism and sexism. To assume that other genders and races having similar power and responsibility will be intrinsically better is to be blinded to actual competences of individuals by a moralizing and almost certainly self-serving myth. Wokeism treats whiteness or maleness or cisgenderedness as unities, as monovalent essences. These labels are then used to enable judgments and assignment of guilt—and that makes their opposites innocent. The irony is that this is exactly how racism works. Hard-core wokeism works in just the way that it objects to in what it attacks: it reproduces its own bogey.[66]

Paradoxically, while wokeism has championed and encouraged "intersectional identities" whereby male and female, black and white, straight and gay, are no longer binaries, or at least not mutually exclusive, it has consolidated the component monovalent identities and intensified attachment to and reckoning by them and, in effect, reinforced their divisiveness. This has been documented in disturbing detail by Joshua Mitchell in *American Awakening* with its analysis of the effectual working of identity politics in the USA.

Certain groups, like white male heterosexuals, may feel that their own core beliefs in equality and the inviolable dignity of all people are being appropriated by new and rising elites and turned against them. While these groups may think of themselves as generally disposed to stand up for the underdog, and many members may in fact be among the least well-off, they now find themselves reproached and attacked for being a privileged group and an oppressor. This provokes some of them to want to defend themselves as a group since other groups, especially now privileged elites, seem to be on the attack against them.

---

[66] John McWhorter's book *Woke Racism: How a New Religion Has Betrayed Black America* effectively brings out this paradox.

I wish to make clear again that my aim is not to blame or vituperate wokeism but to understand it and to affirm what may be right in it. Paradox and contradiction are in the very nature of speech and making sense. Wokeism is very much about making a lucid, irrefutable kind of sense and about making it easy to discriminate between right and wrong. However, this evident sense is always but a surface, and we need to probe beneath it. In the end, we have to understand why we need what we condemn and reject. We have to account for how it always still belongs to us.

The *Tao Te Ching*, Chapter 38, teaches that when the Way (Dao) was lost there was virtue; when virtue was lost there was humaneness; when humaneness was lost there was morality; when morality was lost there was ritual, etc. The wisdom of Taoist philosophy, especially as distilled by the philosophical interpretation of Wang Bi (226–249 CE), emphasizes how intentional virtue undermines itself because it is about its own self-glorification and misses the real goal of virtue, which has to be disinterested. For this purpose, it must even be unconscious of itself.[67] Robert Musil's novel *The Man Without Qualities* (*Der Mann ohne Eigenschaften*, published in three installments in 1930, 1933, and 1943) develops an analogous doctrine whereby making a rule and requirement of morality paradoxically corrupts and perverts it. Wokeism, by requiring public profession of certain principles of social justice as recognizable formulas and mantras ("equality, diversity, inclusion"), forcibly engenders hypocrisy in the same way as institutionalized religions tend to do.

---

[67] See Romain Graziani, *L'usage du vide: essai sur l'intelligence de l'action, de l'Europe à la Chine* (Paris: Gallimard, 2019), 66-77.

13.

Woke Bipolarity: Reified Groups and Absolutized Individuals

While treating enormous, amorphous groups—blacks, women, heterosexuals, or gays—as if they were essential entities with consistent valences and attributes significant in themselves, wokeism at the same time engages in the contrary action of absolutizing isolated individuals. Wokeism, in many connections, practically deifies the individual choice of the single self. In the transgender debate, for instance, which has moved into the limelight after the culture wars of previous decades waged over the literary canon, we have the stubborn position insisting that no one can say that I am a man or a woman just by looking at me and my biology: being male or female or some other gender is my personal choice. This approach absolutizes the subject and its freedom of self-determination even with regard to the self's natural endowments by refusing to recognize or acknowledge any externally conditioning factors.

Woke culture swings wildly between what we can call "racialist" judgment of groups as unities based on abstractions, such as blackness or femaleness or non-binarity, and the reduction to an isolated self with no responsibility or connection to others prior to its own conscious decisions. The latter reduces the self to an empty cipher that arbitrarily determines itself by its own choice or self-will. Hence Joshua Mitchell's diagnosis of wokeism's addiction to "bipolarity." These seemingly opposite extremes of uncompromising individualism and amalgamation into monovalent collectives have in common an absolutization in concrete terms of some value (whether personal identity or a group identity) that can in truth be constituted only by relations. The theological archetype for this transmogrification of value is idolatry: the divine is conflated with some positively identifiable concept or phenomenon and thus becomes idolatrous.

Whether as a reified group or as an absolutized individual, an idol takes on sacred status and becomes inviolable: it is not to be conditioned or compromised by relations or subordinated to anything external or other. The innocent victim, the Lamb of God, is identified with supposedly innocent social identities, while presumably dominant identities become guilty transgressors to be expelled or sacrificed. Whether an individual or the group, the scapegoat serves to create a common aim and consensus among all others. The majority discharge their own guilt by attributing all guilt to one party who is punished by common consent in order to diffuse tension and hostilities among themselves.[68]

We have all done wrong, as Jesus's handling of the scene of the woman taken in adultery poignantly illustrates. But, as Joshua Mitchell argues, "In identity politics, the unrelenting loathing toward the transgressor, the white, heterosexual man, is the precondition of the innocence of everyone else."[69] While the sentiment here is painted with a very broad brush, the function served by these identity markers in the scapegoating mechanism is all too accurately flushed out. We are divided into guilty transgressors and innocent victims on the basis of our social identities. This is empowering politically—at least for some. It becomes possible then to "change things" by changing the identities of those who are in power. Whether that really changes things or only gives the illusion of doing so while actually perpetuating the politics of scapegoating such as racism and sexism have always been based on is another question.

Identity, in certain woke conceptions of it, is supposed to be the absolutely free choice of individuals with godlike powers of self-determination. Individuals invent themselves *ex nihilo* in defiance of anything given as not subject to their will or choice. History, on the other hand, is taken to be hard fact, and there tends to be one indisputable reading of history as oppression in woke perspectives. Wokeism is based

---

[68] This mechanism is constantly at the core of René Girard's work. See particularly *Le bouc émissaire* (Paris: Grasset, 1982), trans. Yvonne Freccero, *The Scapegoat* (Baltimore: The Johns Hopkins University Press, 1989).

[69] Joshua Mitchell, *American Awakening: Identity Politics and Other Afflictions of our Time*, 40.

on an odd mix of asserting objective fact and arbitrary self-determination at the same time. History made up in terms of identity categories is actually an exercise in political manipulation precisely in the facts that it chooses to present and emphasize. No human reparations can ever make up for a sin such as slavery, however heavy the reparations exacted. In Mitchell's view, it has to be forgiven, like all human wrongs, or else we will never get over it and never be able to be frankly decent to one another.

Todd McGowan's analysis in Chapter 5 ("This is Identity") of *Universalism and Identity Politics*, similarly to Mitchell's argument, demonstrates how, when one's politics are based on identity, one is always required to find a new enemy. The logic of identity politics is revealed, explicitly and paradigmatically, by Nazism. Since it must eliminate the victim (Jewish identity) that it requires for its own constitution (German-Aryan identity) as the "chosen people," it undermines itself. For it to succeed is to fail. Nazism eliminates the indispensable condition of its own existence (Jews). Without this victim, it collapses. This is exactly the inverse of the logic of universality: here to fail is to succeed. Only the inevitable and necessary failure of any identity to include all possible identities preserves the openness to all which is constitutive of universality.[70]

In different but complementary terms, Mitchell's analysis of identity as essentially rivalrous in its core suggests why identity politics and the wokeism that it has bequeathed us are doomed to eternal repetition of the scapegoating mechanism. This scenario requires an always new victim. There is no essential guilt in any victim—certainly not in any victimized identity. It is the very nature of identity as differential and invidious, or as based on envy as the very generating source of desire, that produces the presumption of guilt or innocence as effects that are simply inherent in the struggle for power in the polity. Construing identity in this way sets it up to be illuminated by Girard's theory of desire as originally and fundamentally mimetic, even though Girard's thought was articulated a little before the cultural trend baptized as "wokeism" became prominent.

---

[70] Todd McGowan, *Universalism and Identity Politics* (New York: Columbia University Press, 2020), 160.

Part II.

Mimetic Rivalry versus Ordered Diversity

14.

Mimetic Desire and Rivalrous Identities —The Scapegoat Mechanism

Today, in our late modern or postmodern liberal and individualistic culture, we have become witnesses to a total crisis induced by mimetic desire generated by rivalrous competition more than by search for that which is really good for oneself and thus potentially for others, too, in a society and a community positively productive and supportive of all in their pursuit of happiness. Mimetically produced desires aim at the success of individuals relative to—and in rivalry with—others rather than at the fulfillment of all working together in a collaborative fashion. Desire for any type of worldly values, by its imitative nature based on models, as discovered through René Girard's theories, is revealed as inherently rivalrous. Rivalry produces winners and losers. This divide is then intensified to a rift between perpetrators and victims. However, this dialectic can be turned on its head when claims to being a victim become a powerful weapon wielded against adversaries.

The path to power in a culture saturated with wokeism passes by way of declaring oneself the victim of the dominant group in society and identifying oneself with an oppressed minority. All sorts of new identities are invented mimetically by imitation of this model of accession to the power coveted by all. All clamor to be recognized and valorized on grounds of certain specific identity characteristics that so far have allegedly kept them in a subaltern and marginalized position. Rights and recognition are now accorded, or at least claimed, on the basis of particular identity criteria that justify the right to compensatory treatment, which is to be rendered possible by penalizing those who have profited historically from the injustices of the past. In these circumstances, everyone desires and aspires in one way or another to present themselves as victims having rights to preferential treatment—on the basis of their social identities.

The logic of the scapegoat mechanism, which can be verified across cultures ever since human community began, turns on the isolation of a presumable culprit. The one culpable identity in the woke system is that of the cisgender white male, along with certain optional add-ons (Western, Christian, etc.). All other identities are represented as victims of this group alone. Unanimity in designating the guilty party responsible for all the violence that afflicts an entire society is the means of defusing the rivalries among the other groups. They are all in destructive competition, desiring for themselves the legitimacy and privilege that they attribute to the group perceived as dominant. They make this group, on which they have unconsciously modeled their own desire for liberty and power, responsible for all that is wrong in society and history. This enables them to stop fighting with one another. One group alone is blamed for having monopolized power and privilege hitherto.

White cisgender males are not generally considered a minority, but *as an identity group* they can be constituted as one among a great number of other alternative identities of all sorts. This single identity as such can then very well become the victim of an assault of all against one. This group's presumed predominance and superior power destined it for this role, just as, in the anthropology of James Frazer, the kings in archaic cultures become victims sacrificed for the salvation of their communities.[71] In the psychology of the unconscious, murderous revenge can be vented against a construction of identity such as kingship or any other supposedly privileged identity—a phantom image serving in the role of the victim.

At first glance, it seems implausible to us that groups as numerous and as apparently advantaged as men or whites or heterosexuals could suffer victimization in the manner of the poor isolated scapegoat, but by substituting an abstract identity for the complex sociological reality, all men or all whites or all heterosexuals can find themselves somehow represented as one particular identity among numerous others. This identity alone is accused and isolated by all others in order to trigger the type of lynching to which Girard incessantly recurs. He sees in murder of

---

[71] James Frazer, *The Golden Bough: A Study in Comparative Religion* (1890).

the scapegoat the very foundation of human society as revealed universally by anthropology.

The resonances of this lynching at a symbolic level can then cross over from the sphere of the typical and abstract to provoke real consequences for those who share certain identifiable characteristics. Thus a whole class of individuals can find itself affected by the lynching of a single identity type alone deemed to be responsible and guilty among all others and inscribed at the symbolic level in the cultural imaginary of a society. Furthermore, white male cisgendered men themselves can join ranks against their own identity group and attack it in mass, shoring up the unanimity of the attack.

Let me be clear that I do not mean to complain about injustice against men, against whites, against heterosexuals, etc. (even though it does exist), but rather to underline the irony of reinforcing the principle of discrimination in the name of abolishing it. We can admit that, on the whole, "woman," "black," "homosexual," "trans," etc., are vulnerable categories and ones susceptible of being subject to discrimination. This, however, is not a good excuse for becoming blind to, or not wanting to recognize, victims who are (intersectionally) male, white, or heterosexual on the pretext that it cannot be as bad for them as for a woman or for another generally disfavored category—even if that may often be the case. To see injustice as a one-way street defined in terms of privileged and subaltern categories pretends to be an objective analysis of sociological fact but actually contributes mightily to a polarized structuring of society and to invidious construals of its components. Rigid identity politics hypostatize and reify categories, blending out the radical relationality of being human, in which all categories are reciprocally determined. Fundamentally, the blind and constant assignment by wokeism of the role of privileged culprit to a single identity sets in motion a racialist logic and the mechanism of the scapegoat. This is the way, since time immemorial, that human communities have dealt with their endemic violence, but it is based on insidious falsehoods and unconscious self-deceptions that Girard's thinking single-mindedly aims to expose.

Girard describes the astonishing efficacity (at least historically) of the "victimary mechanism," the "mimetic all-against-one," for pacifying communities by purging them of internecine violence. The mechanism consists of passing from a situation of all-against-all to a new configuration of all-against-one. Based on wide-ranging anthropological documentation, Girard explains how the war of "all against all" seeks its resolution without fail in the selective violence of "all against one."

15.

Mimetic Desire Turns Divine Comedy into Human Tragedy

The mimetic desire for identity, for self-affirmation as belonging to a valorized group, undoubtedly motivates the current movements thriving in the general climate of wokeism. One supposes that white cisgendered males possess an identity that is universally respected and puissant in all its relations, and this legitimacy is coveted. One would like to have the same legitimacy for oneself and for one's own identity. However, having a socially defined identity becomes desirable only in and through this type of projection—such an affirmed identity is desired because it is seen to be desired by others. One thinks that those with affirmed, valorized identities are at ease in the world and confident because their identity is recognized, and one desires this same security for oneself. This sort of mimetic generation of desire is based on illusion and perverts our social conduct, as Girard's theories demonstrate with anthropological perspicacity.

Proliferating identities (whether straight, gay, bisexual, trans, queer, or other) do not know what they desire except through imitating others. What is to be desired? All want to affirm their own desire, but all actually imitate others in desiring to affirm themselves and in feeling themselves to be victims whose desire is not recognized as legitimate. Other identities seem to successfully affirm themselves and their desires, and each group desires to achieve this same self-affirmation, but none knows how to assure it except by imitating others. It seems that certain groups' having secured their desire and identity deprive others—those who have a different identity—of theirs. The true object of their desire escapes them if it is not confirmed by others. This mechanism, according to Girard, is not conscious. Nonetheless, the fundamental errancy and arbitrariness of desire, its spawning of variants from a model, has perhaps never before become so conspicuous as now with the multiplication of declared social identities. This becomes evident in a strikingly literal manner in the mushrooming genres of sexual desire with LGBTQI+ . . . At least surreptitiously, the whole host of identities compete among themselves for self-affirmation and recognition of the legitimacy of their desire. None is simply sufficient unto itself, secure in the intrinsic desirability of its own object of desire.

According to Girard's theories, the resolution of this mimetic crisis consistently and almost inevitably takes the form of a single victim's being held responsible for all the violences and aggressions of all throughout a society. The victim designated by all the diverse minorities allied under the rainbow banner of wokeism is punished as the representative of patriarchy or of white privilege. All can agree that this is the source of their own malaise and victimhood. All appetites for violence converge and aim at the destruction of this supposed source of all evil.

The description that Girard gives of the scapegoat phenomenon in general finds a completely convincing instantiation in the explosion of mutually differentiated social identities and their common opposition to the patriarchy or heteronormative identity of the white occidental male. Although Girard writes about the figure of mimetic violence in general, his analysis applies accurately to the current tension catalyzed by wokeism: "This victim therefore effectively replaces all those who opposed each other a little earlier in the thousand scandals that were dispersed here and there and that now are all gathered in a single target" ("Cette victime remplace donc effectivement tous ceux qui s'opposaient les uns aux autres un peu plus tôt dans mille scandales éparpillés çà et là et qui, maintenant, sont tous rassemblés contre une cible unique").[72]

The analysis of sociologist Nathalie Heinich demonstrates how woke ideology gives birth to a war of all against all.[73] She documents how the different minority identities of the rainbow coalition turn against one another: black feminists against white feminists, differentialist feminists against universalist feminists, these latter revendicating justice and rationality rather than communitarianism and sectarianism. Even

---

[72] René Girard, *Je vois Satan tomber comme l'éclair* (Paris : Grasset, 1999), 66.
[73] Nathalie Heinich, *Le wokisme serait-il un totalitarisme?* (Paris: Albin Michel, 2023).

neofeminists find themselves contested now by intersectional feminists. Intersectional identities, as hybrids compounding liabilities, are able to elevate themselves above the suppressed groups that they are made up out of so as to position themselves as the true victims among victims and to understand themselves as victims even of victimized groups. Transgender spokespersons oppose homosexuals as well as heterosexuals.

This scene shows signs of degenerating toward a war of all against all. Heinich concludes: "The alliance of the battles between categories of victimized minorities decomposes by the force of identitarian segmentations into a sordid intestine war of all against all" ("l'alliance des luttes entre catégories de minorités victimisées se décompose, à force de segmentations identitaristes, en une sordide guerre intestine de toutes contre toutes," 27).[74] Let me be clear that I do not intend to adjudge any groups as more fractious than others but simply to admit that all are subject to the same universal mechanisms of human social psychology, including the mimeticism of desire.

Rather than try to suspend or neutralize sexual difference in the interest of universal liberty, the most recent feminists accentuate this difference and condemn and alienate women who do not share their own radical opinions.[75] Similarly, the new, more radical forms of antiracism, now "decolonialist," do not aim to surmount racialized perceptions and practices in society in order to affirm universal republican values and norms. Instead, they make race the center of their revendications and do everything they can to fight against the current republican model of society and its presumable beneficiaries. Some finish by no longer respecting the state of law and promote a regime of the strongest and most violent. Heinich protests: "it seems legitimate to some to deprive a 'dominant white male' of the right to speak, without seeing this as sexist and racist at the same time" ("il paraît normal à certains de priver de parole un 'mâle blanc dominant', sans voir ce que cela peut avoir de sexiste et de raciste à la fois," 38-39). Their immediate objective is to crush the domination of

---

[74] The intense friction between trans and feminism and gay movements is documented also by Douglas Murray in his chapter on "Trans" in *The Madness of Crowds: Gender, Race and Identity* (London: Bloomsbury, 2019).

[75] Bérénice Levet, *Libérons-nous du féminisme* (Paris: Editions de l'Observatoire, 2018).

white cisgendered males rather than to share in a power that would admit no reference to race or sex.

Everything concerning the republic and its egalitarian ideals is rejected as tainted by the white masculine culture against which the new wave of confederated woke minorities wage war. In light of the analyses of Girard, such a focalization on the culpable race and sex would be a manner of masking the rivalry between those who condemn the victim held to be responsible. All are actually rivals for exactly what they reproach the white cisgendered male for possessing—power, prestige, wealth. Behind this consensus about the guilty party are concealed tensions between the rival accusers that are produced by their own mimetically generated desires. These tensions are dissimulated while their own mutual latent violence is unleashed against the victim held to be responsible for having engendered all the violence that plagues the community.

According to Girard, the generation of such reciprocal hostilities is precisely the work accomplished by "Satan" as described in the Bible. In the Gospels, this violence is manifest in the most dramatic manner in the Passion, which Jesus announces in declaring, "the hour of Satan has come" (Luke 22: 53). The role of Satan is to sow discord and violence in the community. Yet the "prince of this world" also uses the mechanism of victimization that attenuates tensions in order to keep the world under his control. Still, pacification each time is short-lived. Thus, the repeated cycle of violence remains governed by the power of Satan. This is all the truer in our modern, or now postmodern, world, with its conditions of accelerated communication and constant social mutation. Today the multiple successive repetitions of the cycle of mimetic violence are telescoped and superimposed on one another such that cause and effect can no longer be clearly perceived and distinguished in their real temporal order.

Girard describes how "Satan" or mimeticism takes control of hysterical crowds exactly in the manner observed by Heinich in certain incidents of violent opposition. The violence is directed even against causes normally considered liberal but represented by lecturers of the wrong race or gender. Judged to be ideologically unacceptable by woke criteria, white male speakers can be silenced and barred or banned from college campuses. Heinich cautions against the "totalitarian" tendencies of wokeism. They are leading not to a totalitarian state but rather to a "totalitarianism of atmosphere" (129-69). The actions of violent masses in public places are possible to the degree that such crowds, like the KKK formerly, feel themselves backed up by the cultural sensibility dominating powerful institutions and notably the judicial system.

16.

The Woke Revolution
and the Risk of Its Betrayal

An ethical and political revolution requiring equal recognition for minorities and for all subaltern groups is far advanced today in Western countries. It is an integral part of the profound self-critique that characterizes and distinguishes the democratic culture of the West in its Judeo-Christian descendance across centuries and millennia. This moral base of wokeism is a leaven of truth that demands a constant purge of our all-too-human tendency to exempt ourselves and protect our own from culpability by projecting it onto others. A necessary and salutary shaking up of complacencies by critical questioning of systematically biased histories of race, class, and gender is currently underway propelled by wokeism. Revisionist woke histories have exposed horrors such as slavery and colonialism (not to mention sexual abuse of children in boarding schools often in the headlines today) with a vivacity seldom reached before. They have the power to convert hearts and transform our humanity in its moral and ethical sensibilities.[76] But this penetrating critique is at risk of being betrayed and coopted into another institutionalized establishment which dissociates humans, raising them against one another and obscuring their complex relations, separating them into guilty and innocent groups as a function of their social identities.

In assigning roles of oppressed and oppressor according to social identities, wokeism judges humans as if from the height of the position of God. However, only the exposition in mutual vulnerability of all human beings to all others can begin to heal the wounds and accumulated mistrust

---

[76] A celebrated author fostering such revisiting of racialized history in America is Ta-Nehisi Coates, author of *Between the World and Me* (New York: One World, 2015).

engendered by a violent history. We have to recognize ourselves, without prejudice, as beholden to one another, each one assuming their part of responsibility, in order to begin to construct a common future. The first step cannot but be to empty oneself of oneself in a movement of kenosis, of self-sacrifice. Required to heal our conflicts in the world is an ethic based on the acceptance of our vulnerability in a hospitable spirit of openness and responsibility to one another. This entails avowing our relativity and radical interdependence. Such mutual recognition and acceptance is prerequisite for erecting organic structures of ordered diversity.

17.

Constructed are Our Identities, not Our Natural Endowments

We are all equal if and only if we avoid assuming divisive identities. You have the same rights as everyone if you are just a person and do not separate yourself from others on some identitarian grounds. Claiming rights specifically for one group or another, typically as victims of one history or another, effects such a separation that alienates us from common human rights. It sets us against one another vying in desire for something that is claimed as a right for women or blacks or LGBTQI, or whatever group, and no longer simply as a common human right. In the Middle Ages, no one was stigmatized as a homosexual. All were equally persons, with the same rights and responsibilities and potentials, at least in theory and from the point of view of religion. There were just some persons who engaged in "sodomy." In accordance with evolving social sensibilities, this activity was redescribed, reevaluated, and exonerated as same-gender sex, but to use it to define a distinct category of identity, personal and social, is already to fall into a divisive politics and will surely generate claims of inequity on one side or the other and in all probability on both. Only having rights that belong to all equally as persons enables us to be free and equal and responsible to all.

The only tenable ethics today is an ethics based on accepting our mutual vulnerability in a hospitable spirit of openness to one another. This approach has perhaps more affinity with a deconstructive attempt such John Caputo's to suspend and surpass ethics than with traditional foundational ethical theories.[77] However, I believe that transcendent or

---

[77] John Caputo, *Against Ethics: Contributions to a Poetics of Obligation with Constant Reference to Deconstruction* (Bloomington: University of Indiana Press, 1993).

absolute foundations for values can and should be recognized, even if their formulation in language is always culturally relative. Cross-cultural discourses can help to relativize all our specific vocabularies and make us see that they are all aiming at something else beyond themselves. Caputo's negative-theological manner of thinking ethics issues from Judeo-Christian thought and culture, with the Bible at its origin and with Derrida as its high priest or prophet. A large number of researchers and thinkers, including Marcel Gauchet, Jean-Luc Nancy, and Tom Holland, also demonstrate this negative-theological derivation in divergent ways.[78]

A deeper, more metaphysical problem that I see behind wokeism (looking at it from a Girardian perspective) is the loss of any sense of transcendent foundations for culture and society. Wokeism belongs to the secularizing movement of modern culture whereby we undertake to remake, on our own strictly human terms, everything that touches our lives. Nothing of our language or even our bodies is to be taken simply as a given. Everything is to be run through an ideological filter and is no longer subject to any criteria outside or above our human free will and arbitrary "choice." The cosmos is recast in the human image. Our own personal "identity" becomes the key—the sovereign key—to the universe.[79]

This dimension of personal identity can certainly be a liberating discovery of a new domain of individual freedom and fulfillment, but it should not be absolutized. Gender distinctions and racial differences become no longer gifts from a Creator, nor are they then grounded in nature or in anything objective or transcendent or in any way "given." Even the natural biological differences between the sexes are treated as an invidious imposition of power by a dominant oppressor gender and therefore as calling to be overturned. Thinking ourselves superior to our biology and setting ourselves up as the masters of nature is an illusion. Our cultural relations, when not grounded in natural difference but rather on

[78] In *A Philosophy of the Unsayable*, chapter 4, I construct a genealogy of negative theology from Neoplatonism to postmodernism.

[79] I develop a reading of Western cultural history as a progressive realization of self-reflexivity, of which the obsession with identity is one outcome, in *Dante's* Paradiso *and the Theological Origins of Modern Thought: Toward a Speculative Philosophy of Self-Reflection* (New York: Routledge, 2021).

ideal or posited sameness or equality, lead us directly into the mimetic crisis of all desiring the same things and thus vying against one another.

To live in this world constituted by human contending for power without grace from outside or "above" and without love of something other than oneself, other than one's own comparative and competitive advantage, is dire poverty, not to say tragedy. Many woke stances seem at first to express an ethical sense of the other and of the claim of the Other, but typically a managerial drive can take this impulse over and make it a token for manipulation within the ambit of boundless appropriation and covetousness, leading inevitably to our perennial human rivalries.

Refusing religion, especially monotheistic religion, and rejecting everything tainted by tradition in a patriarchal society is often required for being deemed "progressive." Rejected wholesale, along with patriarchy, is any form of "hierarchy," but this, too, is a marker of alienation from our human nature and its innate potential. *Hier-archy* is literally "sacred order." Paul describes the body of Christ as an organic whole of hierarchically related parts in I Corinthians 12: 12-27. Nothing in nature or society functions without order and subordination based on differences. If we lose sight of this, we will disintegrate into mobs of rivalrous individuals not even realizing why we are inculpating certain individuals or identities in a masked war of all against all.

18.

Hierarchy is not all Invidious: it is Functional and Forestalls Mimetic Crisis

There is a kind of inevitability of power imposing for its own advantage over those it oppresses only if we accept a view of humans as all pursuing their own interest at the expense of others. This is what modern individualistic society has produced, and wokeism is a characteristic product of this neoliberal society.[80] But such an individual-based society, where all vie to define and valorize their identities against those of others, is not the original template on which humanity is forged. More primevally, the model of an organic society is constituted by differentiated roles and responsibilities. Having more power means having more responsibility for the good of others in this more grounded interpretation of humanity. Relations of power should not be reduced to motivations of seeking only individual advantage rather than devotion to the general good. The discourse of victimization is all based on a vision of warring individuals. This produces conflict no matter who is on top or on the bottom.

We lose, moreover, in this modern abandon of a more traditional model of organic society, our grounding in a nature and destiny beyond our own arbitrary and self-willed whims. Who we really are is lost to vagaries of trying to feel good or at least OK about ourselves. Feeling that is centered simply on the self is bound to be uncomfortable since it isolates the self from everything that confers true meaning and purpose on the lives of individuals through their relations with others. This relatedness to others is a primordial given prior to any of our own choices. Such is the ground

---

[80] A lucid analysis in this vein is Hans-Georg Möller, Reply to Jordan Peterson: Individualism, Wokeism, and Civil Religion - YouTube. Accessed 7-14-2023.

of ethical being in Levinas's thinking. Ethics is more basic than metaphysics or any psychology of selfhood.

It serves useful purposes to have certain qualitatively distinct groups assume the lead and responsibility in particular domains requiring specific competencies, talents, and dispositions. This is also necessary to allow a society to avoid succumbing to generalized mimetic crisis. We need to be educated to desire different things and need to be valorized for different capabilities in order not to become rivals and enemies of one another. These differences sometimes correspond to gender characteristics or to other identity criteria. These are qualities that permit or facilitate authentic and not just imitative engagements of oneself.

For example, the gift of sexual difference is crucial for forming couples and families with a nucleus of complimentary desires that can work together in love rather than in perpetual competition. Such cooperative coupling is certainly not limited to heterosexual pairs, but such couples are endowed with specific given resources for cooperative activity, notably in engendering children. Our language itself recognizes procreation or "engendering" as a gendered activity. The Latin word *generare* means to cause to exist, to generate, and it is linked with the word *genus* for origin or kind. Language is, of course, cultural, but its etymological roots reach to a depth at which nature is not yet clearly distinct and separate from culture.

Erasure of all such given, natural differences is producing the society of generalized mimetic crisis and hostility that we are experiencing more and more brutally every day. These differences are not matters of more or less, of superior or inferior, but of differentiated roles and functions in a shared purpose and common endeavor. Matriarchy has proven every bit as necessary and efficacious in many domains as has patriarchy in others. This is true notably in the education of children. I experienced in my own childhood a widespread pattern where the father serves essentially for providing the household with income while the family is managed and governed, to all effects and purposes, by the mother. Her sovereign will determined all important decisions concerning the life of the family. This division of responsibility, moreover, corresponded to the dispositions and desires of the individuals concerned, at least according to my mother, whose views in any case were more vocal and more vehement. This did not make my father or males in the family feel oppressed but was received gratefully as the offer of a valuable service for all by the party most disposed to deliver it.

Girard's thinking is a monumental warning against forcing or incentivizing all to desire and aspire to exactly the same type and degree of recognition and success. Modern liberal society and its media promote a model of success that tends toward quantitative measures without qualitative differentiation. It all just boils down to money in modern America, where the trend for a certain liberal modernity and for wokeism is set. Cohesive society is disintegrating under wokeist influence by its application of the acid of "democratic" egalitarianism in every respect and at all costs. Commerce and advertising promote lures for ensnaring the desires of all. As all value is reduced to money, qualitative differences cease to matter. Exchange value substitutes for real value and all is measured in purely quantitative terms of dollars and cents. When the watchword "democratic" becomes an ideological marker used to condemn other societies as authoritarian or fascist, it too succumbs to the instrumentalization of every nominal difference in the ideological war of all against all. Societies, too, whether socialist or whatever, need to be respected in their qualitative differences.

We need to get back in touch with who we are qualitatively as women and men with characters and psychological components that are both feminine and masculine rather than comparing ourselves to others quantitatively, as if our worth and value were determined by social ranking or a salary. There are, in many cases, justifiable reasons why certain categories have higher wages and higher expenses than others. Women, notably gay women, have taken over running the university in my own local experience. They have more of the responsibility, more of the work, and earn the higher salaries they receive as department chairs and deans. Not gender equality but human equity is the true goal. Young and old (or senior in service) are also natural criteria determining certain salary differentials, although many complexities enter into the equation: and it cannot be treated simply as an equation. Younger employees may have greater needs than those who have been able to work and save for a sustained period. The elderly, too, may have special needs and justifiable seniority privileges tied to lesser prospects for seeking employment elsewhere and a foreshortened career horizon.

Looking at statistics on differentials in income in relation to racial or gender characteristics assumes that if whites or males are earning more it is because they are white or male and not because of other factors relevant to income that may also correlate to race or gender—like dependents supported or other financial responsibilities or career continuity or performance. Do we assume that all categories should earn equally? There may be rational grounds for preferring individuals of certain races or genders for certain roles and functions, to which greater or lesser monetary compensations pertain. Thomas Sowell, in *Social Justice Fallacies* (2023), dismantles the fixed assumptions about race and gender inequality that have been nurtured by generations of reformers up to current-day woke crusaders.

In any case, these social identity markers should not themselves be used as grounds for making distinctions of merit or desert. Any justifiable differentials should be related to performance and possibly to other functional criteria such as need or whatever is of concern to those who are actually paying salaries or wages or paying for products or services. I believe that women have higher salaries in my own academic department, and I accept that as justified because they have risen to power and have more of the final responsibility, which is a type of work and worry that is incalculable in hours. Historic shifts in gendering of work forces in certain professions such as college teaching and administration have consequences for gender disparities that should not simply or automatically be erased in order to force a superficial gender equality that can be statistically verified.

In my profession and career at the university, especially in languages and literature, women have progressively moved into positions of leadership and power at the heads of departments and schools. I feel grateful to them for taking over control to the extent that they have. At their stage of evolution as a social group, they tend to be, on average, more motivated and better equipped in certain ways, to do this than men. The latter often are in the career for different reasons and are likely to have a different focus: for example, certainly in my case, less pragmatic, more speculative. It was appropriate and served the general interest that individuals of certain genders (especially Lesbian among my own superiors) moved predominantly into the hierarchically superior positions. This was not to my advantage personally; on the contrary, my own career rather suffered as a consequence. But the fact of having people willing to devote themselves to tasks of administering programs and feel rewarded for it as an accomplishment for themselves personally was more important for the institution.

If politics for us is a matter of some group gaining power and dominating others rather than of composing a whole of functionally differentiated members each contributing what is best for the whole, it becomes vicious and invidious. The problem with wokeism is not its aims and ideals. The problem is that it fosters a divisive politics rather than a holistic and harmonious attitude and atmosphere. Looking at history in terms of perpetrators and victims divided up according to group identities is inherently invidious. We need, instead, to analyze how society and humanity lose their wholeness and sense of common purpose. Radically politicized viewpoints are partial and tend to render mutual understanding and respect and even communication among social partners difficult if not impossible. In this age of widespread wokeist activism, as well as of frequent woke bashing, the social climate has become almost intolerably toxic.

The problems of "systemic" racial, gender, and class discrimination need to be recognized. But correcting them will require us to become less, not more, conscious of racial, gender, and class differences. These are differences that are (or should be) no differences before the law of the land and in the tribunal of social justice. They can be culturally significant but should not be grounds for assigning benefits as deserved or as due because of supposed handicaps.

Wokes or woke ideology already hold the preponderance of power in many institutional contexts. Heinich (130-36) demonstrates this for what might be considered the banner year of 2023 in France, which is only a reflex or echo of the situation in the United States. The bitter irony is that this power all too often is being used, as has always been the case with institutional and social power, to augment and consolidate this very power by suppressing or silencing opponents. This is the age-old logic of power. It is hardly new or surprising. But the woke coalition came to power by claiming to defend the rights of the disempowered—much as in the messianic message proclaimed in Christian revelation and in other ethical systems. The woke revolution has not really changed this perennial logic of power but in regrettable ways reasserted and reinforced it.

Revolutions often end in totalitarian regimes, as did the Russian and Chinese revolutions in the 20th century.[81] Decolonialization in African countries sometimes tragically aggravated social oppression, as Frantz Fanon himself recognized in chastising certain indigenous elites corruptly controlling post-independence governments.[82] The woke discourse of race, gender, and class, too, participates in the propagation of violence on the model of mimetic desire cogently outlined by Girard. I have attempted to show that this theory can open some penetrating insights into aspects of the wokeist phenomenon. At stake in the revolution that is now being designated with the perhaps ephemeral label of "wokeism" is the fundamental and enduring issue of universal emancipation for the sake of social justice.

---

[81] On this subject, see Hannah Arendt, *The Origins of Totalitarianism* (New York: Harcourt Brace Jovanovich, 1973).

[82] Frantz Fanon, *Les damnés de la terre* (Paris: Maspero, 1961), trans. Richard Philcox as *The Wretched of the Earth* (New York: Grove Press, 2004), 45-47.

Part III.

Identity versus Universality

19.

Politics of Diversity versus Universal Emancipation

Karl Marx (1818-83) and the world-historical revolution that his thinking brought about proved to be profoundly right and wrong at the same time and in ways prefiguring the ambiguities of wokeism. Marxism was right about the screaming injustice and intolerable human misery produced by industrialization in the age of unregulated and unrestrained capitalism but wrong in producing or justifying systems of violence and totalitarian tyranny in the name of combatting this evil. At least this appears now to be so to our historically enlightened reason in hindsight. It was not always evident at the time, not even to many leading twentieth-century European intellectuals such as Jean-Paul Sartre or Alain Badiou, who supported, for a time, Stalin and Mao, respectively.

The betrayal of the Enlightenment ideal of universality by the current politics of identity is lucidly displayed and analyzed by Todd McGowan in *Universalism and Identity Politics*.[83] McGowan emphasizes that genuine universality can always only be what is lacking in every particular. When particular political systems claim to actually realize the universal, they become oppressive and demonic and typically totalitarian. They impose some particular form of presence and power, identified with certain defined principles and icons—forming an ideology—as if that were truly universal. True universality is never present among the things of the empirical world and cannot be identified with any party or faction in opposition to others. True universality is without identity. Any particular, any defined identity, runs up against its limit and collapses as

---

[83] Todd McGowan, *Universalism and Identity Politics* (New York: Columbia University Press, 2020).

such because of being nothing in itself but only in relation to others. The universal is thus revealed (as already by Hegel's dialectic) to be the negation of any and every particular.[84] Identitarian politics limiting their focus to particular races or genders or classes betray and pervert the necessary universality of the struggle for emancipation.

The difference between a universality that could even in principle be fully achieved and one that remains infinitely open as a project stands behind Todd McGowan's penetrating analysis of how many current versions of identity politics actually betray the universalistic aspiration of the historical Left. The identitarian turn of the modern project of emancipation, by giving up the demand of universality and, instead, promoting particularist identitarian agendas, turns into a repetition of the disastrous totalitarianisms of the twentieth century. The same disaster results from egalitarian revolutions betrayed in this manner by the Bolsheviks in Russia in 1917, by Mao's communism installed in China in 1949, leading to the cultural revolution of 1966-68, and by the Khmer Rouge, with its ethnic cleansing in Cambodia in 1975-79. McGowan comments:

> In the twentieth century, universal emancipation turned into butchery at the moment when the political projects betrayed the universality that animated them. Stalin, Mao, and Pol Pot all believed in the possibility of total belonging. To that end they tried to create societies in which everyone could belong, failing to grasp that universality exists because everyone cannot belong—through the failure of a social order to become all-inclusive. We cannot invent universality as fully realized and present but must discover it in the internal limit that every society confronts. But these murderous projects viewed equality as a value to invent rather [than] as a value to discover. This is the formula for the gulag. (5-6)

Equality that is humanly defined and imposed rather than discovered as an absolute existing already in the nature of things is oppression. McGowan outlines the alternative, which is based on what is lacking from any definable identity, on what does not belong in any falsely defined and apparently realized universal:

---

[84] Another crucial influence on McGowan is Jacques Lacan and his logic of the "not-all" (*pas-tout*). For a rapid orientation to this non-concept, see Franke (2021b) 68-69.

When we root universalist projects in the embrace of lack, they look far different than the purportedly universalist projects that led to the gulag or the killing fields. They do not try to impose a particular idea of equality but instead pay attention to the equality of what doesn't belong. They ask that we treat those who don't belong as the bearers of universal equality rather than trapping them in the dream of total inclusion. (195)

McGowan recognizes that certain movements under the woke banner transcend identity politics can successfully assert universalist claims. Black Lives Matter and Gay Marriage Rights in principle aim at universal emancipation. These specific identities serve as tokens for more generalized struggles. They simply start where violations of equality are most evident and egregious. Still, the inclusion of more and more identities, "coalition building," can never produce true universality. The very nature of universality is to be negatively defined and to remain infinitely open. Any kind of inclusion or belonging is based necessarily on nonbelonging and recognizing exclusions. Only by not demanding that everyone belong can violent, invidious nonbelonging likewise be avoided: "the solidarity organized around a shared absence does not necessitate the nonbelonging of some because it accepts that no one really belongs. We can discover universal solidarity only through what doesn't belong, not through the act of belonging" (186). McGowan explains that in this sense it is what does not belong that is crucial to universality. The universal is revealed as essentially absent and unidentifiable. Concretely, when we are at odds with one another and discover the gap between us, we are translated into the truly universal dimension that we cannot define or circumscribe. This is the truly universal openness that alone can found a non-exclusionary community. It begins by acknowledging this situation of our being beholden to one another.

I take this analysis to be completely aligned with my apophatic ethics based on non-identity. Rather than trying to fit everyone into some identity or other so that all can belong, true universality consists in admitting that non-identity is the truly universal that is shared by all. By developing his own original logic of universality as lack, McGowan effectively criticizes "the particularist politics of representation" and "diversity" that prevail everywhere in wokeist culture (196). He credits the "most forceful attack" on use of such purportedly neutral DEI (diversity, equality, inclusion) terminology that covers over real discrimination, oppression, and exploitation to Karen and Barbara Fields. Their analysis exposes "racecraft" whereby politics of racial inequality actually engender the phenomena that are socially perceived as race.[85] In this perspective, race is produced by racism rather than being an independent, natural ground for it.

This analysis is corroborated by the historical research, punctuated by personal experience and testimony, of Kenan Malik. Malik documents the historical construction of the concept of race and insists on the necessity of its being transcended into a universalist perspective that has been betrayed by contemporary identity politics based on race.[86] Racism is a structure that is produced systematically across societies and their diverse ethnic and socioeconomic compositions. It is produced in contemporary history not least by identity politics. But what is entailed by designating such insidious forms of racism as "systemic," as identity politics does?

[85] Karen E. Fields and Barbara J. Fields, *Racecraft: The Soul of Inequality in American Life* (London: Verso, 2012).
[86] Kenan Malik, *Not So Black and White: A History of Race from White Supremacy to Identity Politics* (London: Hurst, 2023).

20.

"Systemic" Racism as Symptom: The Violence of Gendering Violence

We often hear in our woke-inflected culture about "systemic racism." This phrase has become a kind of battle cry for the social justice constituency. What exactly is in the charge of "systemic"? Those who accuse a society or its institutions of systemic racism presumably are saying that the system is wrong and that they want to change the system. Yet the newly empowered classes that we are calling "wokes" endeavor to exert their own sense of what is right through the power of the system. They have sought and attained empowerment in institutions such as the university and have successfully taken over and imposed woke views in myriad domains ranging from the media to business and government. Wokeism seems, in the end, to be augmenting the subjection of us all to "the system" rather than challenging or attenuating it. Woke practices are now commonly accused of being dictatorial and totalitarian. The title of Heinich's book, literally translated: *Is Wokeism a Totalitarianism?*, succinctly encapsulates this theme as a spreading concern and sounds an alarm.[87]

A similarly solemn warning is issued by Susanne Schröter to defend democratic society from trends currently transmuting it into a "surveillance state" ("Überwachungsstaate") in which the moral code of the politically correct infiltrates and takes over especially the "pre-political

---

[87] A similar alarm is sounded by Mathieu Bock-Côté, *La Révolution racialiste: et autres virus idéologiques* (Paris: Presses de la Cité, 2021). See, further, his videoconference: Qu'est-ce que le wokisme ? Décryptage d'un phénomène mondial (youtube.com).

spheres" of education and culture. [88] Children's books like Pippi Longstocking and comic strips or Cowboy and Indian films are banned or bowdlerized and rewritten so as to avoid alleged offense to protected identity groups. Theatre programs and museum exhibitions and media representations of all types in democratic countries like Germany are regularly subjected to vetting and censure by a culturally woke establishment. Such public venues, as well as high-profile sports events and film festivals, are turned into showplaces for moralizing representations that instruct the public in political positions, including being anti-Russian or anti-Israeli. Participation by those nationalities is banned. The mass media constantly disseminate this moralizing revindication of political positions and prejudices based on group identities that are held up as principles universally right and unquestionable.

There are many measures and mechanisms which censure public and institution-specific discourse by woke standards of political correctness. Heinich reviews examples of strongly muscled forms of censorship in which speakers are shouted down or assaulted and cultural events are canceled because of protests especially by young wokes acting as mobs, often on college campuses (93-127). Cultural institutes have ways of intimidating anyone who would dare to propose a discourse challenging or contesting the consecrated values. Less violently and insidiously, yet still rather intrusively, my computer's spell-check warns me indefatigably as I write that, "This term may imply gender bias." Just the terms "men" and "women" provoke this admonition.

Anything systemic becomes oppressive for unique individuals. We all need to be liberated from systemic racism, but anti-racism, too, which in practice can mean anti-whiteness, has become systemic. It then becomes in its turn a form of censorship, imposing some establishment's prejudice as to what is politically correct. All these filters dehumanize us, as does whatever discourse that sees human individuals as tokens of generic identities. Treating individuals in terms of categories within a system is pernicious, and this is the problem with identity politics which Girard's

---

[88] Susanne Schröter, *Der neue Kulturkampf: Wie eine woke Linke Wissenschaft, Kultur und Gesellschaft bedroht*, 12.

theories enable us to unmask as inevitably invidious, self-deceived forms justifying rivalrous passions of envy.

These distortions accruing to the phenomenon of wokeism force us to face the fact that even the highest ethical ideals and principles can be instrumentalized for all the same old practices of taking advantage of weakness and vulnerability in the interest of enhancing one's own power and prestige. Wokeism is a perfect case study of how saying all the right things and defending moral ideals can be a way of covering over unscrupulous exploitation of a system of values and its principles. The ideal content of our discourses can be performatively contradicted by their actual applications. An ideology that nominally promotes fairness may actually achieve the opposite. In Girard's terms, designating a certain identity as systematically privileged and therefore the culprit makes a certain category of individuals responsible for the violence produced by the system itself. Talk of "systemic racism" should be understood to inculpate the system that produces rivalrous strife, but it is commonly taken to justify putting down one category of participants in the system in favor of others on politically fabricated grounds of moral judgment and condemnation. Such is the scapegoat mechanism. It actually blinds us to the systemic nature of racism by focusing all blame on a certain race and rendering the others innocent by presumption.

One says, "systemic racism" and thus presumes to have a higher angle of vision on the whole system through the realization that, in fact, racism is a system and does not consist simply in isolated individual phenomena. But then there is the further presumption of knowing exactly who the guilty party in this system of oppression is. There is the guilty race and the innocent race, the perpetrators and the victims. Rather than speaking of "systemic racism" one could almost speak of the racism or injustice of the "systemic" as such. This would open the way for Girardian insight into how violence and oppression of victims is produced through mechanisms of mimeticism in society. In fact, the woke outcry against systemic racism is a mimetic production. It entails taking the high ground and claiming to have just the kind of superior right against which it is protesting. By treating specific identities as systemically guilty or innocent, wokeism works and moves within the system of race and gender discrimination rather than challenging it. Such an application of identity does even less for unmasking it as another repetition of the millenary mechanisms of victimization.

We hear constantly today about "the violence of men against women." Women's Studies programs and forums at most universities are one type of amplifier for this discourse that is everywhere to be found also in the media. The evidence of such violence is also macroscopic and omnipresent. However, already this description is compelling because it activates the conviction that we have *identified* the cause of the violence and can now work to root it out. The scapegoat mechanism, belief in having found the culprit, kicks in with just this minimal yet fateful description of the problem as one of *male* violence. We think (justifiably): There must be a masculine culture of violence lurking in the background that causes the tsunami of feminicides and the plague of domestic aggressions and abuse. This masculine aggressive tendency then needs to be identified, arrested, and corrected or destroyed.

Genderizing, even in this seemingly obvious and almost unavoidable way, however, is not quite as innocuous or objective as it may seem. It can defame a whole gender, making men as a group guilty. Yet only individuals are actually guilty of crimes of violence. They may themselves be victims in turn, victims of a toxic "male" culture, for example. One could be even more specific, like Ayaan Hirsi Ali, and identify the violence against women intersectionally as viral in *Muslim* male culture.[89] Still, in the end, responsibility can be assigned only to particular individuals acting with free will. That is the only basis juridically on which someone can be held responsible for violence against women or against anyone else.

At this level of individual responsibility, we are all morally and juridically equal and all, at least formally, capable of free choice. Treating domestic violence as "male" targets a certain gender as guilty and effectively scapegoats it. One protests, but they *are* men. Yes, but is the solution to isolate and punish or stigmatize a gender? Or is that not likely to provoke more violence by men who feel that they are being demeaned

---

[89] Ayaan Hirsi Ali, *Prey: Immigration, Islam, and the Erosion of Women's Rights* (New York: HarperCollins, 2021).

or suppressed *as* men? It may seem that gendering violence ("of men against women") is the only way to get at the roots of the problem, but this method runs the risk of making a certain gender a victim in its turn. Men are made guilty because they are men instead of as individual transgressors. Frequently, one hears that men are complicit by their silence and that it is their fault as men for not taking a stand to denounce violence against women in particular. Is it not comprehensible if some of them feel that dictate as a "micro-aggression"?

Responsibility can and must be assigned to free individuals. Banding together to protest against "male violence" enacts the mechanism of all against one: one guilty party identified by amalgamation as "male" is run out of town or tarred as the guilty party. Symbolically, violent action is taken against the archetypal male aggressor. The energies released are those of stomping out a menace to the community. But psychologically, this is just how scapegoating always works. Blame does have to be assigned to individuals responsible for their acts, but the systemic problems can only be dealt with by refusing to set any part of the community over against any other. Only this refusal can stop the victimization mechanism, with its cycle of violence, and recreate an organic whole in which all are recognized as having their positive part to play.

Certainly, there are reasons why men or why immigrants, for example, are more susceptible on average to becoming violent. These reasons relate to specific vulnerabilities—and also virtues—of these groups. Called for is understanding rather than blaming such differences, along with appropriate preventative measures. Aggressive and passive sides of human behavior need to be fostered to work together. Judging, condemning, and suppressing either pole perpetuates rather than parries violence.

21.

The Enlightenment Heritage
and its Dialectic: The Limits of Knowing

Authentic individual and group identities alike are not things that can be posited or asserted as such. They are constituted by complex relations that escape the abbreviated, ideologized forms of reasoning which have become more and more commonly recognizable as "woke." A certain absolutization of the self as the possessor of rights fails to allow for the fact that every individual's rights and freedom are delimited by the freedom and rights of every other individual. This mutual conditioning is enshrined in Hegel's concept of freedom as reciprocal recognition.[90] Such freedom for "spirit" in the sense of Hegelian *Geist* is achieved socially through a dialectic of mutual self-transformation, not merely by a fiat of self-will. Freedom pertains properly to society, not to individuals freed from social bonds. Only a society that is infinitely open and inclusive can be completely free. Otherwise, it is limited and constrained by its outcasts and enemies.

Broadly speaking, wokeism stands in the trajectory of the Enlightenment for which history is a progressive story of emancipation of all human beings from domination by religion and authoritarian government in the name of affirming autonomous, sovereign individuals. There are ironies in this heritage, however. As Peter Harrison observes, the progressive views of leading Enlightenment thinkers such as Voltaire, Hume, Locke, and Kant, envisaged a natural progress from the putatively inferior, more childish races of Africa, India, Asia, and America to more

---

[90] This much is commonly underlined by contemporary interpreters of Hegel as diverse as John Milbank and Slavoj Žižek and Catherine Malabu. Human spirit is poly-gendered and multi-racial and transcends all class lines.

fully developed, intellectually mature, races of European types.[91] Harrison points out, moreover, that the abolitionist movement in England was spearheaded not by Enlightenment philosophers but by evangelical churches, Methodists, and Quakers. Similarly, the Civil Rights movement in the United States, as led exemplarily by the Reverand Martin Luther King, owed much more to Christian churches than to critical philosophy. These might seem to be oddly conservative sources for the progressive agenda, but radical Enlightenment philosophy, too, is inextricably entangled with various forms of conservatism.

Public intellectuals such as Jordan Peterson and Roger Scruton, among others, have profiled wokeism as a radical leftist movement, but this interpretation is sharply disputed by many like Susan Neiman, who portrays wokeism as a betrayal of leftist ideals.[92] Like Neiman, Hans-Georg Möller ascribes wokeism to a neo-liberal or conservative turn in the politics of the university and of Western, especially American, society in general.[93] This would account for its accentuated concern with race and gender but not class, which is central in Marxist thinking. Wokeism serves the universities for profiling themselves as moral institutions actively engaged in anti-racism and gender equality and inclusion of minorities. Rather than following their vocation to educate in critical thinking, universities have become training grounds for conformity to neo-liberal ideology as key to social acceptance and career success. They have become enterprises serving as supports and pillars of capitalist society. Touting their progressiveness in "diversity" and "inclusion" serves them for promoting their public images. Corporations do the same for purposes of attracting their clientele and for marketing their products.

The Enlightenment sources at the root of wokeism unconsciously intuit, as a basis for ethical action, acquiescence to and conservation of *what is*, at least as a start. Alexander Pope, the poet of eighteenth-century English classicism, put the premise of this approach most succinctly:

[91] Peter Harrison, "Enlightened Racism?" Enlightened racism? - ABC Religion & Ethics Accessed 13/01/2023
[92] Susan Neiman, *Left is not Woke* (Cambridge: Polity, 2023).
[93] Reply to Jordan Peterson: Individualism, Wokeism, and Civil Religion - YouTube. Accessed 7-14-2023.

"whatever is is right" ("Essay on Man").[94] However, we do best to hear this in a metaphysical register such as Hegel expressed in his *Philosophy of Right* in the context of his general metaphysical philosophy of the whole and of the progressive evolution of history: "whatever is reasonable becomes real, and the real becomes reasonable" ("Was vernünftig ist, wird wirklich und das Wirkliche wird vernünftig").[95]

A version of this dynamic and evolving realism, based on analysis of *what is* in its revolutionary becoming, results in accepting whatever is as the necessary starting point for all interventions and attempts at amelioration. In a certain sense, whatever *is* has to be accepted, and our judgments on it—presuming that it ought not to be—are irrelevant. Metaphysically speaking, that anything at all exists is a sheer gift and simply to be gratefully accepted prior to all evaluations. Nevertheless, everything that is represents only a starting point for change and a stimulus for our active and critical engagement. That said, neither do we know a priori or possess the objective or ideal that could or should guide us in fostering that change. The universal good for society and the world is not a given. We cannot simply posit it based on our own preferences. If it is to be truly universal, it can only be sought out by an effort coordinated with and considering all concerned.

Existence itself is ontologically prior to our judgments about it. Nietzsche, as a thinker of tragedy, challenged our presumption to dare to judge by our own lights whether anything deserves to exist or not. While this attitude does not mean *simply* accepting everything as it is, it does mean starting from that acceptance as the right way to find our proper role and cues for acting within the situation in which we find ourselves. We ought not just to posit our own subjective feeling of what is right or wrong as the standard and demand that everyone else conform. We have to open

---

[94] Cf. Sean D. Moore, "'Whatever Is, Is Right': The Redwood Library and the Reception of Pope's Poetry in Colonial Rhode Island," *Slavery and the Making of Early American Libraries: British Literature, Political Thought, and the Transatlantic Book Trade, 1731-1814* (Oxford, 2019; online edn, Oxford Academic, 17 Apr. 2019), https://doi.org/10.1093/oso/9780198836377.003.0002, accessed 13 Jan. 2023.
[95] Georg Wilhelm Friedrich Hegel, *Die Philosophie des Rechts. Vorlesung von 1821/22* (Frankfurt a.M.: Suhrkamp Verlag 2005). Hegel reiterates this premise of his thinking in the Preface to the *Philosophy of History* (1837).

ourselves to a collective search and determination in which we are at least as conditioned by others as they are by our ideas of what is right. This embrace of mutuality, this renunciation of unilateralism, comes with the rigorous demand of universality.[96]

The social justice agenda based on identity politics believes in imposing what it takes to be its own just principles rather than relativizing its own values in discovering together with other and even opposed factions and parties the values that can be shared universally. It compares equality of outcomes among different social identity categories as the measuring stick of justice and is willing to brand as immoral and retrograde whoever is not willing to actively apply this standard.

This unself-critical type of wokeism claims a moral power with rights to revolutionize society and redistribute wealth across the globe. It looks away from what individuals themselves do in order, instead, to claim compensation based on nationality or race or genderized criteria from others for wrongs committed historically. A constant redistribution of wealth is certainly necessary, but can this be controlled and regulated by racial, gender, and class criteria and be directed by human beings' judgments as to who deserves what? Can humans calculate and create a total system assigning each their own, or is that usurping a task fit only for a god?

In the *Inferno*, Dante envisions the goddess *Fortuna* with her constantly turning Wheel serving as a handmaid of God redistributing goods in arbitrary, or at least in humanly incalculable, ways. Fortune constantly mutates so as to foil all human attachment to worldly goods and benefits (VII.73-86). As this image suggests, we can only build on what is already given to us. We play out the hand we are dealt. Metaphysically, this means that we can shape our existence, but we cannot create it in a theological sense *ex nihilo*. It follows that we cannot sit in judgment over existence as a whole but can only assess our part in making and influencing

---

[96] I have taken this approach to universality as a loadstar ever since *Poetry and Apocalypse: Theological Disclosures of Poetic Language* (Stanford: Stanford University Press: 2009), with its "Critical Negative Theology of Poetic Language," particularly "Being at the Mercy of Others," 3-8, and "Negative Capabilities for Peace," 83-96. I expound this topic in *On the Universality of What Is Not: The Apophatic Turn in Critical Thinking* (2020).

what it is (not *that* it is in the first place). We can evaluate certain aspects of *what is* in order to fashion it into what they *could* be or *ought* to become.

Who could judge from a perspective taking everyone's grievances and constraints and conditions into account without presuming to play God? Any human divisions of humanity into the clean and the unclean, the innocent and the guilty, are steered by self-deceived political agendas and thus participate in the continuing fight against others, which often means wishing vindictively to inflict harm on them as some kind of compensation for the harm one esteems one has suffered in the past at their hands. Are these judgments not always partial? Is not any human pretention to total vision capable of assigning each their just reward or condign punishment folly? If the criteria are opened to question—as they must be—then sweeping, blanket change by fiat becomes impossible because there are always questions and objections. Total conformity can only be coerced.

What many have observed in recent decades is that these so-called "progressive" judgements harden into a "liberal orthodoxy" that becomes coercive just like dogmatic religion. They are articles of belief and are enforced by the power of opinion and sometimes even by law. It is not possible, or at least not correct, to disagree or call them into question.[97] Former congresswoman from Hawaii, Tulsi Gabbard, left the democratic party because she felt that its wokeism was imposed with coercive power and punished anyone who expressed an honest opinion that diverged from party lines.[98]

Africa Brooke, in her open letter "Why I am leaving the Cult of Wokeness," describes in detail and with disarming honesty just this sort of experience and how it was making her and her whole black community sick.[99] Brooke protests that "This absolutist, authoritarian world is being fiercely crafted under the guise of 'social justice,' and I want no parts in this." She finds that, as a young, black, progressive women, she was

---

[97] Anne-Sophie Chazaud, *Liberté d'inexpression: nouvelles formes de la censure contemporaine* (Paris: L'Artilleur, 2019) elaborates in detail on this situation in our current social milieus.
[98] 2020 presidential candidate Tulsi Gabbard is leaving the Democratic Party: NPR. Accessed 7-4-2023.
[99] An open letter: why I'm leaving the cult of wokeness by Africa Brooke (ckarchive.com). Accessed 7-31-2023.

expected and was even being "forced to comply with ideologies and practices that don't make sense to me" and that egregiously misrepresent and misuse her actual experience.[100]

Certain tenets are enshrined as unassailable, and to oppose or deny them is to risk tarring oneself as a "negationist" and in any case as retrograde and immoral. Certain views are imposed forcibly on all, and differing opinions are not allowed or, at least, not respected. Any ideology that takes itself for true and wishes to exert power to impose its way of being and ordering the world is liable to fall into the self-righteous delusions that are clearly manifest in many forms of wokeism. Atrocities are justified by the supposedly just denouement envisaged within such a logic in which the end justifies the means.

---

[100] See further Leaving the Cult of Wokeness with Jordan Peterson | Africa Brooke - MP Podcast #120 - YouTube. Accessed 7-31-2023.

22.

Rectification of History
Along Lines of Identity

Among the irrecusable verities of woke religion is that the West has robbed the rest of the world through colonialism and other oppression and should pay indemnities for the wrongs it has committed throughout history. Imagine if, furthermore, other animal species, or the earth or forests, should have to be granted reparations by humanity for centuries and millennia of uncontrolled, uncompensated exploitation.[101] This fact, too, of the unscrupulous, forced exploitation of all other beings by human beings is glaring. It is only a matter of what categories of others we are willing to recognize. And here political choices, even among sympathizers with the woke cause, will be various.

The overall picture may be evident and undeniable as to the massive injustices committed, but to reason abstractly in identity categories and draw consequences in generic terms can nevertheless hardly help but be invidious. It can encourage scurrying for entitlements and claims against others rather than self-reliance and concentration on dedicating one's own effort and energies to constructively building one's own life in conjunction with one's communities. Generic judgments depend on our *pre*-judgments, our prejudices, concerning the categories in question based on our previous life experience, and the latter can never be gathered into a conclusively reasoned judgment with exhaustive and explicit justification. Our judgments are formed and reformed in the midst of our living and are, therefore, always partial and provisional. Monolithic moral judgments in identitarian terms turn ethics into politics and lead to pogroms.

---

[101] Corine Pelluchon, *Manifeste animaliste: Politiser la cause animale* (Paris: Alma, 2017) thinks in this direction.

Politically considered, would it ever be possible to claim reparations for massacres of ancestors by Indian raids? The suggestion is sacrilegious, but it is worth pondering why. Is it not because the whites who were killed are now taken to be prosperous and their race is stained as the aggressor while the Indians are seen as the losers of history, finding themselves in an impotent and often abject condition? The pre-history of how the Indians once occupied the land is not addressed and any possible violence before the violence brought on the scene by settlers of European origin is not even imagined. My point is that the history we choose to consider is always selective. We can only make punctual rectifications based on limited knowledge and partial perspectives. We need to avoid confusing our judgments with divine judgment that would require total cognizance. Identity categories, because of their abstractness, entail uninflected judgments of responsibility or entitlement that seem to rectify whole macro-histories but operate prejudicially as applied to particular cases.

Wokeism is aligned with restitutions and rectifications that open a thrilling new chapter in the never-ending struggle to restore justice on earth—only fantasizing, of course, that the world ever was just. We cannot but warm and resonate to this cause. Yet the cause needs to guard itself in every way from becoming a self-righteous pretext for substituting one's own purportedly better morality for that of others, one's antagonists, because just that kind of pretention to a moral high ground is behind most all the injustices of history that need to be admitted if they are ever to result in any kind of reconciliation.

I realize that for some I am undoubtedly tarnishing my own image by not unqualifiedly endorsing the so-called progressive agenda as unequivocally the right side. My purpose is not to retain a spotless image but to sacrifice my own claim to innocence for a realistic understanding of the opaque nature of conflict and tension between self and other in society in the hope that mutual recognition may be fostered. Simple recognition of the other as other, as not at our disposal to play the part we wish to assign them, needs to precede any of our judgments concerning them. Wokeism, as an ism, has become a politics of the image committed to taking sides and condemning those on the other side. But precisely this is what has proved to be poisonous in contemporary politics, which no longer function to criticize and compare in common discernment but to shame and blame others from an inflexible position of presumed superiority and righteousness. As long as each side claims to be purely right and innocent, productive dialogue is hardly possible.

23.

Being One's Incommensurable
Self and Assuming Blame

My fundamental reservation concerning wokeism, then, has to do with its grounding in identity politics and its treating identity abstractly in essentialist terms rather than as relational and dialectical. More often than not, what makes us free and equal is not jockeying for power among social determinations but much more our evasion of them, our making them not count, our becoming color and gender blind, or rather neutral, in order to focus instead on the performances and capabilities of individuals. Wokeism's identity politics are about redistributing power and wealth among rather arbitrarily defined races and genders. This kind of sectorial or oppositional identification, I feel, in any case, as an enslavement. Only by *not* defining our identities in social terms and by treating these categorizations as indifferent—or as equally valid and enriching cultural backgrounds—are we free to be ourselves. These identificatory labels are socially constructed identities that constrain our necessarily inconclusive efforts to delineate our true and authentic being and potential for developing freely. They confine us to being equal and identical with others as amalgamated into groups rather than freeing us to be our own incommensurable selves. We are all truly equal and free only in being absolutely incommensurable.[102]

Once we are free of identity categories brandished as if they were inescapable fates assigning us our place among either the guilty or the

---

[102] I am extending my critique of identity politics argued in "A Negative Theological Critique of Postmodern Identity Politics," *Religions* 10/488 (2019): 1-15, and taken up again in *On the Universality of What is Not: The Apophatic Turn in Critical Theory* (2020), 291-314, chapter 11: "Postmodern Identity Politics and the Social Tyranny of the Definable."

innocent, we are free to redeploy our colorful and richly historied heritages as women or men, black, white, yellow, or brown, queer or straight or gay or whatever, and use them creatively to discover and invent ourselves and disclose ourselves to others. [103] Religious or cultural backgrounds, experiences of belonging to national, ethnic, or other social communities, when appropriated in personal ways by individuals, can immensely enrich the unique personalities that we become—but only when these identities stand as resources for creative use in reflecting facets of our unique personalities and the relations and influences that make us up rather than assigning us fixed valences in a static social taxonomy. If they are not absolutized and polarized and so set into conflict with one another, differentiated identities can be an enhancement for each individual and for humanity as a whole.

Only by being one's own unique self is one free and equal with everyone else striving in their turn to be fully themselves in relation to others. Becoming entrenched in our social identities divides us from others. This kind of social self-consciousness is also highly susceptible to veering into narcissism. A new generation of individuals with diversity markers are being trained, or at least encouraged and induced, to feel themselves "unapologetically me." [104] This seems right, at one level. Why should anyone feel that they need to apologize for who they are? Yet personally, and I am not alone, I feel ashamed of all of my social identities—white, male, straight—undoubtedly because of the vaguely woke culture *avant la lettre* in which I grew up and was educated. These identities were blamed for the worst atrocities and were made guilty of the whole history of oppression from colonialism and cutthroat capitalism to slavery and race and gender discrimination, Klu Klux Klan lynchings and the rest.

I feel I have to apologize for being me in every respect of my social identities. Only by not allowing myself to be reduced to those identities

---

[103] Exemplary here is Rachel Khan, *Racée* (Paris: Alpha/Humensis, 2021), drawing on all her diverse ethnic, religious, and national backgrounds and invoking Romain Gary as guiding light, notably his *Chien blanc* (Paris: Gallimard, 1970).

[104] This phrase is taken from a CIA recruitment video designed to whitewash the agency well-known for such dubious and immoral activities as torture and political assassinations. cia unapologetically me - Recherche Google. Accessed 7-4-2023. See analysis by Hans-Georg Möller: Wokeism - YouTube. Accessed 7-4-2023.

and retaining a more fundamental sense of my non-identity as a free and responsible person am I able to affirm and sustain a will to be me at all. Theodor Adorno's thinking of non-identity, or the non-identical ("das nicht-Identische"), offers resources for further elucidation of the philosophical grounding for my transversal thinking through and engagement with wokeism.[105] I invoke Adorno alongside Levinas as the thinker of infinite obligation to the other. Both of these thinkers of alterity furnish elements for thinking philosophically the notion of kenosis, or self-emptying, modeled by Christ in the Scriptures. Christ's self-humbling even unto death on the cross (Philippians 2: 5-11) to expiate the sins of all represents a radical alternative to blaming and shaming others. Such an act indicates a way to interrupt otherwise fatal cycles of retaliation.

---

[105] Theodor Adorno theorizes the non-identical, among other places, in *Negative Dialektik* (Frankfurt a.M.: Suhrkamp, 1966). I interpret his contribution to what I call "apophatic thinking" in *On What Cannot Be Said*, vol. 2, 260-70.

24.

Personal Testimony of Shame —And Moving Beyond

Since childhood, I have internalized constant cultural messages that have made me loath my own given social identities. I felt that I belong to the guilty and violent sex, the uncaring and egotistical gender, the oppressive, suprematist race, and the arrogant and irresponsible nationality. Personally, I found myself ashamed to be American. This has been the case ever since my first sojourns in Europe in the 1980s while the open wound of the Viet Nam War was still rankling in memory—no less than nefarious CIA operations in Chile and elsewhere in South and Central America, of which the European left, unlike the American public, was acutely aware and outraged. I have sought and acquired another citizenship (French) and have immersed myself passionately in the study of foreign cultures and religions. My social network is constructed predominantly on the basis of non-English-speaking Europeans, Latinos, Chinese, Muslims, and indigenous communities. It seems I have even become ambiguously gay in my tastes and preferences in clothing, manners, etc. This is unintentional on my part, but I am made conscious of it through the observations of others.

I must say that I feel torn asunder by the ideological battle and culture wars that wokeism provokes and sustains—to such a degree that I was seriously contemplating, as I wrote my initial lecture on wokeism, whether my logical conclusion should not be to leave the university and the academic profession altogether. This ambience, with the constant pressure of accusation against white-male-hetero-Occidental humans, has broken down my own self-respect. I find myself inhabited by shame on account of the social identities that fall to my lot. Or perhaps the shame comes from what I sense as the indignity of treating humanity in such invidious categories at all—assigning victim roles and presumption of blame based on belonging to generic social groups. These are the messages I unconsciously imbibed as a boy—parallel to the cultural conditioning to which girls are subjected, as feminist research (notably Carol Gilligan's) has so abundantly documented and displayed. Maybe the wrongs of history are now being rectified. It is hard to find an external position from which to judge that. My gut feeling is that we are also in many ways spiraling deeper into ideological divisiveness and violence.

When I was a child, I was taught by my parents and teachers that it was my duty as a boy to concede a certain priority to girls after the motto "ladies first." This was demanded of me as a kind of nobility to qualify as a "gentleman." As I pursued my more proper schooling all the way through the educational system, the same sort of concession has been demanded, yet no longer through an appeal to my innate sense of kindness and nobility but rather as a matter of guilt and of entitlement due to the other, the historically wronged, gender. Women have been cheated and oppressed throughout history by my gender and its high-handed injustice towards all others. I have stood throughout my adult life under the accusation of belonging to the guilty side of every identitarian dichotomy. All that I might do would amount to only a small measure of reparation for the untold wrongs which have been inflicted on others by my kind and purportedly for my advantage since time immemorial. The same guilt applies to me for my race and socioeconomic class as for my gender and sexual orientation.

If I say I find it regrettable that humans are treated according to these classifiers, I receive the retort: now that *I* am being typed racially and sexually, I find it uncomfortable and object. I am told that it is high time that I suffer what women and non-whites and other innocent victims have suffered for centuries and millennia. Finally, the stigmatization is landing where it is well-deserved—with the truly guilty gender and race responsible for all of these atrocious histories of oppression.

This reproof seems prima facie valid since the assumption is that there is one dominant race and gender, but a lot is ignored in such monovalent, grievance-driven versions of history. Relations of domination are almost never completely unilateral or monopolized exclusively by one race or gender. They are multi-layered and ambiguous and can even prove reversible—as with the trade of white Christian males as slaves in the Mediterranean centered around Algiers during the early modern period. The usual one-sided accounts also ignore all the equivocations of "domination" taken uniquely as privilege and erased as obligation and even as bearing the duty of self-sacrifice for the benefit and preservation of others. The duty to serve as soldiers in war is one example, traditionally demanded predominantly of males.

A word like "domination" is a brilliantly obscurantist invention that focuses all sorts of disparate phenomenon around a single, intelligible sense. This illustrates the great resource and also deceptive power of language. It enables us, ironically, to *dominate* the world. But like every abstraction, such a concept, however powerful, erases untold ambiguity and complexity. The very genius of language also makes it our pitfall. We have to learn to use these powerful abstractions without being duped by them.

Every victim story tends to absolutize and monopolize evil as all directed against an aggrieved party. These narratives can easily become narcissistic.[106] This sort of interpretive excess is characteristic of almost any totalizing narrative, which is what the social justice narrative has become. In contemporary America, it has become the dominant meta-narrative in universities, as well as in corporations, as is shown especially by their advertising. The same narrative dominates in government agencies and throughout the social media that have become such powerful means of communication in our time. (At least this was the situation up to Donald Trump's second presidential mandate now spearheaded by an aggressive attempt at its reversal.) Hence Nathalie Heinich warns against the "totalitarian" tendencies of wokeism, which result not in a totalitarian state but in an atmosphere of totalitarianism ("totalitarisme d'atmosphère").[107] Such leanings have provoked the often vehement, sometimes even violent, backlash against wokeism.

---

[106] Bérénice Levet, *Le Courage de la dissidence: L'esprit français contre le wokisme* (Paris: L'Observatoire, 2022), 30, 68-69 launches a sharply focused attack. A broad and prescient analysis is Christopher Lasch, Th*e Culture of Narcissism* (New York: Norton, 1979).
[107] Nathalie Heinich, *Le wokisme serait-il un totalitarisme ?*, 129-69.

Wokeism's thoroughgoing penetration and control of US institutions is outlined by Rod Dreher as the left's "colonization of every institution of civil society." Dreher has fled the USA to Viktor Orbán's Hungary in order to continue a career as a writer with a right to free speech in a "normal" country, as he puts it.[108] The country's relative homogeneity consisting of over eighty percent ethnic Hungarians (Magyar) enables it to maintain a certain coherence and stability that then allows in turn for traditional differentiations among individuals along functional lines. Or so Dreher esteems. Individuals are not required to reinvent themselves *ex nihilo* with no natural or inherited basis to go on.

In our current cultural climate in most Western, highly woke-influenced societies, every differentiation of roles is bound to be felt to be invidious. Someone always feels that they are cheated by being the "other" gender or the "other" race. However, legislating indifferentiation of social roles triggers what René Girard terms a mimetic crisis (as spelled out in Part II). All individuals of whatever type become competitors for exactly the same desired objects or distinctions rather than each attaining their own different goals in a mutually complimentary fashion. If men and women are not differentiated in terms of their function, nor even in terms of their nature, they are bound to become rivals with each other rather than partners aiming at a common, symbiotic fulfilment comprising different objectives and attainments for each.

We are living today in an acute crisis of total self-determination—and therewith of over-determination or indetermination. If we determine everything completely for ourselves, we lose entirely the orientation and meaning or sense of our existence. Only by accepting some things as given are we saved from having absolutely everything subject to rivalrous acquisition and to contradictory claims and revindications destined to degenerate into poisonous bickering among competing opponents. We have to be able, at least in part, to discover and accept our nature and destiny—rather than having to arbitrarily decide them ourselves—in order to maintain a healthy equilibrium and work constructively toward self-realization within a supportive framework and in common cause with

---

[108] The Exact Formula That Helped Hungary Beat 'Wokeness' | Rod Dreher | INTERNATIONAL | Rubin Report - YouTube. Accessed 7-14-2023.

others. If not, we have nothing to build on as a foundation that is not itself already undermined by having no stable ground. Paradoxically, our primary or premier self-determination has to be a self-surrender to what is given to us and gives us our foundation. This necessary fact of the givenness of our being is enshrined, for example, in the biblical doctrine of Creation. It is contemplated metaphysically in the classic question: Why there is something rather than nothing? This question was famously raised by Gottfried Wilhelm Leibniz ("Principles of Nature and Grace," 1714) and is treated as the fundamental question of metaphysics by Martin Heidegger ("What is Metaphysics?" 1929).

We exist not purely by and of our own will. Transgender activists who say "Only I know who I am" could perhaps learn something from twentieth-century philosophers, such as Ludwig Wittgenstein, who demonstrate that we cannot know anything for ourselves alone but only in the context of a community that establishes the meaning of language—and therewith also of thought—inter-subjectively.[109] We learn who we are from others and their reactions to us more than by doubling down narcissistically on the definition or image that we wish to hold of ourselves. That does not mean that trans people should not have the right to decide who they want to be. It is simply to recognize that this is a highly social affair—as indeed the trans movement implicitly acknowledges by its publicly displayed determination to gain legal and social recognition: social identities are all about how one is seen by others. Parading pride risks reduction to vulgar narcissism, which is a reason why some manifestations are provoking all types of outraged criticism from females and males, straight and gay, left and right.[110]

The groundlessness of current debate, resulting in mutually recriminatory virulence, is due to our having evacuated our own cultural heritage. Not everything in history is just or right, and many rectifications and restitutions are certainly in order. But the wholesale condemnation of a culture because it does not meet the standards of political correctness set

---

[109] Wittgenstein works this thesis out in proving that there is no private language in *Philosophical Investigations* Part I, paragraphs 243-314.
[110] What is the point of Pride? Douglas Murray & Julie Bindel – The View from 22 | Spectator TV (youtube.com). Accessed 1-5-2025.

up by those currently in positions enabling them to set these standards is stifling. We are better advised to accept ourselves and love our heritage, even while acknowledging its wrongs and imperfections. Placing everything in question is what this sacred tradition itself has taught us to do.[111] Arrogating to ourselves a prerogative of unappealable judgment is the assertion of the old power-grabbing autocratic greed that we have been constantly warned against—if we have receptively cultivated the knowledge offered to us from the past experience of untold generations.

---

[111] Something of this style of apophaticism is captured in original terms by my former student David Dark in *The Sacredness of Questioning Everything* (Grand Rapids: Zondervan, 2009).

25.

Historical Revisionism: Containing Hate and Hypocrisy

The question of our attitude regarding wokeism involves the enormous issue of what stance to adopt in relation to the revisionary re-writing of history that is currently underway in our society. Particularly the histories of well-known and not so well-known colonialisms and genocides have been subjected to searching and contradictory revisions. This is a necessary discussion and debate but one that also risks re-igniting burning resentments that can threaten to destroy a society and its much-needed cultural cohesion. Rather than focusing on condemning and alienating whatever is abhorrent to us—and ascribing it to those social categories and opponents whom we hold to be responsible for it—we should concentrate on understanding how such uncomfortable legacies nevertheless belong to us as our past and remain latently violent within us at present.

We all owe a debt of gratitude to wokeism for pointing us toward the moral challenges that we face. It is right to rectify obvious wrongs of the past and to restore, where possible, what belongs to those who have been dispossessed. These are noble goals and actions that should belong, as a joint effort, to all who are moved to pursue and achieve them, not excluding whites, men, or heteronormatives. These latter groups—if they must be amalgamated into groups—have also done some things to advance humanity that also deserve to be publicly recognized. More exactly, not groups but individuals belonging to these groups deserve recognition for outstanding achievements. Such achievement is not really a matter of the group, but wokeist perspectives tend to make that primary in determining what is to be recognized or not. No group can be treated only in terms of their crimes and not their accomplishments without creating resentment, especially when other groups are treated as only innocent and virtuous victims. In fact, the sources of wokeism are to be found in the exacting critical spirit so unflinchingly developed by innumerable Western thinkers generally strongly influenced by Judeo-Christian culture.

When I am expected to turn against white Western straight men in order to proclaim myself one of the *good* white Western straight men who denounce this group and its crimes, I cannot help but feel this as a blatant hypocrisy. By enacting such a denunciation, I raise my own self-definition above what I have been given to be. I pretend to be better by my intentions than others with whom I share socially identifiable characteristics. And I thereby reinforce the social condemnation of a certain group as guilty. I condemn them further as guilty of not owning up to their guilt, like me. By redeeming myself individually, I rubber stamp the stigma attaching to the collective identity to which I belong but from which I distance myself in word. I become one of the "elect" in the woke religion discerned by John McWhorter.

I do not want to use identities and their labels as weapons to attack others or as instruments of power or of pride for self-promotion. I want to let them become powerless in themselves and, instead, markers only of vulnerability. We are all vulnerable and all, under whichever of our identity tags, beholden to others and even infinitely obligated to them in Levinasian terms. Wokeism forces all of us to face the extreme moral challenges that our history and our privileges entail, but these are moral claims to which each individual person needs to respond in ways respectful of the incalculable differences of any real person's concrete life.

Species of all types and climes constantly colonize. Only humans moralize about it. This moralizing, too, exerts a will to power. Often it wills to colonize in its turn, aiming to make all the world submit to its own universal moral judgments. Nominally dedicated to defending the powerless, wokeism has become a well-nigh incontestable power in our universities and corporations and governments. In certain of its incarnations, it brooks no dissension or disagreement. Use of power to dominate and degrade others is a constant of history and perhaps as close as we can come to defining evil universally. Any identity category whatever—man or woman, slave or free, fundamentalist or liberal, Catholic or Protestant, Tutsi or Hutu—can be used by one group as an excuse to subdue and destroy another over which it has the power to exercise its superior force.

26.

Rectification of History and Cancel Culture

That certain genders or races or classes should be protagonists for certain aspects and periods of history and take the lead over others is not automatically reprehensible or necessarily oppression. We are not all equal in our capabilities and predispositions. Race, gender, or class can correlate with differentials in competence, not universally, but in complex, delimited, and situated respects. When I look at the French national soccer team, I am led to suspect that some non-white ethnicities may have a leg up in playing soccer. Is it wrong that soccer players on the French national squad are almost all non-whites of North African heritage and in this respect not proportionately representative of the demographics of the nation? These players have the competence and talent required. Perhaps they are also fit by physical or cultural affinity to play well together. Identifications such as that of the nation with the "French" team is a choice that is not dictated by ethnicity. It can be motivated by the desire to support and root for a winning team. This example suggests how natural characteristics remain decisive even when their cultural appropriation is steered by willful choice and passion.

Inclusion and diversity are relative, like all other humanly defined values. Abstracted from actual ability and natural fitness, they are not necessarily what is most salutary and useful in every historical moment or in every respect. I have experienced in my own career that the preponderance of women and nonbinaries in roles of department chair and deans and heads of schools has been effective for allowing leaders to work together on an agenda suited to a peculiar moment in history. Any group has its biases and particular character. They typically exclude and alienate their opposites and are not truly inclusive or thoroughly diverse from the moment that they articulate and define themselves inevitably in some specific, partial, exclusionary language. Indeed, the differential logic of language is per se oppositional. This principle is best demonstrated by Saussurian linguistics after the motto: "In language there are only differences, *without positive terms*" ("dans la langue il n'y a que des différences, *sans termes positifs*").[112]

There is in these disproportions and in the articulations of policy that they produce a factor of appropriation, but it can be by mutual consent of concerned parties and in the general interest. If women are no longer satisfied to stay home in war time but want to take part directly in the horror of the fighting, change is warranted, and the image of the warrior will evolve accordingly to accommodate feminine versions. But that does not mean that it is an egregious injustice that it has not always been that way. Technology has so profoundly altered the capabilities demanded of humans that the distribution of gender roles to be played by the sexes no longer has the same rationale or grounding that it once had. Of course, even in the ancient world, the figure of the feminine warrior, the Amazon, was a formidable reminder of a certain arbitrariness about human customs and conventions, which can be reversed.

Restoring, or perhaps rather constructing, the history of women is a great achievement of feminist historiography. But if done in a militant spirit of crushing the scoundrel men who have for centuries and millennia denied women their rightful place, it runs the risk of making bad guys out of a whole gender. Then it is bound to provoke resentment and resistance. Militancy is sometimes necessary, but it can also be counterproductive. The pursuit of inclusiveness would do best to avoid smearing groups generically and provoking division into oppositions of reputedly good and bad categories of humans.

The mentality or strategy of attacking whatever groups have been successful invites the worst excesses of a kind of opportunism exploiting cultural trends. The Cultural Revolution of Maoist China played out catastrophic tragedies on this scenario.[113] Such upheavals are basically

---

[112] Ferdinand de Saussure, *Cours de linguistique générale*, eds. Charles Bally and Albert Sechehaye (Paris: Payot, 1955 [1916]), 166.

[113] John O'Sullivan works out this parallel in detail in "Where Wokeness Leads the Way: A Brief History of Cultural Revolutions," in *Sleepwalking into Wokeness: How We Got Here* (Washington: Academica Press, 2024).

destructive in tenor. They focus on what they aim to destroy, without having much of a positive nature to offer in its place.

Cancel culture movements and claims are based on the pretention to substitute for the unjust cultures of the past the just ones which we create in the present. As I discovered after several years absence on a stroll through Nashville's Centennial Park built for the Tennessee Centennial and International Exposition in 1897, with a one-hundred-per-cent-scale replica of the Parthenon, the statues of civil war heroes have been replaced by female figures of suffragettes. I salute this new recognition, but I feel uneasy about the erasure of the confederate past now treated as an evil, white, Southern male culture to be expunged and covered over by heroic female freedom fighters.

The women's movement (in passing from first- to third-wave feminism) has in its turn fallen victim to critique for its suppression of minorities within its ranks. Not all women were recognized equally.[114] Voices of those whose skin color or sexual orientation was different or queer were often suppressed. Great women leaders accepted living in great privilege while masses of their sisters suffered excruciatingly. These women were sometimes slaveowners in their own right. When these more recent critiques come into vogue, are the newer monuments going to be deracinated and swept away? Once men as a group have been thoroughly discredited and have disappeared from power, will these heroines in their turn be stained as guilty in relation to new groups of innocent victims. Something like this is required by the scapegoating mechanism at work in identity politics.[115] But do we not want to remember the heroines or heroes that at least certain cultures formerly have venerated?

We have some choices to make about what history to preserve, but to undo the choices of our predecessors and substitute for them all our own preferences and prejudices smacks of a delusion that we can stand outside of history and judge it rather than only play our role and limited part within

---

[114] Kimberle Crenshaw, "Demarginalizing the Intersection of Race and Sex: A Black Feminist Critique of Antidiscrimination Doctrine, Feminist Theory and Antiracist Politics," *University of Chicago Legal Forum* 1989, no. 1, art. 8, 139–67, critiques "single-axis analysis" of discrimination against women as erasing black women.

[115] See Joshua Mitchell, 38-39, on the internal cleavages of women as a group. Likewise, Schröter, Chapter 6.

it. The civil war figures were commemorated not for being men or slave owners but for sacrificing their lives in order to defend their people and their ancestral civilization. Cannot history be preserved even when the values of those in power change? The figures now monumentalized as heroines in Nashville's Centennial Park, and other distinguished individuals to whom monuments are now being erected, belonged to a society nourished by eating meat procured through systematic exploitation and mass slaughter of animals. One day this will surely be recognized as heinous, an unacceptable crime against subjugated species. Are we, at that point, going to condemn anyone complicit in a society that practiced carnivorism as not worthy to be remembered?

In southern cities, Robert E. Lee statues are torn down in the name of not celebrating anyone who defended the institution of slavery, given its unimaginable horrors. What about eliminating all monuments to American service men who gave their lives to defend a nation that dropped the atomic bomb on Hiroshima and Nagasaki, the only incident to date of this incomparable crime against humanity? Of course, this is to ignore the incalculable horror of protracted war that the use of the A-bomb was designed to avert, as well as the potential for imposing peace throughout the world that the bomb seemed to many at the time to promise. But this blending out of the whole of history except for one's own supposedly moral focus is simply the standard method of the type of moralistic reasoning that wokeism tends to embrace and exemplify. Do we not have to consider what the people who erect monuments intend to honor in their past rather than count only our own evaluation of what is right and wrong and judge all others by our own standard? One characteristic achievement of Western and Judeo-Christian culture has been that it preserves history for its own sake and not only to serve its own ideological purposes.[116] Can this outstanding virtue of respecting and preserving otherness in Western cultural tradition, with its acknowledged exterior origins, not be preserved and valorized, even though its provenance is not from identity categories currently enjoying consideration as politically correct?

---

[116] Rémi Brague, *Europe, la voie romaine* (Paris: Critérion, 1992) demonstrates the distinctiveness of this achievement of European civilization among world cultures.

27.

Restitution of Stolen Art and Indigenous Lands

Related to the revision of history is the issue of restitutions that inevitably arises in the wake of new and revised perspectives. Should museums automatically "give back" every artwork hailing from "elsewhere"? Why should artworks of Egyptian provenance belong to the Louvre in Paris or to the Egyptian Museum in Turin? And why should the Elgin Marbles that originally adorned the Parthenon on the Acropolis in Athens be on display in the British Museum in London? Do we consider the fact that many such works are extant today only because they were preserved in these museums rather than being left to perish or be plundered in the desert? These works would have been subjected to another history if they had not been overtaken by the history of appropriation by museums in the West and elsewhere. Abstracting them entirely from any history whatever gives a distorted picture of what is necessary for their survival. Were they acquired properly? Who, after all, has rights to sell properties of a whole culture and ultimately of human culture, or even of the inspired genius of humanity?

Are perhaps all property rights established at some point arbitrarily, or even by stealing, as anarchist thinker Pierre-Joseph Proudhon (1809-65) and proto-revolutionary Jean-Jacques Rousseau (1712-78) argue? What right did Napoleón Bonaparte have to sell an enormous portion of the North American continent to President Thomas Jefferson and the USA for 80 million francs (about 15 million dollars) as the Louisiana Purchase in 1803? Was this not a steal on the part of both seller and purchaser? Should it, then, be given back? And to whom? Even more radically, how can any human being have a right of property over the land on which countless species depend for their livelihood and very existence?

The Indian chiefs were much more lucid in declaring that they could not sell their land to the US government because it was not theirs to sell. Their peoples were tolerated like other species as long as they protected the land and its manifold forms of life rather than exploiting and degrading it. Ownership of art and of land alike should be viewed as stewardship rather than as an absolute prerogative and lordship. Property rights over such goods are not a license to do whatever one wishes with what is one's own. Whatever we may possess in such genres of property is to be protected and used for purposes that are not only our own.

I would apply a similar logic to the issue of *Raubkunst*, literally "art robbery." Certainly, there are some articles of property that were stolen and should be returned to owners. However, to make everything simply private property of a legally specified owner is itself the greatest steal of heritage from the whole of humanity. Artworks exist, apart from whatever other purposes, to radiate the human spirit universally and without limits. To reduce every human artifact to an article of property, which someone has exclusive rights over and sovereign power to dispose of in whatever way they wish, is the greatest of human hefts. Other species do not do that, though some of them do certainly fight to defend their own territories. However, the control exerted by animals is generally only an interdiction against other individuals of the same species and does not mean sealing the district off from all exchange with the outside. Such exchange of living interactions is necessary in order for any territory to remain alive. Only humans absolutize their sovereignty over "property," reducing living reality to "things" in order to practice their brand of proprietary totalitarianism.

That selected articles of a certain cultural heritage should find their way to exalted positions in museums for the admiration of publics worldwide—today more than ever thanks to the moveable feasts of online galleries—is perhaps more serving of humanity and of art, and of the artists or artisans that produce it, than are narrowly trumped up proprietary rights based on racist criteria, especially when any original producers (giving a right to ownership) have been deceased for centuries or millennia. The Native American Graves Protection and Repatriation Act (1990) requiring museums and universities to give up bones and other sacred objects has been used as a woke weapon to the detriment of science.[117]

The purpose of protecting and displaying artwork to the public, even globally by the internet, ought ideally to be agreed on and concerted by all concerned parties. If there are profits, as well as expenses, in providing such a service, they should be appropriately shared. The aim has to be to concordantly serve the common good rather than to vie for ownership in selfish antagonism.

Custody and curatorship of art entails much more than simply exercising property rights. Beyond any human agents and their legal rights or claims, there is a more universal and metaphysical dimension to a people's heritage. Letting this be considered changes the issue to one of how best to share cultural goods rather than simply of who has legal rights to exclusive possession. Open access rather than hoarding serves everyone and can be more important to safeguarding the life of an artwork than determining its one rightful possessor. One could fancifully imagine an argument for the future emancipation of all artworks from their jealously possessive masters.

Recognition of the wrongs of the past such as resulted in the custody of bones of native American ancestors in museums on university campuses needs to be taken up inclusively in a spirit of collective mourning that enables all races, skin-colors, and genders to share in the grief. We need not only to acknowledge our own guilt but also to recognize a guilt that extends to humankind and invests the human condition. Such is the burden of biblical passages declaring that all have sinned and gone away backwards (Psalm 53: 3), or indeed that all have sinned in Adam (Romans 3: 23-24). Identitarian divisiveness will naturally make the processes of negotiating restitutions issue in further culture wars, and we see all too clearly in current history how such wars run the risk of becoming not just cold wars. These are occasions for collective identification and for recognizing wrongs of the past that all of us have an interest in rectifying.

---

[117] Elizabeth Weiss, *On the Warpath: My Battles With Indians, Pretendians, and Woke Warriors* (Washington: Academica Press, 2024) delivers a compelling personal testimony to how woke politics can obstruct research and lead to persecution of sincere devotees trying to preserve and illuminate this heritage.

The very universities most charged with incubating wokeist ideology and militancy have produced the new elites that speak out and aggrandize their own power with this agenda. But when the university is confronted with Indigenous claims to restitute the land on which it stands to peoples whose treaty rights were violated, suddenly the president's ear becomes deaf. Or so I hear on public radio: the presidential voice, together with the chorus of obliging echoes of the group of "leaders" who orchestrate the wokeist chant around the president, suddenly grows dumb.

Should the college campus, then, be turned into an encampment for teepees or a hunting ground? Or more realistically into a casino for legal and profitable gambling? Would this serve the common good and be in the general interest? But maybe that is not the right question. Maybe those identifying as indigenous should not be expected to honor any so-called common public purpose. At least they should be the ones to say if they care to or not. Anyone's construal of the public good is apt to be tendentious. Only a gesture of abnegation can create a space of freedom for the other to decide to make common cause or not.

Or would such a gesture of renunciation on the part of universities or governments more likely satisfy certain resentments, excite *Schadenfreude*, and invite further overbearing exactions of the will to power? That is a risk, but still it is what we can and need to do in order to work to restore community and mutual respect and even love. Whatever is done to restore and restitute will be positive and productive only if performed as a generous gesture of respect for one's fellows and love of their precious heritage. If restitution is exacted as a punitive measure, it will mean the continuation of class conflict and culture wars that are about vying for advantage among different identity groups rather than about constructing an inclusive and open society. Maybe certain violent clashes and ugly conflicts were necessary in order to bring us to the point where we are now. But now—the now in which and toward which we speak and write—it is time to speak peace and compose harmony. This "now" is always a possibility and indeed an imperative for us.

In apophatic terms, my approach to this topic is to recognize a type of ownership prior to that of various human claimants and to recognize a duty to serve a purpose beyond any definable rights of human parties, a higher purpose to which all are equally beholden. The psalmist says, "The earth is the Lord's and the fullness thereof; the world, and they that dwell therein" (24: 1). And native American Indians sing their own belonging to the land and not the land's belonging to them. These perspectives open a dimension beyond confrontation of interests of human constituencies and agents. They are necessary to encourage and promote cooperative and peaceful action on behalf of all. It is imperative to appeal to the human compassion and generosity of all in working toward a common good rather than dividing humanity along color lines or other identitarian cleavages into opposing camps of those who are condemned to owe and those who are entitled to receive compensations.

Responsibility is productive when taken up and assumed freely rather than being assigned by the animus of others. We are all endlessly responsible for one another. Any human definitions and delimitations are partial and biased. Justice cannot be reduced to a human calculus because it is global and infinite. To sit back and expect the world to "pay up" is to pretend to have a God's eye view and to know absolute justice. But this is idolatrous. It helps keep this in focus if we do not lose sight of the absolute justice that norms us but is never determined by us.

28.

Compensations for Climate Change

Paying cash compensations to countries or individuals who have suffered damage from climate change, as demanded at UN global climate change conferences (last held in November 2024 in Azerbaijan), purports to rectify injustices in the global order and bring the responsible parties to account. It relies on some human authority's determinations and quantifications of guilt and innocence. Such reckoning is apt to count some countries as criminal and others as innocent because of their lifestyle. My reservation about this approach is that human judgment in these matters is inevitably politicized and thus determined again by the play of power and superior force. As with war, different parties will emphasize totally different aspects of the situation in their respective narratives and come to opposite conclusions as to who is responsible for what. As in war, each side always says that the other side started it. Each claims only to be defending its legitimate interests against the aggression of the other. In order to work together rather than against one another, we have to avoid this schism into the innocent and the guilty and treat the problem as our common concern and seek solutions that involve all caring for each in the manner of which they are most capable rather than holding some peoples to be totally responsible for all damages and others as absolved of all responsibility. Determining guilt focused on the past is a very messy business and will not create the cooperative spirit necessary for coping with the future.

The question should be what resources and capabilities, given our newly emergent priorities and imperatives, do developed countries have for countering disasters rather than who should transfer their wealth to those who have suffered most visibly through climate change. The operative analogy in the latter case is a kind of settlement by lawsuit. The judgment is based on a determination of guilt and damages suffered. But on the world stage there are myriad other causes of suffering out there already. To single out one cause, as human judgment inevitably does, and settle on that alone, inevitably leads to distortion and disequilibrium. When a court judges a criminal, it focuses on certain aspects of the crime and all too often forgets the whole social context out of which the crime arises. This, too, often leads to invidious results—the more so when it is politicized, as has become so clearly the case with wokeism and its claims vehiculated in our age by media culture, with its image-making and unmaking.

All humans and all living creatures use natural resources for their own advantage. Certain technologies have been used to exploit natural resources with phenomenal success, resulting in enormous benefits for human comfort and what we cannot but call the modern world. The result has also been depletion of and damage to these resources. Claims for compensation for these damages are now being asserted by some against others. Yet all countries are eager to profit from the advantages of technological development and industrialization. The moral accusation against some typically comes from those who are themselves striving to do exactly what they are blaming others for doing. Nationalization of industries, for example, in Africa and South America, has sometimes made them even more ruinous of those countries' natural resources than they were when controlled by foreign entities. I think we need to change the terms of the debate from blaming some to acknowledging the complicity of all in pursuing common goals which need also to be scathingly critiqued and severely controlled by common consent.

We need to motivate superpowers and sovereign states to do all that they can and employ their resources to stem humanly induced climate change and the consequent damages. Dividing the world into opposing factions will worsen the problem, not resolve it. There are weaker and more vulnerable nations and regions. They were not created by the other, better endowed countries, although all countries do influence each other reciprocally. Demanding that they should all be made equal by fiat is going to fracture the world further. We need to inspire, instead, generosity in all to care for the world as a whole and to assist each part with its peculiar challenges. Resources need to be devoted to making the most advantageous adaptations working in concert for the future more than to assigning blame and indemnities for natural changes in the past. The constant complaint of virtually all critiques of wokeism that I have come across in journalism and social media is that it divides us when exactly the opposite is required to deal with the problems needing to be addressed.

If we continue to try to deal with compensations for climate change in terms of litigation determining guilty and innocent parties with conflicted interests, we are doomed to fan the conflagration and produce further controversy rather than cooperation. We need something more like a family model where we all feel responsible for our collective well-being and take on very different roles according to our capacities and relations.

29.

Monarchy and
the Incalculable Power of Symbols

Dante's (1265-1321) prescription for uniting humanity and for stemming the factional warfare among city states that was tearing his world apart is monarchy in the form of world government or what he calls "empire," meaning the Holy Roman Empire (*De Monarchia*, circa 1318). Today, however, monarchy, not to mention empire, is more likely to be taken as the epitome of unjustified domination, of privilege and oppression that the modern ethical rationality of fairness and equality for all will not tolerate. The British royal family has been subjected to merciless critique and has been felt by many to show how outmoded and retrograde the institution we call monarchy is in today's world. This is so particularly in France and on the left. The ideology of rational equality would certainly sweep this institution away as inegalitarian and as steeped in complicity with all the horrors of history that we are now supposed to overcome and put behind us. Nevertheless, the peripeties of history are always full of ironies that mock those inclined to dismiss as outmoded such traditions and institutions.

The enormous worldwide event provoked by the death of Queen Elizabeth II of Windsor in September 2022 was unexpectedly eye-opening. In principle, it changed nothing whatever in the governance of the country and had a purely ceremonial impact. Yet the power of symbols showed itself in this instance to be more consequential than any of the practical and functional decisions made by the prime minister and parliament. People's hearts and attention the world over were far more captivated by this simple decease of an individual monarch without political power than by the nearly simultaneous change of political regimes in Great Britain (to Liz Truss's government). The symbolic is more powerful than the real—

or, rather, reveals itself as the deeper source from which the real is apprehended.

The rationalization of life in society in the interests of equality for all and democratic affirmation of rule by the people can tend to make monarchy repugnant. Yet this symbolic event made many realize that the role of figurehead of state, even apart from actual political power, still counts an enormous amount. It can count no less, or perhaps even more, than in the past, with our totally massified and mediatized societies in the (post)industrial age now dominated by digital technology. If we have only prime ministers or presidents succeeding one another in rapid succession, people and nations have difficulty cultivating and maintaining their sense of identity. National identities are, under any circumstances, changing, malleable, ambiguous entities. But still we form them with reference to guiding ideas and personal icons as orienting points of reference. Something or someone serves this purpose, whether intentionally or not.

In effect, heads of state such as Xi Jin Ping and Vladmir Putin (to name just two) have collapsed together the office of making the decisions of policy that fall to any sovereign power and the symbolic role of representing the soul of the nation. There is a powerful tendency of peoples to loyally adhere to their recognized leaders, even when and where they may be revolted, in their heart of hearts, by their leaders' politics. The image of the nation and the identity of a people itself are at stake. Even North Korea's Kim Jong Un provides a symbolic rallying point of great emotional force for a people ruthlessly oppressed by his dictatorial rule.

What counts most in such cases, quite apart from controversial decisions, is simply continuity of presence. The office of head of state for life has an important power in it far beyond the political. Whether people agree with the leader's ideas or not, through this figurehead they have a sense of identity for better or worse, and this gives them a sense of stability and groundedness. That, too, is crucial for making responsible decisions to which one will be willing to own up.

Dictators can stand for the nation. And even those among their subjects who hate them, as most Iraqis did Saddam Hussein, can feel violated by the use of external force against their leaders. An overwhelming majority of Iraqis were desperate for Saddam Hussein to be deposed and yet found themselves bitterly resentful toward America for destroying their government. Especially since the US was not capable of imposing an effective governance in its place, the country experienced as trauma and national tragedy what the US administration presented as a triumph of liberation. Leaders, revered or reviled, prove to be key to the sense of identity of peoples.

If we take into account the psychology of nationhood and popular sovereignty, the British system, with its tenacious monarchy (not to mention Sweden, Denmark, Belgium, Spain, etc.), is not necessarily so completely archaic and retrograde as might otherwise be assumed. Near the origin of the theory of the modern liberal state, Hegel, in his *Philosophy of Right* (1821), was a monarchist who appreciated the fundamentally symbolic importance of the Prussian monarch as the embodiment of the State—the body politic represented in a particular biological body.

On completely different grounds, ignoring the modern nation-state system, Dante saw monarchy or empire as the only way to pacify the world. Dante's *Monarchia* is conceived in a thoroughly medieval perspective but is not without relevance to the challenge of world government in an age oscillating between globalization and the threat of war between major blocks East and West.[118] The monarch's authority in Dante's political theology is thoroughly secular, requiring no papal sanction. Yet, as universally human, it is grounded independently in divinity—or in transcendent non-identity. Evoking Dante here and his symbol for a universal political order serves to suggest that we need to cultivate the ability to think symbols like monarchy as beyond identity, as infinitely open to divinity or to whatever would be our (indefinable) common Ground with all others. This negative theological perspective locates the incalculable power of symbols in their surpassing all our own prejudices pro or con.

---

[118] Cf. Claude Lefort, "La modernité de Dante," introduction to Dante, *La Monarchie*, translated from Latin to French by Michèle Gally (Paris: Belin, D.L., 1993). English trans. Jennifer Rushworth as "Dante's Modernity: An Introduction to the *Monarchia*" (Berlin: ICI Berlin Press, 2020).

I bring up symbolic, ideological expressions and formations like "monarchy" as examples of how rejecting the old symbols for new ones shifts power from one party to another but does not undo the dilemmas of its exercise. I accept the old just as well as the new—perhaps the old ideological formulas are less likely to delude us into thinking that they are per se right and that others should necessarily conform to them. Whatever beliefs and backgrounds we embrace need to be held with a self-critical awareness of their limits together with a willing openness to accept others with their different beliefs.

Is it incontrovertible that unalloyed democracy embodies the best (not to mention the only) means of fostering and realizing this societal openness and inclusivity? Our Western democracies are currently breaking down into irreconcilable factions of political parties that cannot even communicate with one another. The competition in fabricating popularity by media representation and fake news in the battle for promoting images hardly inspires confidence. Such trumped up promotion is the flip side of smear campaigns manufacturing repugnance. The circus of the democratic political process has fallen prey to all manner of corruption and mediatic manipulation in Western countries and looks like a farce to many living in much less democratic systems. The democratic process often seems apt to produce results that, paradoxically, are blatantly unacceptable to most of the country concerned, not to mention the world.

Necessary to govern wisely and justly is not so much popularity, which degenerates into populism in democratic electoral systems, but virtue and competence. These qualities might have been better cultivated even in a caste or dynastic system. Required is a strong sense of responsibilities beyond one's own personal goals and ambitions. Right and virtuous governance demands a sacrifice of self to be learned by rigorous training and breeding over generations. It is not likely to be assured by winners in a popularity contest. I say this not to undermine or abandon the democratic ideal but rather to underline that it should remain respectful of other forms of government and open to valorizing and learning from them and not try to impose its own credo on all others, presuming itself to be the only right way for all.[119]

Our liberal systems of government are based on seeking fulfilment as individuals rather than on dedication to serving a people and purpose beyond oneself. A sense of responsibility to collective destiny and purpose might serve for putting the public interest first more than a feeling of personal triumph as earning or deserving power to do one's own will. In the end, we owe allegiance to one another more than to any system or ideology, whatever we prefer to call it: "democracy" or "socialism" are no exceptions. Responsibility to the people is not just doing what the people want and demand, often in great ignorance and irresponsibility. I am not advocating a return to hereditary rule, but I want to escape the myopia of a narcissistic age that cannot see beyond itself nor learn from a past that it compulsively condemns and rejects, blindly deeming itself to be superior.

---

[119] For historical perspective on democracy's close association with tyranny, which today frequently takes the form of populism, see Montserrat Herrero, *Filosofía política. De la antigüedad al mundo contemporáneo,* 15-26, chapter 1: "Tiranía y democracia en el origen del fenómeno político."

30.

Self-Righteous Certitude versus Risky Openness to Others

Human beings having the pretention of correcting the wrongs of history are too often blind to the wrongs in which they are themselves entangled and which repeat history. We cannot step outside history and start all over again on an equitable footing—as if history had never happened, or as if we knew better now how it all should have happened and were going to make amends and do it over again now on our own unimpeachable terms. Those who pretend to do this are posturing more than engaging in the real challenges of their own particular historical moment. Wars of religion involved staking one's life on one's convictions. But culture wars more often than not involve taking positions and profiling oneself and one's righteousness through virtue signaling without real commitment or investment or risk to oneself.

Don Quixote makes judgments based on power differentials between those he attacks and those he defends. He perceives immediately a disequilibrium of force, and he acts with no knowledge of particulars such as a judge in a tribunal would have to examine in order to try to come to a just verdict. Don Quixote's justice is impromptu, for example, when he defends the servant boy Andrés, who, tied to a tree, is being savagely whipped by his master, Juan Haldudo. We learn much later on that this intervention has completely backfired and led to even more severe punishment for the victim. However, Don Quixote does not claim that his action is complete or final. It is a determinate intervention or rectification and relies expressly on God to do the rest. Likewise, when he frees the galley slaves, Don Quixote says that their virtue or vice will bring its own punishment or reward upon each of them once they are free to act. We have to let life have its way with us and with others rather than presume to regulate it by our moral standards. Our acts have to be predicated on acceptance of the conditions life offers us.

Wokeism aims, like Don Quixote, to defend the oppressed, but it can quickly become a kind of bullying in reverse in the way it exercises its power over others. What are we silently accepting and assuming when we acquiesce to politically correct, "woke" positions? What markers are confirmed as in place and operative as standards? Are we arrogating to humans the position of final arbiter rather than leaving it to life to deal each, finally, their deserts beyond any human calculus, which should be designed, at most, simply to level the playing field?

Joshua Mitchell comes to just this conclusion concerning identity politics and its claim "to put justice within man's conceptual grasp" (30). He also contends that the purging of guilty identities in the attempt to enact the woke concept of justice is never final but requires finding always a new scapegoat to serve that function once each purge has been carried out: "there will be no end to trouble if that scapegoat is mortal rather than Divine" (xix).

> Those who believe they have a grip on it, who think they can put it to political use on their behalf, do not understand that identity politics will turn against *all* who seek to enlist it. "They that sow the wind, shall reap the whirlwind" (Hosea 8:7).[120]

Mitchell's analysis is that the scapegoating mechanism of identity politics, which is currently turned against white heterosexual men, will have to find other, always new groups to scapegoat. That is how scapegoating deals with guilt, which is never forgiven. There is always a guilty history among humans of whatever category, contrary to the recurrent pretention to have found the one guilty caste enabling the dominant party or group to undertake to effectuate the necessary purge and rectify and redeem history.

Jean de La Fontaine's verse fable, "The animals sick with the plague" ("Les animaux malades de la peste") suggests that guilt and innocence are generally assigned in accordance with the power of those doing the judging and with the flattering acquiescence of all the rest who are

---

[120] Mitchell, *American Awakening*, 30.

joyously relieved that it is not them on whom the ax falls. The lion, the tiger, the wolf, the bear, the fox, are all eager to excuse themselves of killing their prey and by common accord condemn the ass for eating someone else's grass.[121] The "guilty" victim who is to be sacrificed in order to appease the gods and hopefully end the plague is actually less, rather than more, guilty of the "crimes" in question, but the entire process of judgment is governed by the dynamics of power. It may even be impossible for us to see all the way around and behind our own drive for power, although it steers us in our assignments of blame.

The all too frequently verified fact that "history is the history of the victors," as Walter Benjamin formulated it in his "Theses on the Philosophy of History" ("Geschichtsphilosophischen Thesen," 1940), is exactly what woke voices are protesting against. Yet woke activists often are attempting to do the same with their own narrative and its newfound power and still within the same logic of domination. They are liable to do unto others the wrong that has been done unto them, and they do so only as proxies, not really as the offended parties. Most typically, those pushing woke agendas tend to be privileged white academics taking up and championing publicly the cause of the minorities and marginalized.

Wokeism can provide a salutary interrogation, but it contains also a lethal politics when it becomes self-righteous and arrogates to itself the right to systematically deal out to each their due on the basis of social identities. Wokeism can serve well to provoke significant reflections and reactions and gestures—if it can avoid self-righteousness. But to right all the wrongs of history is beyond any rational calculus. It is the pretention of total control and regulation of justice that leads afresh to injustices and reverse discriminations. Things are as they are, and we must always start from there to work to make them better and more equitable. When we try to pass judgment on everything through some schematic prism of our own, we fall into the same faults and delusions that have marred the history of our predecessors. Social justice is not any formula that we can conjure up and impose. Life takes its course, and we have to work acceptingly with its results and its struggles. We can, like the Knight Errant Don Quixote,

---

[121] Jean de La Fontaine, *Fables*, 1678-1679 (Paris: Aubert, 1842), Livre VII, Fable 1.

make some restitutions, but we are also, inevitably, deeply steeped in our own history of errancy.

31.

Don Quixote and Justice

Don Quixote revives the tradition of chivalric knight errantry. He is an icon of how any agent of justice or avenger of wrongs stands up out of some specific history—in fundamental ways mythologized and misunderstood—and carries it forward into a new situation in the present. He, of course, at least in his own conceits, represents the noble tradition and lineage of knight-errantry.[122] These legendary figures were essentially armed vigilantes roaming the country on horseback, looking to rectify any situations that they perceived as injustices by challenging and defeating the presumed evildoers in duels. Considerable cultural context is indispensable in order to be intelligible as such an agent of justice, and there is always a good deal of fiction and fantasy that goes into its construction.

In one typical and telling episode (I, 22), Don Quixote frees criminals condemned to be galley slaves, thereby making himself an outlaw and the object of a warrant for arrest issuing in a sweeping manhunt on the part of the King's Holy Brotherhood. Since galley slaves were the Spanish king's property, Don Quixote's freeing them is directly an offense against the king and an infringement on his royal rights. But Don Quixote is answering to a much higher authority than that of the king. The justice he seeks to execute is absolute and divine. Of course, the former slaves and convicted criminals are liable to wreak havoc on the country in which they are set loose, yet Don Quixote takes no responsibility for that. He says that they will be punished or rewarded according to their deserts by God. He

---

[122] Miguel de Cervantes Saavedra, *El Ingenioso Hidalgo Don Quijote de la Mancha*, eds. Salvador Fajardo and James A. Parr (Asheville, North Carolina: Pegasus Press, 1998). A good English-language translation is by Edith Grossman, *Don Quixote* (New York: HarperCollins, 2003).

restores to them the liberty of which no power on earth can rightly deprive them. Human justice cannot be total and autonomous. It can operate only within a context of some other, higher tribunal of right and wrong or of life and death. Wokeism, at least in its vitiated forms, erases this higher court or larger context and takes justice into its own hands. But no human hands can suffice to prevent justice from becoming tendentious and politicized and turning unjust.

The lesson I am trying to draw from Don Quixote is complex. On the one hand, we do have to take justice into our own hands. Don Quixote courageously confronts those he perceives as taking advantage of weaker parties. At the same time, we cannot do more than perform delimited acts of rectification or generosity. We must ourselves be subject to a higher justice than our own: Don Quixote's dedication and consecration of himself to the service of God and his lady acknowledges this. Precisely this unconditional service to an Other as a higher power is what frees Don Quixote from himself, his personal desires, and enslavement to his own fixed ideas of justice. "Social justice" in the secularized modern world, lacking any sense of transcendence, in contrast, is liable to be instrumentalized to absolutize one's own relative judgment. It will be subject to influence by one's own interests in scarcely conscious, untransparent ways.

Beyond our social identities, there is, of course, something absolute about each individual and their free will. Spanish philosopher Miguel de Unamuno, in commenting on Don Quixote, notes that the knight, even when humiliated and caged (at the end of Part I), remains, nevertheless, entirely free. No one can cage his spirit. The will as such cannot, in principle, be coerced. Don Quixote stands as a reminder that we are often more apt to demand liberty of thought and action from others who are supposed to concede it to us than simply to exercise our inalienable faculty of thinking freely ("pedís libertad de pensamiento en vez de ejercitaros en pensar").[123] There is an absolute dimension envisaged in human thinking

---

[123] Miguel de Unamuno's works, including his *Vida de Don Quijote y Sancho*, are cited from *Del sentimiento trágico de la vida y otros ensayos* (Barcelona: Debolsillo [Penguin], 2020), 171. All translations, unless otherwise attributed, are my own.

and willing that is not manifest on the social scene, with its relative distinctions into different categories by outward appearances.

There is, of course, also literal slavery that absolutely deprives persons of all outward forms of freedom based on external criteria. Cervantes's own life as a slave in Algiers is reflected in the episode of the Captive (*El Cautivo*) intercalated into Part II of *Don Quixote*, Chapters XXXIX-XLI. Especially from the fifteenth to the eighteenth centuries in the Mediterranean basin, Christians, especially men but occasionally also women who were traveling with them, were kidnapped by pirates and sold into slavery to Muslim masters in North Africa. Algiers became the hub of this slave trade, which was the mainstay of its economy throughout the era. The captives, who were enslaved in great numbers, were held for ransom, if that seemed possible and profitable. Otherwise, they became domestic slaves or else were delivered over to be worked to death as galley slaves for the short lives that remained to them.

This was a form of enslavement particularly of Christians. Conversion to Islam was in certain cases offered as a means of redemption. Those who renounced the Christian religion and converted to Islam and were circumcised could be accorded the status of renegades and therewith recover their freedom. Of course, they would be persecuted by the Inquisition if they attempted to return to their own countries, particularly Spain, as is recalled by Miguel de Cervantes in his various fictional treatments based on these historical facts, which he lived through personally and survived to write about. Cervantes reflected on this experience also in his largely autobiographical comedy *Los baños de Argel* (1615).

Cervantes delivers fictionalized filters of his personal experience of being such a captive in the possession of a master from whom he was finally ransomed after four unsuccessful attempts at escape. Miraculously, he was spared crippling punishments and execution for his repeated attempts to escape, thanks also to certain interventions by religious authorities on his behalf in recognition of his exceptional qualities and character. He was finally ransomed after over five years of captivity through great sacrifice by his family, which went into debt in order to raise part of the ransom. The other part was paid by a religious order, the

Trinitarians.[124] The ransom came about only in the eleventh hour when Miguel de Cervantes was about to be shipped as a galley slave to Constantinople—almost surely a death sentence.

In thousands of documented cases like Cervantes's, being Christian was cause for enslavement. Conversion to Islam was a way of redeeming one's life out of slavery. Does that give Christians some kind of right to compensation from Muslims for past persecutions? No one would think so. I mention this absurd hypothesis only in order to raise the question of how far the liability for past wrongs on the basis of generic identities can be stretched. The illusion is that we or anyone, especially as generic identity groups, can be responsible for everything that is and that is unjust. We always play only a delimited role. Almost everything that happens in history can be very plausibly construed as damaging someone. Many people are prone to devoting themselves entirely to the cause of seeking reparations for some past harm. Of course, this too belongs to the constant struggle for political power and advantage. Cervantes's case is an important reminder of the endemic contradictions of history and a warning against our oversimplifications of it. Generic social identities are no basis for assigning penalties or reparations. Guaranteeing equal, or even compensatory, opportunity in the present seems to me a more productive approach. Compensatory measures should be contemplated but on condition of being constructive rather than vindictive in spirit.

Woke revisionary histories tend to impose a reading in which slavery is absolutely monovalent and completely racialized. Being black identifies one automatically as victim of the Atlantic slave trade. Being white means participating in guilt for that horrible history and being liable to pay compensations for it. That there was a slave trade for centuries in which European Christians were enslaved is simply erased because it does not conform to the recognized stereotypes. The slave trade is widely considered the original sin uniquely of America, although more African slaves, some 18 million rather than 11 or 12 million in America, were actually sent eastward to mostly Muslim countries, with all the men

---

[124] Aaron M. Kahn, Introduction, *The Oxford Handbook of Cervantes* (Oxford: Oxford University Press, 2021), xxviii.

castrated.[125] Enslavement of members of one's own tribe or of enemy tribes in Africa was often at the origin of export to foreign countries of those already enslaved by other Africans. The British Empire was first to abolish slavery within its borders and spent much blood and treasure to stop it elsewhere, too, thanks especially to abolitionists driven by Christian convictions.[126]

---

[125] Egon Flaig, *Weltgeschichte der Sklaverei* (München: Beck, 2009) covers this other history of slavery as world-historically the most extensive ("Die islamische war die umfangreichste der Geschichte," 12). The transatlantic slave trade, on the other hand, was the most contested from its inception and led to abolition worldwide. The error of making enslavement of black Africans a uniquely or even especially Western and white atrocity is contradicted also by the historical research of Tidiane N'Diaye, *Der verschleierte Völkermord. Die Geschichte des muslimischen Sklavenhandels* (Reinbek bei Hamburg: Rowohlt, 2010).

[126] Douglas Murray, *The War on the West: How to Prevail in the Age of Unreason* (London: HarperCollins, 2022) helps to place into a world-historical context the one-sided revisionary history of slavery that much woke ideology has fostered.

32.

Colonialism, Modernization, and Multiculturalism

The cultural revolution spearheaded by wokeism insinuates that the West colonized and subjugated the rest of the world because its people, or at least its dominant white males, have been more unscrupulous and more immoral than any other race or sex or region. However, a more objective analysis might be that the West colonized vast regions of the globe in past centuries because its inventiveness and industry produced the power to do so through large-scale development of technological and material means of unprecedented efficaciousness. These are also the same means that ushered in the modern style of life together with its almost universally coveted material improvements in living conditions for human beings around the globe. To abstract colonialism from this history of modernization sets the stage for moralization that selectively focuses certain aspects of that history and is liable to project a false dichotomy of good and evil races and genders.

Any race or gender, or any species, for that matter, tends to use its power, when superior, to dominate and subjugate others. Rather exceptional, if not unique, in historical perspective, about European or Western versions of this universal pattern has been the marked determination to reflect self-critically on the ethically questionable aspects of such domination and to judge it and condemn it and attempt to rectify it. Wokeism is the product precisely of this culture of critical self-reflection. Such reflection, however, shallowed out, can also be truncated and aborted in our current woke culture. Rather than being preserved as an instrument of critique, superficial self-reflection can turn into another weapon used for exerting power. The history of modernization and its attendant subjugations is turned by ideological abstraction into a pernicious mythology projecting images of an evil race and gender. Douglas Murray analyzes such a false understanding of history as propelled by systemic, deliberate injustice perpetrated by a dominant race and gender or region (the West). Such a falsification is produced and propagated wholesale through ignorance on the part of masses of people who adhere to emotionally captivating or comforting narratives from which self-critical reflection and knowledge of the historical facts has been evacuated.[127]

Much domination, especially in our modern world, is, to some degree, self-inflicted and self-imposed. Whether perversely or not, humans often demand domination. Rare are the peoples who have not shown themselves ready and willing to submit to domination by the global economic order out of desire for Coca-Cola or MacDonalds or iPhones and all the conveniences and comforts of modern living. Mahatma Gandhi in his classic work on "Indian Home Rule" (*Hind Swaraj*, 1909) appealed to the Indian people simply to begin governing themselves, to stop depending on anyone else besides themselves, and then the British would have nothing more to do among them and would go away.[128] With this guiding belief, he orchestrated perhaps the world's most massive and successful non-violent independence movement.

Wokeism can quickly land us in a logic in which one party is responsible for all the ills that befall any other because their race, gender, or class has been dominant in certain respects, while others are simply innocent victims, no matter what. Much of what happens in life is unpredictable, and we are all subject to all manner of contingency and ultimately to death. In our most narcissistic modes, we want to assign the responsibility precisely to another party for any adversity. Our wounded egos start, unreasonably, from the benchmark that anything bad that befalls us should not have happened and is someone else's fault. We blend out the intrinsically vulnerable nature of our existence and unconsciously assume that without the malicious interference of others who do us wrong

[127] Murray's books, including *The War on the West* and *The Madness of Crowds*, are supplemented by numerous online appearances, such as Douglas Murray: Why conservatives will win the war on the West (youtube.com).
[128] I explore this argument in "The Ethical Posture of Anti-Colonial Discourse in Said and in Gandhi," *Journal of Contemporary Thought* 25 (Summer, 2007): 5-24.

we would live forever in perfect health and happiness. We act as if everything in a right world ought to serve to enhance our own well-being. With today's means and sensibilities, it is possible to make quite a career out of claiming indemnities from others for whatever goes wrong in our lives.

This way of reasoning from the position of the victim is bound to provoke resistance to a kind of "unlimited liability"—as Germany and other Western countries say in resisting certain claims for indemnity on the part of developing nations due to damage to the environment from industrialization. No one could ever pay enough for loss of life and well-being due to climate change. Our industry and consumption are certainly responsible for the dramatic degradation of our global environment and must be drastically curtailed. Instead, we bicker about who should pay indemnities to whom. Human assignments of causality are always very relative and partial—they do not and cannot take account of the total context. The dinosaurs evidently perished because of climate change, which happens no matter what.

We have an unlimited responsibility to others, as Dmitri Karamazov in Dostoyevsky's *The Brothers Karamazov* poignantly realizes. But it is always in a context that reaches beyond our control, as Don Quixote's escapades illustrate. Such responsibility operates not in the same sphere as finite, determinate, human claims. For these novelistic protagonists, total responsibility is regulated by God, not by humans, even though that does not prevent Don Quixote in act—and, only less conspicuously, Dmitri in conviction—from being ready to intervene at their own risk in the attempt to set right every situation they perceive as wrong or unjust. It is just the pretense to have a total system or formula that proves to be illusory.

We live in a world of screaming injustice. Activism has an important role to play in challenging and changing that. But it is not by tarring certain social identities and whitewashing others that justice can be served. In calling to our attention how social identities have been used in discriminatory fashion in the past, social justice activism should work as a call not to reverse the valences of such discrimination in a cycle of vengeance but rather to desist from judging human individuals on the basis of their skin color or other group identity markers.

33.

Is *Social* Justice a Fallacy?

After all, "social justice" is perhaps something of a misnomer. Society is an arena of struggle among identities whereas justice is transcendent and non-identical, unique and incommensurable. In biblical terms, "The Lord alone is just" (Sirach 18:2). Does justice come from society? Or does its source have to lie elsewhere? Much Marxist thought conceives of justice as a social production, but this is perhaps only a very modern, narrowly secularized view. Prior political theorists seldom expected justice to be social in its origins and foundations. Justice was more commonly thought to be written in the heavens. Society is an arena more of *in*justice. From the height of the starry heaven, Dante sees the earth as "the flower bed that makes us so ferocious" ("L'aiuola che ci fa tanto feroci," *Paradiso* XXII.151).

A lot is loaded into speaking of justice as *social*. The phrase seems to assume that justice should be generated by society. That assumption might itself be a misunderstanding destined to produce injustice. Can society take control of determining justice? Perhaps *adjustment* rather than justice is more properly and plausibly the jurisdiction of the social. The social is a realm of mutual adjustments between forces. It is impossible for an absolute such as justice to be realized socially, except in very partial degrees.

The social is a relative sphere of compromises. It cannot comprehend the absolutes of justice. "Justice" does have to operate in the relative realm of human action and reaction, but justice in the strict sense is never quite attained. It can only be striven after. I think we need not to lose sight of justice as an absolute, even as "divine," in order to keep the compromised human realm from becoming a tyrannical engine of injustice. We take certain principles to be absolute, but when they are refracted and deformed by our own culture and language, they are not truly universal and may become oppressive for others. Only this self-reflective awareness of limits can save us from the injustice of insisting on our own way or right and turn us toward an openness to justice as coming from beyond us. Justice cannot be imposed by anyone: it can only be received through cooperative effort with potentially all others.

The recognition of an absolute justice that exceeds human laws and systems requires an openness to others and their values and to their different sense of justice. An intuition for this verity was demonstrated by the Islamic Mujahideen rebels who recently toppled the Assad regime in Syria and rather than proclaiming their own system of Sheria as the law of the land spoke of establishing a Syria that would be home to all faiths and open to accommodate all ethnicities and genders without forced submission to an alien law. Of course, this gesture might be interpreted as a disingenuous strategic ploy to avert harsh backlash and sanctions from the international community and buy time in order to be able to impose more effectively its own oppressive regime by making it less conspicuous. However, still, the recognition of a sense of justice as referred beyond one's own formula is embodied in this strategy, even if that's all it is.

We can always ask, Whose justice? Society tears the universality that seems to resound in the word "justice" apart. What is just for one faction is not just for another. Can we answer, "God's justice?" Certainly not to everyone's satisfaction.

The truly universal cannot be defined socially, as Todd McGowan convincingly shows. Terms of definition are inherently oppositional. Justice has to be blind to social identity and difference. Justice, like Love (Cupid), is depicted in Renaissance iconography as blindfolded. This image revives and represents, in early modern times, the discovery of the universal that emerges with ancient Greek philosophy and is iconographically represented in Themis, the Greek goddess of Justice. The intuition behind this representation is that justice cannot be safeguarded and delivered by formulas or by a focus on particular identities. There is something divine about Justice that must be respected as reaching beyond all our inevitably limited human perceptions and appropriations. Justice harbors in the *spirit* of the laws, which necessarily exceeds any positive formulation and human application of them.[129]

The law is important precisely for its limits that point us beyond what can be legally determined.[130] This intuition is embodied poetically by Dante, with his figure of the goddess *Fortuna* representing the economic aspect of social justice in the circle of hell where the avaricious are punished (*Inferno* VII. 61-96). Like Sisyphus, the avaricious roll boulders around a semicircle only to have them pushed back by the prodigal over and over in vain for all eternity. *Fortuna*, a minister of God, makes wealth change hands constantly. No one can keep it rolling in their direction for long because fortune is constantly subject to ebb and flow. It seems totally random to human vision, although for Dante the providence of God is accomplished precisely through this apparent chaos.

This traditional insight into the negative nature of universality as represented iconographically by the blindfolded Egyptian goddess of Truth and Justice, Ma'at, as well as by the Greek goddess, Themis, is now being cancelled under the influence of postcolonial revisionism. India's supreme court recently unveiled a version of the Greek statue without the blindfold, with open eyes, accompanied by a statement by Justice Chandrachud overruling the ancient tradition through an ideological stance asserting justice's ability to see all equally.[131]

---

[129] Montesquieu, *De l'esprit des lois* (1748).

[130] Justin Steinberg, *Dante and the Limits of the Law* (2013). I bring this out in my review essay, "Professional Dantology and the Human Significance of Dante Studies," *Diacritics: A Review of Contemporary Criticism* 42/4 (2014): 54-71.

[131] Lady Justice no longer blind: Supreme Court embraces new symbolism

**Figure 2. From the Ancient Goddess Ma'at to Lady Justice with open eyes.
(Photo: Egyptian goddess Ma'at, Wiki Commons;
Lady Justice in Supreme Court of India)**

The pretention of such a ruling is that former ages were blind and that woke judges now see clearly and know what is just. Obscured is the ancient wisdom realizing that total vision for us is an illusion. Justice, *as we know it*, depends, instead, on admitting a certain blindness. "I once was blind but now I see" (from the spiritual "Amazing Grace," echoing the Gospel of John 9: 25) means that I was blind to it but now I see the amazing grace that was guiding me all along.

The goddess's blindfold is primarily a veil between the human and the divine. We cannot see the divine except as veiled. The blindfold is for us. We can and must love justice but cannot pretend to see it univocally. The blindfold is not really for the divinity, who *can* possess the faculty of seeing what individuals merit and demerit in all the infinite complexity and hiddenness of their hearts. This is what humans cannot see. The blindfold is for us, who cannot see concealed intentions with this degree of completeness and accuracy. For us, justice remains in many of its aspects opaque and incomprehensible. Themis personifies divine, cosmic justice, but she has a daughter by Zeus, namely, Dike, who personifies human justice, legal and moral (Hesiod, *Theogony* I, 901). The blindfold is most appropriate for Dike

Dante inscribes this lesson into his vision of Holy Scripture as a spectacle of writing justice in the sky of Paradise. In *Paradiso* XVIII,

Dante sees blazoned across the heavens, in the form of sparking letters, the incipit of the Book of Wisdom: DILIGITE IUSTITIAM QUI IUDICATIS TERRAM ("Love Justice you who rule the earth"). Reproducing Holy Scripture verbatim, this citation of the Word of God (Book of Wisdom 1: 1) is made manifest to Dante as a mystical vision in heaven. The letters speak, but in a way that seems totally random to Dante's sight, even though this is Holy Writ, the Word of God.

The final letter, M, of the phrase in which the sentence's syntax is completed and its meaning is made intelligible, stands for Monarchy as the human institution securing justice for the world. In Dante's conception and political ideal, the Emperor or absolute Monarch of the temporal world was the guarantor of a universal order of peace and justice on earth. The M evokes perhaps also Mary as the correlative principle of mercy (or *misericordia*) in heaven. This association is suggested by the letter M's being garlanded by the Marian symbol of the lily, the fleur-de-lys ("ingigliarsi a l'emme," 113).

Dante sees this gothic M formed by the incandescent souls of the Heaven of Jupiter, the Heaven of Justice. The just souls of this heaven are sparks that form this letter that then explodes into an apparent chaos—as when a firebrand is struck and the sparks scatter helter-skelter. They then shape themselves miraculously into the head and wings of the imperial eagle of Rome, the emblem of justice in the world in Dante's theory. Speaking (*favellare*) and sparking (*sfavillar*), from *favella* (speech) and *favilla* (spark), come to coincide in Dante's grammatology. A divine intention is expressed in the apparent chaos of material combustion. Justice seems to be completely random to our eyes, even though it is guided by divine providence in every minute determination, every seemingly random motion of every spark in the explosion. Heavenly Justice has to appear as blind chance to us in order *not* to be subjected to any of our finite rational schemes of comprehension and thereby be reduced to an idol.[132]

---

[132] I develop this reading in detail in William Franke, *The Divine Vision of Dante's Paradiso: The Metaphysics of Representation* (Cambridge, UK: Cambridge University Press, 2021).

In some sense, I think we need to be oriented to Justice written in the sky in order to avoid the deadlock of endless social strife between our incompatible interpretations of it. Justice could also be written in the land. The American Indians recognized life on the earth as inscribed with a principle of justice. All justice had to be grounded on respect for the ground on which we live and think and act. This is the universal as transcendent or as "trans-descendent" but as, in any case, beyond the grasp of us who are grounded by it. We are normed by our seeking after it. An apophatic vision of being justly governed requires us to respond to a law preceding us. Such a law is higher (or lower) than all that we can legislate, although we alone remain responsible and need to answer to our fellows for all our interpretations and applications of this per se authoritative law.

Figure 3. Dante's Vision of Justice (DILIGITE), Columbia Rare Books

Part IV.

Achieved Worth
versus Socially Attributed Value

34.

Objective Reality and Limits of Moralization

An absolute respect for the other and for otherness is a core value of Western culture. It stems especially from Judeo-Christian roots and the reverence for a wholly other, transcendent God. But such reverence for the Other and for everything other can also become offensively sanctimonious—or can certainly be seen as such. We have already (in section 3) considered Nietzsche's analysis of the denial of one's own vital instincts and therewith the canceling of one's own self—or turning one's aggressive instincts inward against oneself—as "nihilism."

Some of the postures of current woke militants provide uncannily accurate depictions of the sort of denaturing that Nietzsche was diagnosing and denouncing in something like prophetic tones well over a century in advance. In certain transgender ideologies coming under the woke umbrella, biological nature is directly denied in order to absolutize the free and unconstrained choice of individuals concerning even what belongs to the sphere of physical fact. If you do not like your biological sex, you can deny it and identify otherwise, and it becomes a moral imperative enjoined on others to respect this choice of yours for another nature or kind than the one given to you biologically.

Woke ideologues, with their cultural politics of favoring whatever or whoever can be labeled as a victim and as "other" to the supposedly dominant race, gender, and class—with the consequent condemnation of races and genders considered to be strong or dominant—are in some rather striking and paradoxical ways perpetuating the agenda of the "ascetic priests" in Nietzsche's *The Genealogy of Morals*. Wokes are typically, and sometimes rabidly, anti-Christian, but they have substantially usurped the moral and regulatory role played by the Christian clergy in Nietzsche's scenario. They are moral arbiters imposing a system counter to nature based on their own power and its championing of weakness. They declare practically all who are in an inferior position to be victims. By inverting the natural hierarchy and declaring weakness to be strength—that is, to have a superior claim to juridical rights in moral terms—they undermine a first-order system of power and substitute for it another system of their own manufacture. They become the masters of overturning valuations and redistributing entitlements.

In Nietzsche's vitalist view, the struggle to survive is what keeps the species fit and sound and, in the case of our species, even sane. When we entirely moralize life, it sickens and dies. We enclose ourselves in a cocoon of reasoning only in terms of how we think things should be or would like them to be and refuse to confront the necessities of how things actually are. Nietzsche's madman ("der tolle Mensch") laments that we have lost our bearings after the death of God. Standing in for humanity, this madman is reeling with the sense of guilt over the fact that "we have killed God."[133] We no longer respect any kind of absolute alterity, even though we have idolized "diversity" understood in our own identitarian terms. We have made ourselves the be all and end all of existence. This, too, is unnatural. It is not only an overreaching of ourselves and our current state of being but an overreaching of nature and of reality, or the order of things itself, so as to impose ourselves and our own order as absolute. This is no longer a natural and necessary expression of the will-to-power. It is an absurd extension beyond natural limits of a human power or faculty— namely, moralizing—abstracted from its proper use and applicable domain as functional to an order which serves life and not just our wishful fantasies.

---

[133] Friedrich Nietzsche, *Die fröliche Wissenschaft* (1882, 1887) para. 125; trans. Walter Kaufmann as *The Gay Science* (New York: Vintage, 1974), pp. 181-82.

35.

Culture of Resentment
versus Performance and Self-Surpassing

Although liberation of previously untapped energies is the desired end, too often the winning strategy in a culture inflected by wokeism becomes that of complaining against others for the privileges purportedly enjoyed by them rather than applying oneself to using one's unique talents for doing all that one can to produce the best possible results for oneself and for the general good. The way of getting ahead is rather by bringing down someone else who is accused of having had unfair advantages. In this logic, one group advances by making claims against another. This strategy presupposes an agonistic view of history—such as is found also in classical Marxism, pivoting on class struggle.

As modeled by Christians, with their slave morality, in Nietzsche's *Genealogy of Morals*, the strategy is to call the good and successful evil and the weak and ineffective good. This is a reversal of values that gains credit through supporting masses who are induced to reevaluate themselves but not to transform themselves or deliver anything more so as to earn higher esteem. According to such "slave morality," whatever is deficient is deemed to lie not in oneself but to be the fault of others and of what they have done to one. Nietzsche demystifies this Christian moralism—of which woke "social justice" morality is but a thinly dissimulated avatar—as being, like all moralities, "the fruit of a barbarous history of debt, torture, revenge, obligation and exploitation." [134] For Nietzsche, this entails, not least, terrible violence and cruelty against

---

[134] Terry Eagleton, *Culture and the Death of God* (New Haven: Yale University Press, 2014), 165, lucidly outlines Nietzsche's logic in these terms.

oneself in becoming civilized and moral, which means repressed and guilt-ridden.

Some thinkers and analysts have asked whether a healthier approach would be to encourage growth and perhaps even some modeling of oneself on successful groups and cultures instead of condemning successful achievers and thereby fostering a culture of resentment. Alan Bloom, following Nietzsche, penned probing analyses in this vein, and his namesake Harold Bloom carried this torch of "the Western canon" of masterpieces of literary achievement at the cost of being burned by it.[135] If we condemn those who succeed better than others, we condemn ourselves to a perfectly unnatural way of working against our own best abilities and interests. We reward helplessness and dependency rather than a spirit of self-help and efforts of courageously undertaking to confront objectively real problems instead of wallowing vindictively in our own narrowly constructed ideas about our adversaries and oppressors.

It has become easier and far more fashionable to invest one's energies in protest, contestation, and accusation instead of in striving for one's own improvement and perfection. As the familiar saying goes: "The squeaky wheel gets the grease." But, as Benjamin Franklin also observed, "The worst wheel of the cart makes the most noise." The greater challenge is not simply to assert one's own rights and deserts but rather to create resources that are needed and available to be used by all. Still, most people are likely to choose the path of least resistance, which consists, in woke-dominated times, not in achieving but rather in claiming entitlements and complaining that one is not being treated fairly by others.

In protest against the self-flagellation of the West and its worshiping the "sacredness of the victim," Pascal Bruckner writes: "In our age of loudly displayed enjoyment, affliction still runs the show. Anyone who seizes control of it seizes power." What this means is that "Suffering gives one rights, it is even the sole source of rights: that is what we have learned over the past century. In Christianity, it used to generate redemption, now

---

[135] Alan Bloom, *The Closing of the American Mind: How Higher Education Has Failed Democracy and Impoverished the Souls of Today's Students* (New York: Simon and Schuster, 1987). Harold Bloom, *The Western Canon: The Books and School of the Ages* (New York: Harcourt Brace, 1994).

it generates reparations . . . ."[136] This predicament leads to "a new aristocracy of the outcast."

With explicit reference to Bruckner, Bérénice Levet counsels courage to affirm an old type of aristocracy which challenged people to exceed themselves and transcend every kind of static identity in creatively becoming something more.[137] She brings out how, in the traditional Western conception of the human since the Greeks, the human is not just an identity with rights but is constituted more profoundly by the duty to become something more and other than oneself as one presently is (30). We must surpass any fixed or given identity through dynamically productive relations with others. The nearly unfathomable achievements of Western civilization from antiquity through the Middle Ages, the Renaissance, Reformation, Enlightenment, Romanticism, Modernism, etc., are all being taken for granted today and made invisible by an education that teaches youth to view the world through the optics of identitarian victimization. Of course, there are many among immigrant or minority or indigenous or incarcerated populations that absolutely require help in order to begin to help themselves, and hardly anything is more noble than enabling them to become positive and productive in their own right.

The achievements of Western civilization are being maligned and condemned as colonialist and racist, and Levet trumpets a clarion call to the French not to be bamboozled by this American-born craziness into renouncing their own proud tradition for a misguided repentance. Her call is to cherish universalism in the French tradition rather than the navel-gazing obsession with identity in current ideologies. The exacting effort to place oneself in the shoes and skins of others is the constant teaching and discipline of the tradition of art and thought in this precious tradition now being vilified for the sake of adhering to the comfort of victimry and ideologies of "diversity" that teach the young to fixate on their own skin color or gender markers rather than to cultivate a rich sense of their humanity as transmitted by the infinitely complex texts of Western

---

[136] Pascal Bruckner, *La tyrannie de la pénitence : Essai sur le masochisme occidental* (Paris: Grasset, 2006), trans. Steven Rendall, *The Tyranny of Guilt: An Essay on Western Masochism* (Princeton, N.J.: Princeton University Press, 2010), 116.
[137] Bérénice Levet, *Le Courage de la dissidence: L'esprit français contre le wokisme* (Paris: L'Observatoire, 2022), 30.

tradition. This human heritage of inexhaustibly provocative and nuanced thought and literature is being reduced to one monotonous message of domination by patriarchy, white supremacy, systemic racism, and Orientalism.

We should be free to love others, including other races or genders, for what they have achieved for humanity, and sometimes this requires battles for recognition. But that is because of the difficulty of changing how people perceive things rather than because one particular race or gender is more evil or selfish than others. It is perverse to be morally required to favor certain groups presented as victims on pain of being put to shame oneself rather than out of love for them and for what they actually are and do.

Victimization, as practiced increasingly in our present cultural climate, leads not to trying to overcome hardship by bettering one's own lot oneself but, instead, to instrumentalizing one's plight or relative unsuccess and using it as a bludgeon against other groups held to be responsible as transgressors or perpetrators.[138] Heroic activity to resist and overcome objective challenges is avoided as one turns instead to a battle of interpretation and of strategies for assigning blame. The aim is not to create something of value for oneself and others but to claim that what someone else has belongs by rights to oneself and demand that it be handed over. One abandons the field of forces of first-order power in order to exert a different kind of power on a moral plane that trumps physical force. Nietzsche analyzes the revolution of Christianity in something like these terms, as we have already indicated. Of course, for most subscribers to wokeism, Christianity counts generally as part of the establishment and belongs to what needs to be overcome. It is patriarchal, colonialist, racist, etc. But now that wokeism has infiltrated and become the establishment itself, the same logic will soon turn against it.[139]

---

[138] Bruce Bawer, *The Victims' Revolution: The Rise of Identity Studies and the Closing of the Liberal Mind*.

[139] Ani O'Brien, Wokies are the establishment – Redline (wordpress.com). Accessed 7/6/2023. See, further, Joanna Williams, *How Woke Won: The Elitist Movement that Threatens Democracy, Tolerance and Reason* (Wanstead, UK: John Wilkes Publishing, 2022). Christopher F. Rufo, *America's Cultural Revolution: How the Radical Left Conquered Everything* (New York: Broadside, 2023).

In this situation, the game is changed from meeting the real challenges of bettering life for oneself and one's community to claiming privileges or compensations from those who seem to have come out on top and whom we deem to have profited at our expense. Unfortunately, the compensation for contesting and fighting against the success of others is very often much greater than the rewards gleaned from single-minded dedication to achieving success in one's own endeavors to produce useful results for the common good. The latter entails confronting a recalcitrant world or nature and learning how to make it productive in spite of all the risks and unforeseeable comeuppances. It requires engagement without limits of one's ingenuity and perseverance to achieve goals that thitherto seemed impossible or out of reach. More valuable than claims made against others for compensation in the name of equity is the opportunity to be productive and build a productive life of one's own. We own what we create and disseminate of ourselves in a far truer sense than what is deeded to us by some kind of entitlement.

Inequality of means exploited to gain advantage over others rather than to serve them is a blemish, but to think that the solution is for governmental authority simply to take control to ensure that all individuals have equal resources is far too simplistic. Far more important than having resources nominally or quantitatively equal with someone else's is to have something—anything whatever—that is genuinely one's own. Individual lives are unique and not all have the same opportunities. Each individual has a hand dealt them by unaccountable factors of genetic endowment and all manner of circumstances. Not all individuals can or should be made after the same mold. What counts is not how much you have in comparison with someone else but what is truly your own without measure because no one else can be you or have exactly what you have. The focus always on monetary resources makes them become more important than one's own character, one's capabilities, one's outlook, one's upbringing and unique life project.

Cancel culture and cancel history are brought in to determine who gets what, but the effect is to deprive everyone of history and culture and of anything that can be made genuinely their own through the creative work of self-cultivation through time and history. On the pretense that they can produce a more just distribution of rights and privileges, woke agendas redistribute privileges based on identity labels. Life has its ways of dealing out boons and banes, and the attempt to neutralize them cannot but arrest this incalculable process and kill life itself. Wokes typically aim to substitute their own control by their principles and values, but these artifices are not superior to life and its chances. Seeing our worth in terms of our share of the same type of resources that everyone else has already condemns society to dissension and strife. Only when giving as much as one can of oneself is felt and believed to be the highest value does society stand a chance of functioning harmoniously. Native American communities were entirely focused on what one could give to one's community, not on having more wealth than others. In this regard, they could serve as models.[140]

---

[140] *Touch the Earth: A Self-Portrait of Indian Existence*, ed. T. C. McLuhan (New York: Outerbridge & Lazaard, 1971). The anthology has become a fundamental reference for widespread general interest in native American culture in France under the title *Pieds nus sur la terre sacrée* (Paris: Denoël, 2021).

36.

Entitlements and Stigmas
versus Objective Exigencies

The social justice movement has contributed to creating a culture of racialized, genderized, class entitlements and stigmas. At a very crude, schematic level (which is nevertheless operative on people's psyches, just as racism is), favor is formally accorded to those who are black and female and poor, while a presumption of guilt is attributed to those who are white, male, and economically well-off. This polarization actually works to the prejudice and dehumanizing of human beings belonging to all such categories, whether on the good side or the bad, because all are evaluated otherwise than as human individuals. Individuals are treated, instead, as tokens representing general types.

Determining individuals' receipts and resources by entitlements politically fought for or socially negotiated and won rather than being produced by individuals' own creative activity and persevering effort, and not without risk, results in a kind of guaranteed and systemic inauthenticity. We are amalgamated into patronized and stigmatized social groups rather than determining our destinies by our own self-fashioning and free engagements and performance.

That more minorities participate more visibly in power and prestige is absolutely to be applauded. It has become highly conspicuous in numerous institutions such as universities and government agencies in our quickly evolving society. However, that individuals become successful *because* they are members of minorities is unfair to them in the first place, since it deflects attention from their own true merits, and it is unfair to all others as well because all rely on those whose human application and ingenuity qualifies them to take on objectively real and demanding tasks. Much more than political jockeying for advantage based on a "diversity" profile is necessary to manage the chaotic challenges of our societies. It is necessary to confront the untowardness and recalcitrance of the material and social worlds and render them accommodating to human purposes.

Taking issues of race and gender equality as if they were matters that could or should be treated independently of these challenges produces what are aptly called "social justice fallacies."[141] There is no substantive reason to expect all social groups to produce comparable outcomes, and trying to make that happen by controlling results does a disservice to all, starting from those it is supposed to help. Paternalistic and patronizing approaches undermine inner strength and self-reliance. Ralph Waldo Emerson's ringing paean to this special virtue urgently recollects what is at stake here.[142]

Thomas Sowell refutes the nearly universal assumption that dramatic improvements for blacks and minorities are the result of government programs and politics of compensatory aid. The largest gains were made between 1940 and 1960 before the Civil Rights Movement. Treating blacks and other minorities as victims has been a bane to them and distorted the true nature and causes of their rise, as well as of their plight. It also distorts accurate perception of the objective exigencies that society needs to meet.

Recent disastrous bank failures in Silicon Valley, California, as well as looming doom for the American dollar, are being called out by conservative commentators as consequences of placing incompetent personnel in top leadership positions based on "diversity" hiring. Jobs are assigned to individuals unqualified professionally but belonging to certain races and genders for whom "victory" can then be celebrated.[143] In the woke-saturated ambience of government and media and even business today, according to such commentators, we are no longer looking at the actual results of what such personnel are supposed to accomplish (and also ward off, like economic collapse). Their being representatives of now favored identity groups in their newly acquired positions of authority is

---

[141] Thomas Sowell, *Social Justice Fallacies* (New York: Basic Books, 2023).

[142] Self-Reliance.pages (emersoncentral.com)

[143] https://www.youtube.com/watch?v=_1g3I9qyvF8. Accessed 7-16-2023. Stephanie Pomboy (Silicon Valley Bank Collapse) on Tucker Carlson Tonight | Fox News 3/14/23 (youtube.com). Accessed 4-25-2023

touted as success by the hiring authorities—regardless of the fact that the financial institutions they are responsible for teeter and plummet into ruin while driving the economy to the brink of catastrophe. We do not need to view this as the conservative commentators do, but still we should be able to see and understand their point. Detailed and exacting economic analysis needs to take precedence over social profiling. The merciful intervention on behalf of truly disadvantaged people facing abject conditions is a duty and a godsend. Filling quotas to fabricate a façade of political correctness is not.

In certain contexts of explicit bigotry, wokeism, as a militant movement defending minority rights, is certainly called for and performs a necessary function. But it can become counterproductive by supporting assignment of tasks and roles as a matter of right or entitlement whereas such assignments actually require rigorous training and skillful engagement, no less than creative talent and passionate commitment. No one is qualified for difficult and demanding missions simply on the basis of their race or gender. The prominence of these identitarian criteria in woke culture risks dulling our perception of the objective exigencies that do need to be addressed by capable personnel.

37.

How not to Repeat
but rather Redeem History

Race has become a kind of entitlement in the current culture imbued with woke ideology. Being black in America means being a victim, at least by inheritance, of the Atlantic slave trade and carries with it a certain kind of entitlement. Being female means being the victim of patriarchy, of misogyny and discrimination against women, and brings with it a right to compensatory consideration. These revisionary positions are based on penetrating insights into certain aspects of history, but they remain one-sided. While based on a sense of equal justice for all, they are manipulated by certain parties claiming a morally superior or politically more correct position as justification for their own exercise of power. Alternative histories can prevent one history alone from determining and claiming exclusive rights to impinge on our present actions. An alternative history should work to prevent any one authorized history from canceling out all others rather than to replace it in imposing itself hegemonically.

What is right in wokeism is the retrieval of histories of oppression to influence our sympathies toward individuals and groups who have received particularly unfair treatment. But identifying oneself as good because of this recognition and on grounds of representing claims of social justice (in the current jargon, "virtue signaling") has become a way of instrumentalizing these histories of victimhood to advance one's own empowerment. Walter Benjamin's alternative to the history of the victors, in contrast, is radically revisionary on behalf of the oppressed (those whom Frantz Fanon later called "the wretched of the earth"). It is not the history of a certain party or power movement. It has to break all partisan histories open to what none can control so as to embrace a truly universal—what Benjamin calls a "messianic"—history of redemption.[144]

Like most other people, I hate seeing people of any race or gender being bullied or demeaned. As a child, I instinctively cringed and felt mortified by the slurs against women as incorrigible gossips or dangerous drivers or whatever. Simply to disparage or diminish anyone for the race or gender or social class to which they belong is a patently unfair appeal to reigning prejudices, whether they have any general validity or not, to disqualify a certain individual. Of course, not all prejudices are necessarily or completely false. As Hans-Georg Gadamer demonstrates with philosophical acumen in *Truth and Method* (*Wahrheit und Methode,* 1960), prejudice, alongside authority and tradition, is epistemologically necessary for our initial orientation among agents and factors that we cannot yet assess individually. The fact that we work with and from preconceptions is built into human cognition. At best, we can become more critically aware of our prejudices.

We cannot undo the wrongs of the past. They are far too many and too contradictory—too multivalent and interwoven with their opposites. Whichever we choose, we forget others—many others, by far the greater share. This approach of singling out which wrongs of the past are going to become issues in the present is steered by resentment or, in any case, by someone's prejudices. To overcome this legacy, we have to be able to start anew in the present and ask what is fair to all. No one is really entitled to anything except in relation to and in consideration of all others. No entitlements are purely natural: they are granted by recognition, and certainly there are grounds for this in what we do and produce. But we will not be able to advance without some type of amnesty and forgiveness granted in people's hearts.

As long as we blame some identity groups generically as responsible for the world's ills and exonerate others as innocent of any implication in

---

[144] Walter Benjamin,"Geschichtsphilosophische Thesen," in *Illuminationen. Ausgewählte Schriften* I, ed. Siegfried Unseld (Frankfurt am Main: Suhrkamp, 1977), 268-281, translated as "Theses on the Philosophy of History," *Illuminations: Essays and Reflections*, ed. Hannah Arendt (New York: Harcourt Brace Jovanovich, 1968) and "Theologisch-politisches Fragment," in *Illuminationen,* 282-83, translated as "Theological-Political Fragment."

them and use these determinations to redistribute privileges, we are only going to deepen resentments based on class or other group identity markers. We are not going to be able to rise above rivalry and conflict to catalyze reconciliation and affirm our necessary collective stewardship of the world. The necessary premise for justice is action aiming at common goods transcending group or party interests. All races and genders and classes have to be accepted before they can be organized into a collective effort of establishing justice as their common interest. The focus on who has what cannot be the starting point. Material possession is the most concrete given that we have to work with, but it cannot be consensual because it divides us into haves and have nots. Intellectual and spiritual goods, in contrast, are by their nature shared. We have to reason from these common and incalculable goods to their material consequences. Real value is not reducible to identical or measurable terms. Reality lies always beyond whatever we can explicitly express: it is bound up with conditions and contexts that can never be totally gathered into our accounting. In this immediate sense, it is "apophatic."

We are able to recognize some type of value as absolute without being able to specify or define it. This I propose as a necessity if we want to live with others in some law-abiding, normed way rather than only in a Hobbesian condition of war of all against all. We can all recognize an authority of the real that is not merely a human invention or imposition. Whether we intuitively believe in such a reality or not, its hypothetical recognition is rendered necessary if we want to have a regulated relation with others. We cannot make others recognize such a norm. All we can do is live as if it existed and thereby incentivize others to do likewise. There is always a risk that they will not, and certainly many will set up all manner of defenses and denial against such recognition. However, some of us have to prepare the path of peace as well. Charles Taylor's (Hegelian) philosophy of recognition of a plurality of community identities leads in this direction of recognizing the good as an absolute value preexisting human evaluations and interpretations.[145] Such recognition is the source

---

[145] Charles Taylor, *Multiculturalism: Examining the Politics of Recognition*, ed. Amy Gutmann (Princeton: Princeton University Press, 1994)

of morality. The multicultural situation which makes this exigency so acute in our time is in considerable measure a legacy of colonialism.

38.

A Culture of Blaming
the Others One Covets

Our entire culture has fallen into the syndrome of looking for others to blame for whatever irks us and leaves us unsatisfied rather than focusing on what we ourselves can do constructively to change things—first and foremost ourselves—for the better. The mentality or strategy of blaming others and of attacking whoever has been more successful than us invites to the worst excesses of a kind of cultural opportunism. The Cultural Revolution (1966-76) of Maoist China played out this tragic scenario in its catastrophic consequences on an epic scale.

In a typical bourgeois outlook, only social standing and money count in establishing the worth and dignity of people. Once we either reverse or radicalize such an outlook, as in Marxist and Neoliberal movements respectively, which are both principal roots of wokeism, whoever has less of these typically bourgeois commodities has a grievance and a mission to demand that others deal them their fair share. Eventually, all value is reduced to just money. Forgotten is how we generate our own true value by our own creative and productive activity and self-fashioning rather than having it paid out and accorded us through a system of objectivized values, social credits, or rankings. Whatever is publicly expressed or signaled is a calculated, artificial profiling and not real value itself.

Once we begin measuring ourselves against one another and using external, objectified measures of value such as money or prestige, we are bound to become conscious of being *un*equal, and we become slaves to all manner of envy and covetousness. If we are free to be ourselves, the question is not who has how much wealth or power as a thing possessed. What counts is rather what we are capable of doing for ourselves and for one another. We are unequal in our natural and acquired capacities. We are incommensurable much more profoundly than we are equal or unequal by any differences in monetary wealth. Politics and society should make us free to exercise our unique capabilities to the fullest degree rather than justifying the imposition of constraints in the interests of "equality" and conformity.

The focus of the latter sort of compensatory politics is almost entirely on what one has, not on what one is and does. Even if it is for the personal psychological damage wrought by child abuse, seeking monetary compensation drives legal battles and encourages all to consider themselves in terms of money. Are we going to spend our lives seeking compensation for wrongs of the past? Are there not innumerably more such wrongs than can be identified and rectified, and are we not ourselves perpetrators of some of them, at least passively, for example, in our role as consumers? Of course, certain recognitions and restitutions are essential to the ongoing process of reconciliation among humans. But tearing down your fellows, on the pretext of being more a victim and therefore more deserving than they, is not a formula for healthy, affirmative living.

The supposed beneficiaries are put in the position of being passive recipients, victims, needing to be handed special help rather than being challenged by adversity to realize and leverage their own strength and potential to the utmost. Of course, the language specifying that such compensation is "not charity but only justice" is meant to defend recipients from such degradation. Yet the disguise is thin and may be felt to be humiliating, firstly by those who receive money for producing nothing, thanks to a revision of history. The rhetoric that claims to be demanding only justice, not favors, betrays a delusion of holding the keys by oneself alone to what is truly just. Such an attitude signals an abstraction from, or willful ignoring of, the human give-and-take in which alone such "justice" can be negotiated.

Indigenous North American peoples have traditionally resisted playing this game of seeking compensations on the terms of the colonizers and have adhered to their culture and identity as more valuable than any indemnifications that would serve, irresistibly, to assimilate them to the colonizers. Of course, this attitude is far from unanimous, as the reservation casino industry attests. Generally, however, these indigenous peoples have stood for refusing to be assimilated into a system that deprives all of anything that is intrinsically their own.

We can make a relative distinction between what we are and what we have. What we are cannot be given away, nor even be taken away, though it is of course influenced by everything that happens to us and becomes part of the history that makes us up. Our focus has to be on building uniquely productive, engaged selves and relationships instead of on what we possess of the common currency of wealth that is measurable in terms of purchase power and consumption.

Not a forced shift in conventional monetary resources so much as a shift of emphasis to another kind of value exceeding monetary value altogether would be real progress.

What we possess should be considered not as our own to hoard or dispose of but rather as our responsibility to manage in the most equitable and humane way. Anything in excess of basic necessities should be seen not primarily as serving for our own private consumption but rather as a part of the collective goods that we are responsible for shepherding for the good of all, ourselves included. In this scheme, no one has anything for themselves alone as their private possession, even though private property can certainly be recognized as what we have the responsibility to take care of and preserve in its fruitfulness. This is how Native Americans viewed and treated the land on which they lived.[146]

---

[146] *Touch the Earth: A Self-Portrait of Indian Existence*, ed. T. C. McLuhan (New York: Outerbridge & Lazaard, 1971), anthologizes original native testimonials of this attitude.

39.

What is Wealth and How is it Shared?

Changing the structure of incentives so as to appeal to the ethical sense and generosity of those who have resources, rather than shaming and blaming them, are preferable means, depending on the circumstances, of gaining results by disarming otherwise inevitable resistance. What people are attached to may not, after all, be so much material wealth, which is something to be used and shared, not simply possessed. Much more recalcitrant is their pride and unwillingness to accept being assigned the villain's part in history and society and the world. Christian Scripture has been a crucial source for learning to relativize all worldly values and focus on the intrinsic worth of persons. It is too quickly condemned in the wholesale rejection of Western cultural tradition.

The reasons for giving up excess resources and sharing with our poorer neighbors had best be positive appeals to solidarity and the willingness to help rather than withering accusations of robbery directed against all those enjoying a presumably more privileged standing. Such revindications need to be couched in terms appealing for cooperative effort—at least in tandem with the accusatory tones—if they are going to stand a chance of gaining acceptance. The ideological bickering, the attacking and defensiveness, needs to stop if people are going to be pierced by compassion and make radical choices that will make a real difference. It is not primarily a matter of sharing benefits so that others can consume what the rich would then no longer consume. Instead, the task is one of distributing responsibility for administering resources in a way that redeems them from immediate consumption and preserves them for others and for the future.

Everything depends on the vision of social justice that is operating in a given culture. If it is looked at as a matter of results, and we assume that what is fair is that all individuals or even groups in a society end up possessing an equal share of its resources, we consider this merely as a problem of distribution of wealth whose existence is presupposed in abstraction from all the ways and means by which wealth is actually produced and acquired—and also used and shared out. Wealth is taken merely as a possession to be distributed equitably in a zero-sum game. Its production is taken for granted. But the production of wealth, at least in its basics, does not happen all by itself. There are enormous risks and contingencies involved in acquiring from the material world the means of human sustenance and enhancement. These risks are certainly not for everyone. Rare individuals conceive a personal calling to invest themselves in uncertain and unprecedented enterprises.

To look at wealth simply in terms of what people have distorts its nature. Real wealth is very personal, not just a matter of having but of administering and managing, not to mention discovering and acquiring. People's ability to manage wealth for their own advantage and that of others is also enormously unequal. Often people are not prepared or even inclined to provide for anything beyond their personal needs. Disproportionate consumption, of course, is ugly and anti-social. The justification for allowing accumulations of private wealth is not to sanction grossly unequal consumption. But to see all wealth as simply for the purpose of consumption also distorts our view. Constructive projects of all sorts are rendered possible by accumulations of wealth. Most wealth beyond basic consumption serves for some kind of investment. Widely dispersed private interests may be much better at discerning and directing possibilities for productive, life-enhancing investments than government bureaucrats. Private interest is of a different, more directly involved nature than public management. This is the level at which communist countries like Russia and China discovered that the private sector was far better at developing their economies than were government plans.

The relation between real productivity and accumulation of wealth is now, admittedly, blurred and perverted by modern money economies and even by virtual currencies that are entirely detached from real value. In principle, wealth is a product of human engagement of self in the world. It entails and engenders a mutually transforming and reciprocally compromising process. There is something direct and natural in what accrues to me as the result of my work and ingenuity. The individuals who produce something have a kind of natural right to dispose of it as their unique contribution to the goods made available for social use. Even more than any monetary value, one's own work belongs to one; we forge ourselves through what we make and do.

Calculating worth in monetary terms is already a grotesque reduction and travesty of real value. Even difficult and health-compromising work like mining has often been the source of pride and identity to the communities formed around such activity. Miners and their families knew that they served a useful purpose and bitterly regretted the condemnation and the closing of the Bauxite mines in the south of France, in Provence (le Var), completed in 1990. They knew that they were appreciated, as their work had considerable importance, and they had developed their own culture of Stoic virtues and technical expertise. They felt themselves left with nothing but memories when this industry was stopped by company decree.[147] Nostalgic celebrations are held in certain towns similarly in Germany's Ruhr district once dedicated to their coal mining industries.

These examples manifest a form of attachment to a social identity, yet one constructed through work and life commitment and not based on identity markers. Identities are moral constructions, but they can reflect and adhere to real production and performance. Even so, the question is not what are their deserts as a group but rather what does a certain group deliver based on its own capabilities? Identity serves here in the structuring of collective activity rather than for claiming rights and entitlements.

---

[147] Eloquent on this subject is Eric Blanco's 2019 film *Les Gueules Rouges*. ARDECHE IMAGES - Les Gueules rouges (lussasdoc.org).

40.

Distributive Justice and its Counterfeits

Are the well-off responsible for the plight of the poor everywhere in the world? Certainly, equitable sharing of resources is imperative, but husbandry of our resources is also required. We need globally to do everything possible to enable people to be productive and, of course, to be primary beneficiaries of their own labor and endeavors. But it is not a zero-sum game. Having more wealth does not necessarily mean consuming more. Taking away from those who are employing their resources to create something unique and invaluable for all in order that they be spent instead on mass consumption, especially liquor and drugs, or beer and cigarettes, is hardly a gain for anyone. Wealth serves not only, nor even primarily, for consumption.

The more globalized and mediatized the world becomes, the more we feel responsible for contiguous situations. It used to seem that each person or society had their own inalienable destiny, but this becomes less plausible with the increased interconnectedness of human society as it progressively constructs itself. The interdependence of all becomes more and more conspicuous. Still, it is imperative that we avoid depriving individuals of responsibility for their own lives. Many extreme and obscene differences in wealth and especially in rights blight society. But there are also screaming differences in effectiveness and competence and social responsibility in managing whatever resources are controlled by different social players and by distinct individuals. To see resources only from the point of view of possessing and consuming them rather than of creating and renewing them is to condemn them to be abused and wasted.

Inequality of wealth is all too evident and all too often an eyesore. But if we think of wealth purely in terms of consumption, we have an entirely distorted and perverted view of its nature and use. Having control and responsibility for property and managing resources are not the same as consuming goods. To see wealth merely as a claim on and capacity for consumption is a base perversion. Some people have assumed much more responsibility than others for building industries and enterprises and have invested themselves, with risk and commitment and devotion of their vital energy and their whole lives, in specific forms of economic production or resource conservation. Only experience can demonstrate who has the competence to assume leading roles of management and control over resources. I do not see it as a matter of deserts, as do many moralizing commentators with their accusations of inequality.[148] In ancient discourse since Cicero, the *res publica* came first before any and all individuals. On this basis, Cicero expressed unqualified condemnation of the ruinous policy ("qua peste quae potest esse maior?") of equal distribution of property ("aequationem bonorum").[149]

Should what we have be determined by the state? Is the state a possible establisher and guarantor of justice? Certainly not of an open idea of justice. The state can apply formulas and can do so equally for all. Some feel that such application is the main concern of government. But others will feel oppressed by any formula. God, too, is no respecter of persons (Romans 2: 11)—which means no respecter of social distinctions. Surely, a profound respect for the infinite worth of every person is divine. This is a basis for distributive—or, better, non-distributive—justice. It requires an openness to the indeterminate. Of course, not all feel comfortable with forgoing guarantees though insurance policies and admitting that life is risk.

Plato emphasizes that unity in the state results from diversity of its citizens and their abilities. (*Republic* 370 b). People are naturally different, no two are exactly alike. They are suited to perform different and necessary functions. These differences rather than sameness are the basis for the unity of the city (372 a). Difference rather than equality is the key to the perfection of the city.[150] Managing resources is one crucial axis of

---

[148] Are rich different from you and me? Would we be better off without them? — Harvard Gazette.

[149] M. Tullius Cicero, *De Officiis*, Book II, paragraph 73, trans. Walter Miller (Cambridge, Mass. [London]: Harvard University Press, 1913).

[150] This point is effectively underscored by Montserrat Herrero, *Filosofía política,* 80.

differentiation. Of course, all have certain basic requirements for which they need to provide. For this to be their responsibility rather than the state's may be preferable since all are then motivated by their own necessity. Whichever type of "right" is declared, crucial is an economy rendering it possible for individuals to provide for themselves. State guarantees may impose a moral sense that ignores reality as given from beyond human machination and calculation.

I salute all efforts aiming at equity in concrete situations with real human individuals, even while I caution against anyone imposing their formula or definition of what equity should look like. "One Law for the Lion and Ox is oppression," prophesied Blake in the "Marriage of Heaven and Hell." Concretely, equity is a mystery beyond anyone's grasp that we need to seek out together. It is apophatic in the sense that it is not identical with any of our definitions of it or prescriptions for it. It manifests best as a free offering of self for others. Such an apophatic ideal of equity is difficult to advocate because of its being indefinite and always to-be-defined by collective, interactive effort. Unfortunately, defining one's enemy and nemesis is generally an easier route to focusing passions and therewith motivating actions. Resentment is too often the driving force of egalitarian political agendas.

The Gospel of Matthew 20: 1-16 relates the parable of the landowner who hires workers at different hours of the day for one denarius and pays them all equally exactly as agreed at the end of the day, causing those who have worked all day to grumble. Comparing what we receive with what others receive blinds us to the justice of our own lot. We lose sight of our own lot as being in itself infinite. Such, at least, is the gift of life. In this vertical dimension, it is incomparably great. Loss of this dimension of perception of the infinite value of the gift of being itself—and of whatever else is granted to us in our own unique endowments—is sure to lead to a society of greed and a culture of resentment. Obviously, all require access to certain resources necessary for life, but viewing the value of one's life as dependent on one's wealth and possessions and measuring it in this common currency is a disaster. Of course, we need to avoid all forms of hoarding which would prevent others from gaining access to what is truly their own. These are ethical imperatives flowing from unconditional respect for oneself and for equal rights of others to exist and flourish.

In its currently perverted form, property has been reified into something that can simply be transferred by fiat from one person to another following judgments concerning deserts and guilt of whatever social authorities. More profoundly, property is what is made one's own by one's own purposeful, creative activity and labor. John Locke, the great defender of property rights in the liberal tradition would be horrified by the way property has been privatized in contemporary liberal politics. In Locke's definition, property is "one's life, one's liberty, and one's possessions"—all these taken together.[151] Property does not consist in indifferently accumulated wealth which can be shifted around like tokens in a game of monopoly—or like money in our economies. Property is intrinsically connected with one's own being and activity. It does not exist as such without its possessor and is not in principle expropriable.

---

[151] Locke, *Second Treatise on Government*, 9.123. Cf. 5.27 and Montserrat Herrero, *Filosofía política*, 344-48.

41.

Claiming to Defend Victims Justifies All —Vladimir Putin's Example

The woke ideological discourses of victimization work by identifying the culprit—white male Western heterosexual—and from there anything is justifiable in order to combat the universal foe. Vladmir Putin uses an analogous logic in order to justify his invasion of the Ukraine. The source of all the evil in the world is the USA or Anglo-Saxon hegemony working by violence through NATO. He presents himself as acting only to protect Russia and free the world from this neo-colonial enslavement. In this light, the underlying logic of the woke discourse, which he recognizes as Western and attacks, is the basis of his own imperialist geopolitical program in deeper ways than he would wish to acknowledge. The discourse of victimization has become the indispensable currency for political revindications of all types in our times that have become so generally and pervasively woke in their sensibilities for better or worse, like it or not.

The Russian war on Ukraine highlights at least one aspect of the culture war that has been going on for decades. Everything is justified by resistance against the dominant group, in this case the Western powers grouped around the NATO alliance. It is almost unbearably painful and frustrating to observe what is happening all over the world in the name of resistance to oppression that has been newly evaluated as such based on various revisionist histories. Observation of such a vindictive logic of opposing the supposed oppressor triggers for me a replay of the traumas I have directly experienced in analogous power moves in local politics and in my own professional sphere at the university.

The scapegoat mechanism is still operating, albeit in reverse: being a victim is used to exert a kind of unimpeachable right to power and priority.

Yet the violence belongs to and is generated by the community in its often concealed rivalries, and pinning the blame on some particular party is the way of perpetuating misrecognition of the true source of the violence. The solution is taken to be elimination or neutralization of one component of the whole, one of the protagonists. But this only masks the underlying problem of mutually destructive aggression among all competitors in mimetically motivated power struggles.

It must be admitted that there is something correct in Putin's assessment. The current liberal or woke ideology flourishing in the West has grown up to a considerable extent on the ground of a narcissistic "me generation" comprised of individuals declaring themselves "unapologetically me."[152] Putin revealingly identifies some of the self-indulgent aspects of Western wokeism catering to "spoiled individuals steeped in consumerism and feelings of entitlement."[153] We should be reminded that, much more profoundly, whatever we have ought to be viewed as a gift and not an entitlement. As Saint Paul in his First Letter to the Corinthians (4: 7) pertinently queries: "What do you have that you did not receive?" (τί δὲ ἔχεις ὃ οὐκ ἔλαβες;). This means that no one has any unqualified right—not even the right to exist. All rights are relative to the rights of others.

Putin has deliberately taken on the role of being the nemesis of the West, calling out its values for corrupt and decadent. Here he has a point. He can plausibly posture as representing a more heroic, less decadent phase of culture than currently prevails in our self-indulgent, hedonistic Western societies. Putin's atrocities are patent. But so is the American nuclear bombing of Hiroshima taken in itself without a comprehensive context, and the latter can never be complete. Who could possibly have a right to cause that degree of unilateral destruction? That would be to place oneself in the position of the divine judge with the prerogative of deciding who has a right to live and who will be destroyed and maimed or live with a burnt-up skin or without limbs for the rest of their lives. It is not ethically tolerable nor hardly even imaginable that we should deliberately do such

---

[152] This expression is pointed up by Hans-Georg Möller in a video presentation: Wokeism – the leftwing of neoliberalism – Redline (wordpress.com). Accessed 12-20-2022

[153] Home | GUST International Conference 2023

harm to anyone. Yet it happened, and for many, certainly for most Americans, there is no question of remorse. But for many around the world America represents the great threat and evil that it is heroic to oppose by any means.

Whether this act of unprecedented destruction was necessary to end the war and impose peace around the world is not a question on which I wish to sit in judgment. The lesson of history, in any case, is that having a monopoly over coercive power almost inevitably corrupts its possessors, however good they may esteem themselves. Thinking that America could unilaterally hold the entire world and evil in check by its incomparably superior sense of right backed up by incomparable destructive power is to usurp the status of God and recognize no other god beside oneself. God, in Christianity at least, does not quash evil by superior force but endures even crucifixion in order to triumph only by (moral) right, not might.

Destroying others can be justified only by the logic of self-defense. And Japan was determined to destroy the US. *Ergo*, use of a superior and decisive weapon was justified to effectively end the conflict. That was perhaps tragically necessary in the real world. Can we possibly design an alternative to such unconscionable destruction? The fact that contemporary Japan is an ally of the United States and the post-war European community gives some ground for hope. Resentment and mistrust can attenuate and vanish and be replaced by cooperation if circumstances change and motivate it. The key, in any case, is overcoming the deadly oppositional thinking that leads to war and social disintegration into mutually hateful factions and replacing it with a holistic and integrative type of thinking that I find modeled in great poetic classics such as the *Divine Comedy* and *Don Quixote*.

42.

Continuing the Race for Dominance
—or Uniting in Organic Community?

Racialized and genderized optics have blinded us to the redemptive genius in our own intellectual traditions. These traditions are nourished from all sorts of cultural and racial roots, yet they are often appropriated or invidiously misconstrued and used for racial and cultural politics. A single-gendered face and monovalent identity-label are pasted on what is produced by a heterogeneous assemblage functioning as an organic community, with all its internal differentiations.[154] Émile Durkheim, in *De la division du travail social* (1893), defined "organic" solidarity based on division of labor in opposition to "mechanical" solidarity based on similarities of race, sex, religion, etc. Identity differences thus become functional and unitive rather than only formal and divisive.'

Wokeism on the offensive can become an aggressive ideology that aggravates rivalry and resentment between classes and races and genders. It accentuates self-consciousness about which categories one belongs to and assigns them generic merits or demerits. There are guilty and innocent, good and bad races and genders. Some are legitimated in feeling themselves "unapologetically me," while others are summoned by their skin color or sexual morphology to assume the lion's share of guilt for all the horrors of history and the wrongs of at least what is considered relevant in the past. Forcing such confessions is not the way to get all to work together in building a more just society. There is a world of difference

---

[154] Thorsten Botz-Bornstein offers topical reflections in his edited volume, *Re-Ethnicizing the Minds? Tendencies of Cultural Revival in Contemporary Philosophy* (Amsterdam: Rodopi, 2006). I find still valuable and relevant also the analyses by Jacques Barzun, for instance, in *Race: A Study in Superstition* (New York: Harper & Row, 1965).

between assuming responsibility freely out of one's own desire for reconciliation joined with one's own willingness to sacrifice and having guilt and the role of scapegoat foist upon one by others who use it for their own empowerment and for putting down those they have maligned and supplanted.

These valuations depend on how history is read. Which facts are going to be highlighted as determining the sense of all the rest? Exploitation, enslavement, subjugation are elements of human history in arguably all of its manifestations. However, so are progressive elements of mutual help and organization and coordination to achieve common goals and cultural ideals of sharing and generosity, which have been developed in the West in ways that have also impacted human life worldwide. If one looks only at unequal distribution of wealth and blends out how it was created and acquired, the distribution seems unethical. No one as such deserves more than anyone else. Why should the West be richer than other parts of the world?

However, the West, with its technological invention and industrialization, has also done a lot to create the means of material improvement for human lives. I don't see this as entitling anyone to more, but it does have something to do with accounting for inequality, which otherwise might be seen simply as theft. A consideration not just turned toward the historical past, furthermore, must comprehend motivation and incentives for the tough work of discovery and production of the means of wealth. Humans are motivated by seeking gain in the first place for themselves and their families or communities. Grueling work and undergoing daunting challenges simply do not happen without powerful motivations driving individuals to extraordinary attempts and feats. That they themselves benefit in the first instance from such efforts is an essential part of what makes them happen. When society dictates what everyone receives without regard to performance, free agency and enterprise flag and deflate.

The self-sacrificial gesture of kenotic self-effacement, as modeled by Christ (Philippians 2: 5-11), can be offered as an act of renunciation, or self-abnegation and generosity. Of course, it will be taken by others to be weakness, as they triumphantly stomp into the ground the meek and yielding. But are we going to let them dictate the terms of social interaction as constant strife for hegemony? Can we not choose to live and die by a peaceful alternative of our own making—with the kenotic Christ (or Krishna or Buddha, etc.) as model?

Figure 4. Wheel of Fortune, from *Carmina Burana*, Anonymous.

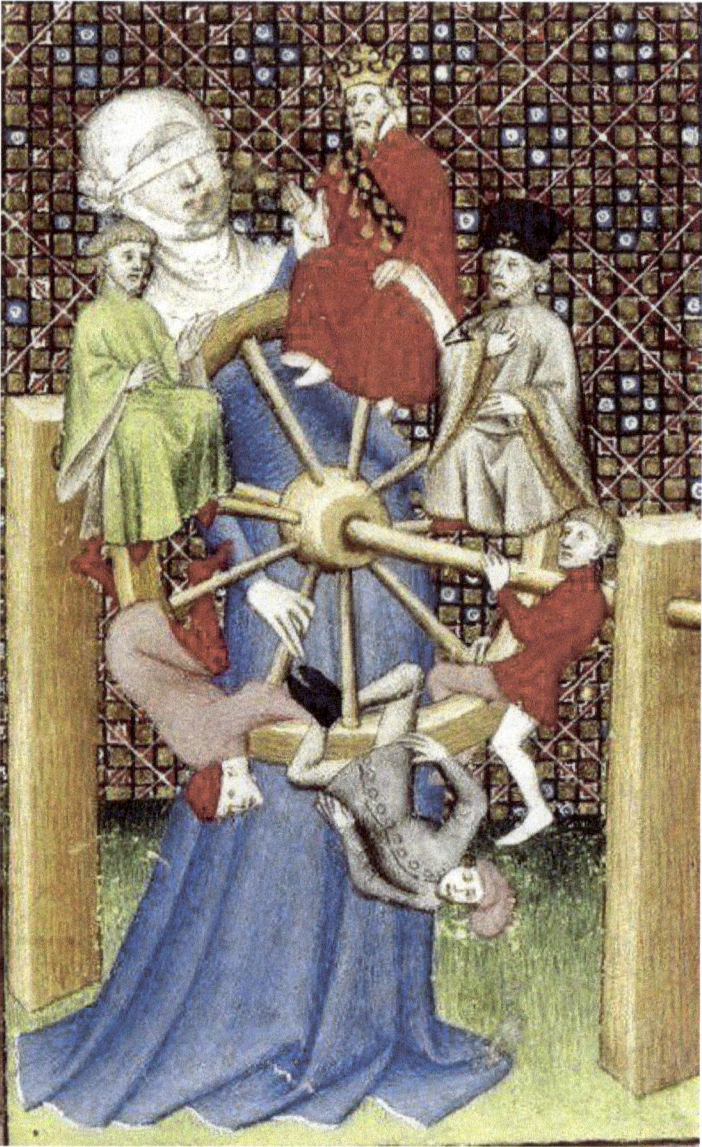

Figure 5. Blindfolded Fortune and her Wheel,
from Sir Thomas More, "Two short Ballads from the Tower of London."

Part V.

The Social Justice Revolution and its Inversion of Christian Revelation[155]

---

[155] This part of the book was adapted to appear as "A Kenotic and Postsecular Approach to Postcolonial Ethics and Politics: The Social Justice Revolution and its Inversion of Christian Revelation," *Postsecularity and Decoloniality: Global Perspectives,* eds. Justin Beaumont and Chris Baker (Washington D.C.: Lexington Books, forthcoming).

43.

A Decolonial, Post-secular, Postmodern Perspective

"Decoloniality" is one moniker for a general, amorphous culture of rejection of Western civilization that has become widespread within Western democratic countries in recent years. It is one of the pillars, along with antiracism, third-wave feminism, gay pride, trans-gender activism, and other movements that are all routinely treated nowadays under the umbrella of the rainbow term "wokeism." The wokeist demand for equal dignity and respect for all, regardless of social determinations, and the rejection of the racist, misogynist, imperialistic, and exploitative practices that have grotesquely marred the history of the modern world, we may hold to be ethically unimpeachable. The equal—or better, the infinite and incommensurable—worth of each individual regardless of skin color, sexual orientation or gender, ethnic heritage, socioeconomic class, nation, etc., is what we might call a universal ethical norm, although this was anything but obvious and universally accepted in pre-modern times and across world cultures.

Such a norm is an exact and literal reprise, though it may also have other derivations, of the ethical doctrine of the Christian New Testament. As summarized in the beatitudes of the Gospels, the downtrodden and despised, the poor and marginalized, are raised to absolutely equal respect and dignity in society, and they are further elevated to blessedness and glory in the eyes of God the Father of all. No longer slave or free, man or woman, Gentile or Jew, all are pronounced by Saint Paul to be equal and one in Christ Jesus (Galatians 3: 28). Historically, the liberationist revindications of today's emancipatory movements and the revisionist program of decolonialist politics owe much to the revolutionary impetus and ethos of the New Testament. It is not accidental that these radical political movements arise historically precisely in those societies that were revolutionized by the Christian religion and are its heirs.

Wokeism has vastly increased awareness of injustices of the colonialist past and has heightened sensitivity to social inequalities still in the present. Revisionary, woke-inspired histories have exposed the unconscionable horrors of slavery and colonialism with previously unimaginable vividness—with pathos and power to convert hearts and transform humanity.[156] However, in the wake of various forms of critique identifying as "postcolonial" that are sweeping across all disciplines at the university and shaking and transforming virtually all sectors of society in the democratic West, the demand for "social justice" has invested itself in social identities based on nation, region, race, gender, and other markers of identity to such an extent as to invert and pervert the force of the ethical imperative of equal dignity and rights for all individuals regardless of their social, economic, cultural, or national classifications. Rather than freeing from the oppression of race, gender, and class used as invidious categories, these inherently oppositional identity markers have been turned into the idols of a new self-righteous "religion" in a broad sense. Human beings are divided into oppressors and oppressed along the lines of guilty and innocent identities, which become the basis for establishing compensatory claims and undelimitable rights to restitution.[157]

Perhaps this divisiveness is inevitable in a wholly immanentized, secularized world in which the transcendent sense lent the world by Christian revelation has been discarded or abandoned. Thenceforth, human beings are perceived only in terms of their biological and social determinations. These phenomena are exhaustively perceptible on a purely immanent plane and material level of existence. Such characteristics are

---

[156] Poignant and readily available examples of such material include Never to Be Forgotten. The History of Colonialism - YouTube and BBC Documentary: The History of Racism - YouTube. The way the US prison system has been used to perpetrate racism is chillingly revealed by the documentary 13TH | FULL FEATURE | Netflix (youtube.com).

[157] Kenan Malik, *Not So Black and White: A History of Race from White Supremacy to Identity Politics* (London: Hurst, 2023) has worked out, historically, how identity politics have been appropriated by right-wing political constituencies to foment division into groups directly against the universalistic aspirations of the Enlightenment and its ideals.

finite and structured by oppositionality (black vs. white, male vs. female, straight vs. gay, rich vs. poor) rather than remaining infinitely open to a spiritual dimension in which opposites finally coincide. In our present predicament, a certain "post-secular" perspective—one capable of peering beyond the merely empirical universe of the secular world—is needed to break out of the impasse of pitting one identity against the other, of dividing society and the world up into oppressors and oppressed by generic labels. On the basis of abstract social identities, individuals are classified as being either victims or perpetrators of colonialism and its legacy. People are separated into those presumed to be either the beneficiaries of imperialism, with its inherent violence and injustice, or else those supposed to suffer from it, at least by inheritance. Such a configuration divides society into presumptively guilty and innocent identity groups that are then destined to fight each other. Each group is defined over against the other. Each becomes a competitor for favor and privilege, a rival, or even an enemy, an "existential" threat to the other that then needs to be eliminated.[158]

To escape this fate, which threatens increasingly to engulf Western, multicultural democracies, we need to recuperate the "negative theology" (knowledge of our ignorance of God[159]) that is the hidden source of the biblical revelation and that makes all of us truly equal in our essential *non-identity*, our intrinsic, inalienable nothingness before God (or the ultimately Real) and one another. The kenotic "self-emptying" of our identity, reducing it to the "nothing in particular" that we all truly share in common and that is deeper than whatever our identifying and distinguishing characteristics may be, is the way forward out of a decolonialism predicated on conflict between colonized and colonizers and the whole culture of resentment that surrounds it.[160] I endeavor to

---

[158] As already expounded in Part II, this logic is worked out in detail in terms of "mimetic desire" by René Girard.

[159] Johannes Aakjær Steenbuch, *Negative Theology: A Short Introduction* (Eugene, Oregon: Cascade Books, 2022), 97 et passim, elucidates this term specifically with reference to my usage of it.

[160] See my *On the Universality of What Is Not: The Apophatic Turn in Critical Thinking* (Notre Dame: University of Notre Dame Press, 2020), particularly Chapter

show how we can inherit finally a post-colonial, but also a post-secular, culture of respect for all people and for all species and for life itself as surpassing human comprehension and control and particularly the oppositional categorizations and social identities that are all too easily instrumentalized for abusive forms of power politics. Such a culture is "post-colonial" in that it takes account of the thoroughgoing critique of colonialism and the dismantling of the colonial systems of the nineteenth-century by European powers in the twentieth. However, it is also "post-secular" because it resists the wholesale rejection of any religious form of transcendence and of all theological thinking that has characterized a central strain of the modernist movement. The type of thinking I propose is thus "post-modern" in its critical turn away from hard-core, reductive forms of modern secularism.

My approach is not simply to reject identity and its politics but rather to reinscribe them into non-identity as the overarching condition and common ground that all share and that needs to remain in place in the background. This refocusing on what is not and cannot be objectively defined or reified brings all groups together as sharing a common predicament even while negotiations between differential identities take place. An unidentifiable absolute is affirmed by each culture in admittedly only relative terms that cannot be imposed on anyone else. Only by acknowledging one's common belonging (or common *un*belonging) to something non-identifiable can *universal* respect for others be upheld. How this form of rationality might intersect with post-secular and decolonial thinking can be thought through in terms of "reflexive secularization." By a self-reflexive act of consciousness, one transcends oppositional terms (such as secular versus religious) and sees both sorts of identifications in their common origin and mutual interdependence. Such thinking, as explained by Beaumont, Eder, and Mendieta, enables us to perceive the "immanent, reflexive, critical postures that aim to elucidate the co-determination of the colonial/decolonial, secular/post-secular

---

11, pp. 291-314. "Apophasis" is Greek for "negation," so negative theology is apophatic theology. "Kenosis," as an "emptying" of self, designates an essential aspect of such theology.

dialectical dyads." [161] This latter type of reflection highlighting the dialectical interdependence of opposites is kindred to my kenotic approach to reconceiving ethics and politics in a post-secular age.

---

[161] Justin Beaumont, Klaus Eder, and Eduardo Mendieta, "Reflexive secularization? Concepts, processes and antagonisms of postsecularity," *European Journal of Social Theory*, 23/3 (2020): 291-309. https://doi.org/10.1177/1368431018813769. Citation 300.

44.

Kenosis as the
Apophatic Solution to Societal Conflict

We are valorized and ennobled, in the final analysis and judgment, not by our degree of power or tyranny over others but by our dedication to serving them. This was the new and revolutionary teaching of the Christian Gospel. Women and minorities have perhaps, in recent centuries, borne a more obvious share of this dedication to others than have privileged white men. The latter perhaps, on average, have some catching up to do. At least in "progressive" social milieus, such a narrative is likely to be recognized as a fair assessment. In any case, this nobler part and role is an essential calling for all. Self-overcoming for the sake of serving others is literally crucial for the realization of each in their intrinsic worth and dignity as human and as called to be remade in the divine image. Of course, this principle in no way justifies holding any group in subjection: the offer of self must be free and not forced. The modern liberation movements and their successful carrying out are presupposed by this kenotic paradigm of self-surrender to God, or to the greater Good. However, to completely reject the model of human fulfillment through service to others and to consider success only in terms of one's own attainments, one's power over others, or one's own wealth as an individual, is to succumb to a false and insidious system of values.

This evangelical teaching still holds and is disseminated today, notably by Pope Francis's 2020 encyclical "On Fraternity and Social Friendship" titled *Fratelli tutti.* This title echoes words of Saint Francis of Assisi, whose journey to meet the sultan of Egypt, Malik al-Kamil, in an intercultural embassy of peace during the Fifth Crusade in 1219, has emblematic value for our own time. Saint Francis's purpose and teaching was to avoid contentious disputes and to "be subject to every human creature for the love God," as he wrote in his *Earlier Rule for the Friars Minor* (*Regula non bullata* 16: 3.6, cited in *Fratelli tutti*, paragraph 3).

The supposedly guilty group, as designated by typical woke narratives, according to today's identity politics, are white heterosexual males. In implementing the biblical paradigm of kenosis, they are called on to assume guilt like Christ in order to put an end to retaliatory vengeance. This exercise of a power higher than any power demonstrated on the field of battle, where one tries to subdue and destroy one's enemies, also reveals, for those who have eyes to see, that women and other supposedly suppressed groups, in many cases exerted far more power—and of an altogether higher, more spiritual sort—than those presumably lording it over them in terms of raw force or of apparent, formal hierarchy in ostensibly patriarchal civilization. Even in some Islamic societies, women may be invisibly in command in vital spheres of family and public life.[162] Christian revelation can serve to render visible this occulted spiritual sovereignty of the supposedly subaltern. In practical terms, the kenotic solution modeled by Christ and the New Testament's proclamation of this event remain today, as René Girard's thinking emphasizes, the way out of the dilemmas that tear our society apart into rival factions that become deadly enemies rather than cooperative partners in testing and feeling out together the common grounds on which to build an inclusive society.

To assume or accept that every individual or group should naturally be hell-bent on seizing as much power and wealth as possible for itself is a wrong orientation guaranteed to lead to frustration of virtually all individuals and to the general failure of society. Unless each person or group perceives their purpose in terms of serving a larger whole, in which they need not hold any more power than is good for all, we are trapped and enslaved in a perverse competition and struggle for hegemony rather than in a cooperative venture of world-building. This is the situation especially in our current culture obsessed with postcolonial revindications. Reclamation of reparations for wrongs long past keeps us divided. We will never right all the wrongs of the past except by building a redemptive future. This will require a spirit of forgiveness on all sides round.

---

[162] See *The Individual and Society in Islam*, eds. Abdelwahab Bouhdiba, Muḥammad Maʿrūf Dawālībī (Paris: UNESCO, 1998).

The seemingly insuperable problem we face today in our multi-cultural societies is that of reconstituting universal community. Any railroading through of a program, woke or otherwise, in the name of social justice, in favor of certain identities, only contributes to the sense of umbrage, if not outrage, of those who feel themselves excluded or, worse, condemned. We need to concentrate not on determining and declaring which identity groups are victims and which are perpetrators but rather on finding the grounds for a consensual society in which all individuals, independently of their labels and communitarian attachments, can participate and believe and identify (which entails also de-identifying).

While individuals and identity groups alike are all equal in rights, they are not all equal in their abilities, achievements, or needs. They are qualitatively differentiated, and certain differences in treatment may, as a consequence, be appropriate. The elderly or the young should not necessarily have exactly the same entitlements and protections as those not in these categories. Moreover, it is a category mistake to treat generic identities as if they were themselves individual subjects requiring equal treatment in every respect. So-called identities are qualities that can count for making relevant distinctions between individuals—but only on an individual basis depending on how they are combined with other characteristics. And if some qualities are better or worse, more or less well adapted for specific functions and purposes, this is not superiority or inferiority in dignity or worth but only differentiation in specific usefulness or functionality.

Rather than emphasizing organic communities, the revindication of racial and gender identities tends to impose the self-interestedness of gendered and racialized egos on us all and to substitute invidious perspectives of politicized factions for a global view of the general interest. Do newly empowered women and non-binaries or other upwardly mobile minorities have to pursue the same egotistical vanity and rivalry that, in woke narratives, has too often characterized masculine culture, pitting one gender against the other? Can we not overcome such an invidious, narcissistic focus on separate, competitive, individual identities and concentrate, instead, on the hybrid communities from which they arise?

An aggressive woke agenda can tend to incite other and often newly formed identity groups to aim to outdo white males in vanity and vindictiveness, at least according to the egoistic image projected onto this group. The others' excuse is that they are only giving back what they have received, but would it not be far better to effectively revolutionize the way social recognition is gained by redirecting it toward an organic community inclusive of all genders and races rather than abstracting individuals from this necessary nurturing ground and background? Gay and queer culture, for instance, should be recognized as one fascinating angle of approach to experiencing the world and being human that has produced some of the greatest art and literature of all time from Virgil to Leonardo da Vinci, Proust, Oscar Wilde, and Virginia Woolf. It should be perceived as an untold enrichment for all rather than as a threat to anyone else's identity.

At stake in the controversy about wokeism are different comprehensive views of history and justice. Do we believe that history is a uni-directional process of evolution from an oppressive past to a fairer future with opportunity for all, or do we recognize certain achievements of the past crystallized in the forms and structures of civilization as a necessary defense against the constant recrudescence of primordial impulses to dominate others that come to the fore still as much as ever in contemporary life, with its resurgent Neo-Naziisms and authoritarian populisms? Welcoming change and resisting wholesale dismantling of the achievements of the past are both deeply ensconced, sometimes contradictory attitudes that need to be allowed to co-exist. In woke culture, in contrast, "The past is anachronistically rewritten in accordance with the playbook of contemporary identity politics."[163]

The decision of the Supreme Court of India to change the traditional iconography depicting Lady Justice as blindfolded is symptomatic. The blindfold symbolized her being impartial to the social categories of individuals as signaled by visible characteristics such as race, gender, and class. The Court's unveiling in 2023 of a new depiction of Lady Justice with open eyes is a measure of the incomprehension into which ancient

---

[163] Frank Furedi, *The War Against the Past*, 3.

wisdom (as relayed by the Renaissance) on matters of justice has fallen in an age saturated with woke sensibilities. [164]

---

[164] Lady Justice symbolise? Ancient origins and colonial impact on global law - India Today. Accessed 12-16-2024. LAW HAS OPENED ITS EYES: REDEFINED LADY JUSTICE STATUE - Jus Corpus. Accessed 12-17-2024.

45.

Wokeism as an Intolerant Religion

Like any religion, wokeism and related militant "isms" making up the social justice movement, can be based on a vision of truth that changes one's life and affects all one's relations. Such is the nature also of personal religious conversion and commitment. But to demand that everyone else share and bow down to the same truth is the mistake that religious dogmatists have always made when they become intolerant. *Re-ligio*, according to one common etymology, means tying (*ligare*) all together and back (*re*) to a common source or origin. However, with phenomena such as wokeism, as so often with politicized religions, revelation of quasi-religious truth veers into partisanship. Wokeism claims universal public validity without recognizing the element of personal passion and interestedness and advocacy on behalf of certain groups and values that mark it as a particular love or faith. It then operates as a sectorial ideology rather than being qualified to reign as a coercive universal ethics to which all should be required to conform.

Exactly as with Marxist regimes, calling out and condemning the injustices in the world between oppressors and oppressed is instrumentalized for the empowerment of those portraying themselves as correcting the wrongs of history in order to place themselves in positions of power and superiority. Just as Marxism, for all its revindication of the rights and interests of all, including especially wage laborers, in a classless society, was perverted to produce ruthless dictatorial regimes, so wokeism, at its worst and in its most perverse derivations or deformations, is producing a class of self-righteous elites coercing society with a self-serving moralism.

This is not fundamentally different from what happens with religions. A blazing revelation of deep, undeniable ethical and spiritual truth inspires individuals to rise above themselves and to sacrifice self-interest for a greater good—just as at the origins of world religions, with Moses, Jesus, Mohammed, and other religious prophets. This revelation becomes coopted into a social project of systematically organizing human endeavor around declared goals. These goals, which are now defined and culturally specific, become progressively less godly and then even ungodly in the measure in which they become ends in themselves. They serve for accumulation of power and wealth by those individuals who succeed in setting themselves up as the defenders and promoters of these movements and their values. An orthodoxy forms to which all must genuflect: its decrees and doctrines are beyond questioning.

Figure 6. Nancy Pelosi and Democratic leaders of the US Congress, Chuck Schumer and Hakeem Jeffries, with Vice-President Kamala Harris, kneeling to honor George Floyd in 2020.[165]

There are certain irresistible revelations of right and wrong that occur in the course of history. They emerge at critical moments—the wrongs of slavery, the necessity of abolition, and the subjugation and liberation of women being conspicuous among them. The dignity of all persons as

---

[165] https://www.youtube.com/watch?v=rYPsDXywyjk. Accessed 1-19-2024.

children of God is the same insight in another guise. The spiritual nature of the free person as Buddha-nature is yet another version. The problem is that the institutional inertia necessary for sustaining these revelations can turn them into something else and even into their diametrical, diabolical opposites.[166]

The betrayal of religious inspiration by objectivizing application of a social project that is more concerned with establishing *itself* than with transmitting what it was originally inspired by is the constant story of religions and, just as obviously, of the modern Western world's liberationist culture (and its betrayal) in a nutshell. We have lost our spiritual bearings worked out over millennia and have fallen into merely mechanical iterations of our techno-maniacal powers. Moralization— demanding from others behaviors that they do not themselves deeply feel—substitutes for spiritual inspiration, or even for just plain decency, in acting as a human being or just as a living creature with an inbred respect for other creatures and for life itself. The blinding revelation of truth relayed by wokeism and by religions alike, at their best, is not that all are flatly equal but that all are infinitely and incommensurably valuable. This entails having equal rights and a certain openness or non-exclusiveness of opportunities but does not imply equality of results or resources. Quite the opposite: all are recognized as fundamentally free in their radically different, concrete circumstances to pursue and realize their own unique and incomparable desires and destinies based on their own endowments and potential.

A problem with wokeism in its more aggressive, ideological forms and expressions is its too shallow and undialectical understanding of human nature, as well as of its own motives. The unethical and even criminal tendencies of the will-to-power toward which wokeism points an accusatory finger are too often the very motives driving its own discourse and ideological program. Ironically, wokeism becomes a religion, even an intolerant religion, one rolling back the gains of the Enlightenment, through which it traces its own venerable genealogy. This movement enacts the ineluctable "dialectic of Enlightenment," in Adorno and

---

[166] Fyodor Dostoyevsky's parable of the Grand Inquisitor in *The Brothers Karamazov*, with its premonition of Stalinist Russia, is a classic analysis of this infernal cycle.

Horkheimer's terms, whereby reason itself, in this case the rational demand for equality, becomes an oppressor in its turn.[167] Having freed individuals and society from the shackles of religion, the power of reason in the phase of enlightenment can hardly keep from imposing its own totalitarian rule. Humans, in fact, reason very diversely, and only coercive power can force all to conform to one uniform rationality. The only common rationality for all is simply the potential for openness, in principle, to dialogue, to reasoning with others and learning from them.

---

[167] Theodor Adorno and Max Horkheimer, *Dialektik der Aufklärung* (Amsterdam: Querido, 1947), trans. Edmund Jephcott as *Dialectic of Enlightenment* (Stanford: Stanford University Press, 2002).

46.

Apophatic Marxism—Proposal for a Reformed Radically Leftist Politics

I wish to recognize and welcome the existence of an alternative form of Marxism that explicitly critiques classical Marxism's pretention to complete knowledge and to a total explanation of the dynamic of history and therewith of the *necessary* course of the future. China Miéville has been writing brilliantly in the vein of an explicitly "apophatic Marxism" now for a couple of decades. [168] Aspects of this radically reformed direction of Marxist thought had been anticipated already by Jürgen Habermas, especially in his writings gathered under the title "An Awareness of What is Missing: Faith and Reason in a Secular Age" (*Ein Bewusstsein von dem was fehlt*). [169] Any formulation of Marxist theory

---

[168] China Miéville, "Silence in Debris: Towards an Apophatic Marxism," *Salvage* 6 (2018): 115–44. See most recently, China Miéville, *A Spectre, Haunting: On the Communist Manifesto* (Chicago: Haymarket Books, 2022). This trajectory began two decades ago with Miéville's *Between Equal Rights: A Marxist Theory of International Law* (Amsterdam: Brill Academic Publications, 2004).

I refereed for *Radical Philosophy* an anonymous article titled "The Dialectic of Nostalgia and Melancholy in Apophatic Marxism" that contextualizes this new approach within a host of radical, Neo-Marxist approaches, highlighting Walter Benjamin, among others. The article effectively brings out what the traditions of apophatic theology (Neoplatonism, Jewish Mysticism, Nicholas of Cusa, etc.) specifically have to offer to this revised form of Marxism that is acutely relevant to our present dilemmas and impasses—over rights to free speech, for example.

[169] Jürgen Habermas, "Ein Bewußtsein von dem, was fehlt," in *Ein Bewußtsein von dem, was fehlt: Eine Diskussion mit Jürgen Habermas*, ed. Michael Reder and Josef Schmidt (Frankfurt am Main: Suhrkamp, 2008), trans. Ciaran Cronin as *An Awareness of What Is Missing: Faith and Reason in a Post-Secular Age* (Cambridge: Polity Press, 2010). Broadly relevant here is the Jewish Messianism backgrounding the Frankfurt School of Critical Theory. See Jürgen Habermas, *Religion and Rationality: Essays on Reason, God, and Modernity,* ed. Eduardo Mendieta (Cambridge: MIT Press, 2002).

must acknowledge that its discourse relates to something beyond all that it can articulate. As in negative theology, the ground (God) is always only present as missing from our grasp. For Neo-Marxists, this missing ground may be nothing but the unfathomable, untotalizable complexity of society and history.

A sense of what is lacking and always in need of further work toward completion is crucial to the Marxist sensibilities of Miéville and others such as Étienne Balibar, who emphasizes that a true Marxist philosophy must actively "incomplete" ("inachever") itself.[170] Such an awareness and sensibility are effectively shown to have belonged very much to Marx himself and to his lifelong working on *Das Kapital* in order to *incomplete* it. The dogmatic visage of Marxist politics in subsequent incarnations emerges as a caricature for which the founding thinker cannot be held accountable. This revisionism helps to motivate a genuinely new look at Marxist theory.

The most radical movements of the historical Marxist Left, like many of its expressions now recognized as "wokeism," have foundered because of a certain overconfident totalitarian tenor and logic.[171] They have made genuine dialogue impossible by their uncompromising character that bespeaks the moralism of their spokespersons but leaves no room for reply or for give and take and for working together toward a common understanding. They present black and white pictures of moral right and wrong. They condemn and exonerate unconditionally and without appeal.[172] This approach polarizes and renders concession and consensus difficult, if not impossible.

The approach of pursuing liberation through and for particular identity categories has been thoroughly exposed as fundamentally flawed in that it fails to understand the universalistic essence of the Marxist movement—

---

[170] Étienne Balibar, "The Infinite Contradiction," *Yale French Studies* 88 (1995): 142–64.

[171] Gianni Vattimo and others develop this critique rallying around the notion of "weak thought" ("pensiero debole") as necessary to counter forms of "strong thought" such as Marxism. See Gianni Vattimo and Pier Aldo Rovatti, eds., *Il pensiero debole* (Milan: Feltrinelli, 2010).

[172] Susanne Schröter, *Der neue Kulturkampf: Wie eine woke Linke Wissenschaft, Kultur und Gesellschaft bedroht* convincingly documents many of these worries concerning left-leaning wokeism.

and more generally of the modern Enlightenment project. Todd McGowan, writing as the advocate of emancipatory, leftist philosophy, clearly recognizes that "Although emancipatory political projects might look as if they are identitarian today, all emancipation is universalist, or it is not emancipation" (9). We have seen (chapter 19) how McGowan clearly explains that this emancipatory characteristic of universality has to lie beyond all particularities of identity and that universality itself cannot as such appear in any social field because it constitutes these fields: "Universality cannot have a direct manifestation because it is constitutively absent and emerges in the form of lack" (10). The same susceptibility of the universal to specific and delimited appropriation for a particular faith or religion or ideology that tries to impose itself on others results in idolatrous and demonic forms of imperialist pseudo-universalism. Stalin, Mao, and Pol Pot are aligned by McGowan as exemplary twentieth-century miscarriages of universalism after this pattern.

47.

Politicized Transcendence: Dialectics of Enlightenment and Despisers of Religion

The constant propensity of religious vision to degenerate into idolatry of finite, humanly manufactured ideals throws a revealing light on the history of culture and on the place of wokeism in it. The occluding and eclipsing of the insight of negative theology into the humanly insuperable unknowability of God or truth or reality absolutely or in itself is perennial and repeats itself from age to age. Wokeism shows up as just our current form of absolutistic humanism, echoing the Enlightenment religion of reason. Wokeism's inevitable devolution readily evinces analogies to idolatrous forms of religion. In effect, I take wokeism as a perennial posture of those who esteem and declare themselves to be the illuminated ones ("les illumines") because of some (likely unexceptionable) principle that they have grasped and are determined to advocate universally.

Enlightenment reason, if followed through rigorously to its own logical conclusions, effectively critiques itself and acknowledges the limits of reason and of all rational knowledge and thereby creates a space for the Unknown of negative theology.[173] This is the step I propose we should take beyond current wokeism. Wokeism, whether or not it comes in its hard-edged secularist version, is in any case quite concrete about social determinations of class, gender, race, etc. It perceives absolute realities or values of justice in terms of socially specific categories.

In the terms of Mark Lilla, we could say that wokeism crosses the line established historically by the Great Separation in which the

---

[173] For detailed reflection on this pattern, see my *Poetry and Apocalypse*, Part 1, and my *Dante's* Paradiso *and the Theological Origins of Modern Thought: Toward a Speculative Philosophy of Self-Reflection*, 193, 251.

Enlightenment turned away from the concrete political theologies that fomented the religious wars between Catholics and Protestants, particularly the disastrous Thirty Years War of 1616-48. Faced with such unconscionable cruelty in the name of the highest principles of morality, Enlightenment thinkers learned to embrace a more abstract and generic notion of God that was compatible with modern democratic institutions.[174] Current concrete identity politics of race and gender risk retrogressing and plunging us once again into something like the sixteenth and seventeenth centuries' wars of religion in the wake of the Protestant break repudiating a corrupt institution (the papacy) but also sometimes erecting a new, humanly defined absolute (like *sola fede*, salvation by faith alone) that could incite or provoke destruction and justify killing.

Lilla contemplates how concrete ideas about God and his intentions for the universe, with their implications for political theology in the West after the Enlightenment, were separated from more generic ideas of the divine that did not interfere with the modern democratic state.[175] This modern achievement, known in the US as the separation of church and state or secularism—and in France as "läicité" or "laicism"—was vitally necessary to the establishment of the American democracy and of the French republic. But it is rolled back by the new religion of identities, which, in effect, identifies divine justice with the promotion of certain socially specific groups. As a purely immanent religion without transcendence, wokeism becomes inevitably tendentious and—worse— idolatrous.

As Protestant political theologian Reinhold Niebuhr wrote,

> Only in a religion in which there is a true sense of transcendence can we find the recourse to convict every historical achievement of incompleteness, and to prevent the sanctification of the relative values of any age or any era.[176]

---

[174] Mark Lilla, *The Stillborn God: Religion, Politics, and the Modern West* (New York: Knopf, 2007).

[175] A shorter version of Lilla's argument is available in "Coping with Political Theology." Coping with Political Theology | Cato Unbound (cato-unbound.org) Accessed 2-12-2023.

[176] Reinhold Niebuhr, *Christianity and Power Politics* (New York: Scribner, 1940), 200.

Such an unwarranted sanctification is taking place with wokeism's identification of the holy and just with only one term of the classic oppositions between races (black versus white) and genders (female versus male) or even queer versus binary. Something similar can happen with rigidly fundamentalist readings of the Bible that identify God with specific human precepts and ideas. However, wokeism is also liable to judge the religious, and especially Christians, as unholy and dangerous because of their believing apparently in other absolutes beside or above wokeism's own construal of the imperatives of social justice. This leads to the Bible being attacked as atavistic and barbaric by supposedly enlightened or awakened wokes. Reading the Bible as a sacrilege against enlightened, politically correct ethical principles has become a commonplace in secular-minded woke culture.

For example, an argument frequently evoked under woke-influenced sympathies condemns the fact that the Creation Story in Genesis makes Man or humankind (*'adam,* אָדָם) the crowning glory of the Creation. Such critique finds here, in the supposed teachings of the Bible, the root of our catastrophic desecration and destruction of our environment. The self-proclaimed ethically enlightened "despisers of religion" (as Friedrich Schleiermacher designated their forerunners in the historical period of the Enlightenment) and particularly of the Bible often point to the language of "subduing" and "dominating" in Genesis:

> Be fruitful, and multiply, and replenish the earth, and subdue it: and have dominion over the fish of the sea, and over the fowl of the air, and over every living thing that moveth upon the earth. (1: 26).

God is seen here as granting man a right to master and dominate nature and as authorizing the kind of exploitation that wokeism sees itself as called on to chastise and combat. A whole culture and religion leading to Christian colonization and domination of the world is routinely judged and condemned by this exposé of Genesis and its Creation myth as scandal.

This reading of Genesis ignores the fact that the mandate is first to "replenish" the earth and render it fruitful. Demanded, above all, is a caring and nurturing husbandry. Moreover, God designates as "good" everything that is created *before* man is around at all. Humanity comes to be only on the last day (the sixth) of Creation and alongside the other land creatures—after the earth and sky, the dry land and the sea, the plants and fowls of the air and numerous other living things have already been created and *blessed*. The message, arguably, is that each echelon of the Creation exists and is valorized and loved for its own sake.[177]

Ideologically tendentious readings identify *the* teaching of the Bible with one proposition and line of thought, ignoring the diversity and even contradictoriness of everything human and especially of anything aiming at expression of ultimate truth or meaning. Such interpretation divides the human against itself and blames one part while protecting and rewarding the other. This is exactly how racism arises. Members of a certain identity group become guilty by definition. Their only option for redeeming themselves is turning on their own group and denouncing it. The most vociferous wokeist protest against racism is itself deeply rooted in racist (or at least "racialist") reasoning (cf. McWhorter on reverse racism).[178] Human nature proves itself contradictory in this way, whereas crude wokeism believes that it can, by generic definitions, separate and champion the good and deserving against the guilty and, at any rate, immoral "oppressors." Trying to make these distinctions is not wrong in itself, but it requires the highest degree of self-critical self-awareness—in order to be as just as possible toward the Other.

---

[177] This is argued at length by Joseph K. Gordon, *Divine Scripture in Human Understanding: A Systematic Theology of the Christian Bible* (Notre Dame: University of Notre Dame Press, 2019, 2022).

[178] A further poignant testimony is offered by Katharine Birbalsingh: Decolonising Shakespeare: 'White guilt will destroy the West' – Katharine Birbalsingh - YouTube. Accessed 3-20-2025.

48.

Justice for All?
Culture Wars and Self-Critique

As in former times and in certain regions a black man accused by a white woman was condemned quite apart from the particulars of a case, today, in some especially woke-influenced milieus, being a male accused by females of sexual predation reads automatically as a case of #MeToo. What is essential, or at least visible from the outside, is nothing of the particularities of the accusation or the evidence but the social categories of the accused and the accusers. Apart from how well the results of a judgment adhere to the specifics of the case, there is a presumption that, in any case, a long-overdue historical rectification is being carried out. Right or wrong in specifics, the judgment makes an unequivocal statement that men have no right to dominate and abuse women—so justice, in this "social" sense, can be said to be served. Such scenarios illustrate how our overarching ideological beliefs and presuppositions inevitably encroach on how we perceive particular cases.

Wokeism, crudely construed, enables a mega-narrative, a *grand récit* of social justice to take over in making determinations of who deserves what on the basis largely of race, class, and gender within the frame of a certain reigning interpretation of the wrongs of history. This makes decisions easy. The grand narrative tells us who deserves to be penalized and who merits compensations in categorical terms, without need to consider individuals in all the detail and complexity of their situations and acts—which are, admittedly, endless and endlessly equivocal. Still, this domination of a certain revisionary narrative is a perpetuation of exactly the sort of injustice that wokeism protests against. And—incidentally—those who pay lip service to the agenda of redistribution of wealth and privilege, aligning themselves verbally with the right side, can thereby

entitle themselves to retain and increase their lion's share of the very
privileges that they are nominally denouncing. Musa al-Gharbi
demonstrates this crushingly about the vast class of professors, journalists,
administrators, legal and financial professionals and technocrats of all
types that he characterizes as "symbolic capitalists."[179]

Justice is without doubt a question at the heart of the Western canon
in books like the Bible, the *Odyssey*, the *Divine Comedy*, and *Don Quixote*.
Odysseus's revenge against the suitors, Dante's Hell, Don Quixote's
freeing of the galley slaves, etc., penetrate to the core questions of what
human justice can possibly be and whether and how it might have divine
sanction or a universally valid warrant.[180] This canonical tradition, which
is often under attack from the wokeist camp as epitomizing the evils of our
racist, misogynist, homophobic, transphobic civilization, does not give pat
answers in terms of racial and gender categories. These texts grapple with
all the excruciating complexities of justice on earth and under heaven that
are never completely resolved by anyone's merely human means. The
sensibility for justice has been cultivated within this tradition of Western
representation and reflection as much as anywhere, yet this immense
thesaurus of wisdom is now being read and taught, if at all, by picking out
things offensive to the sensibilities of the "me generation" or millennials
or other new generational identities (Gen Alpha or Gen Z), while
neglecting to historicize such elements and ignoring their larger contexts.
The tradition is seen globally as fostering and justifying the injustices that
some contemporary woke-attuned groups have the presumption of now
suddenly waking up to and calling out and pretending to reverse.

The difficult and exacting work of discernment has been performed
throughout millennia within this tradition distinguished by the critical
thinking of which we are all heirs and perhaps even beneficiaries in
important ways. No good purpose is served through the summary trashing
of it by those willfully ignorant of all but their own hypocritical, self-

---

[179] Musa al-Gharbi, *We Have Never Been Woke: The Cultural Contradictions of a New Elite.*

[180] I highlight the acute critical reflection on justice in these texts in *The Revelation of Imagination: From Homer and the Bible through Virgil and Augustine to Dante* (2015) and in *Don Quixote's Impossible Quest for the Absolute in Literature: Fiction, Reflection, and Negative Theology* (2025).

serving dictates. Of course, refusal of critique and woke bashing are no better.[181] Like any tradition, it is a mixed bag and inconsistent, but the essential resources for critical thinking and defense of the ideals of justice are rife in the sources of Western civilization—as much as anywhere else—for anyone willing to see them.

It is the Western tradition, and perhaps it alone, or at least chiefly, moreover, that has produced wokeism, with its acute sensitivity to questions of justice and of how social determinants factor into the equitable or inequitable handling individuals.[182] However, particularly this tradition is routinely calumniated by prominent woke voices. They are increasingly parroted by college freshmen and now (more than equally) by freshwomen students in the classroom, as white racist, male chauvinist, and Christian bigoted. Neglecting to acknowledge any of the equivocations involved, the condemnations conspicuously fail to exercise the capacity for auto-critique, which has been developed so vigorously and rigorously within Western intellectual tradition. Wokeism misunderstands itself in turning *en bloc* against the Western canon and tradition. There needs to be acknowledgment and even gratitude toward this tradition in the name of justice if woke culture wants to be lucid about its own genealogy and fair towards those it criticizes.

Against the grain of Western humanist tradition, students today are too often taught to identify with their race or gender rather than to cultivate their peculiar talents and potential as unique persons aspiring to know and foster the universally human. Some are being taught to claim rights and entitlements more than to empower themselves by exacting discipline and cultivation of their humanity as the potential for virtue and vitality. They are encouraged to feel good about themselves because of their belonging to various identity groups and to hate and decry a society that purportedly

---

[181] Particularly insightful critiques of right-wing anti-wokeism are Adrian Daub, *The Cancel Culture Panic: How an American Obsession Went Global* (Stanford: Stanford University Press, 2024) and Tony McKenna, *Has Political Correctness Gone Mad? Interrogating a Right-wing Conspiracy Theory* (London: Bloomsbury Academic, 2024).

[182] The question of how wokeism spreads and is adopted outside the sphere of Western culture is explored in the collective volume *Tracking Global Wokeism*, ed. Thorsten Botz-Bornstein (Amsterdam: Brill, 2025).

wants to put them down (unaware of what it is really like for gender non-conforming individuals in Orban's Hungary or Putin's Russia). This reverses a former tendency of education to inculcate pride in national belonging. Everything depends on the narratives we choose to tell ourselves. In any event, education should teach and train the young to be self-critical.

In sum, among the decisive questions that need to be raised about the claims and revindications of wokeism are the following.

(1) Are these claims inclusive or divisive? Do they stigmatize certain groups and alienate them, or do they motivate all to work together toward achieving a shared justice and a common human dignity? The latter becomes unlikely if such claims are felt as stigmatizing and as seeking revenge on behalf of those assumed to be victims in history. Further bad blood is inevitable when such claims serve for garnering advantages for the self-elected brokers of these grievances.

(2) Is history read with the pretention of knowing who is in the right and with the presumption that one's own present understanding is capable of standing supremely in judgment of past perspectives? Or are we all seeking to submit to one another and render justice to others, even more than we demand it from them, acknowledging the limits and the inevitable biases and distortions of our own point of view?

Justice entails much more than we can comprehend. It involves relations without limit that connect every being in the universe together with every other. We only ever discern and grasp some infinitesimal portion of this inexhaustible interweave of beings. Yet all have irrecusable claims that in the course of universal time come back to haunt us in the guise of the return of the repressed. Always what we are forgetting, willingly or not, is far the greater part of the justice we owe to others. An overconfident wokeism thinking itself the agent of universal justice is another veiled repetition of the imperialist ideologies pretending to establish peace and order for all—on their own terms, of course, which are, as always, those of the conquerors.

This situation of being infinitely surpassed by the claims of justice that could potentially be levied upon us counsels a certain humility and a critical consciousness with regard to our own perceptions and judgments.

We all stand to be corrected constantly by the judgments of others and by the future. Our justice had best avoid the pretention to a comprehensive revisioning and righting of the wrongs of history, arrogating to itself the prerogative to cancel culture of others and substitute what happens to be deemed right at the moment in our own familiar milieus.

Rather than attempting to enact a grand narrative of universal justice, we do better to intervene punctually in specific situations where particular individuals and groups can be accorded greater equity. Wokeism takes up what is undeniably a just cause—to favor the downtrodden—but does so at the price of turning it into a means of placing oneself in the right and bludgeoning down other potentially rival groups as unjust and retrograde. The social justice paradigm imposes on the conscience of society in such a way as to perpetrate a culture war against a certain race (white) and gender (male) or class as dominant and the oppressor. To focus exclusively on the claims of some, as if they had more claim to justice than others because it is fashionable and in the focus of public attention, is a temptation that proves almost irresistible in our media culture based on social profiling, but it is invidious and a perpetuation of injustice.[183]

Generic social identities, by their differential and exclusive nature, cannot take the lead in structuring interactions among human beings without polarizing and alienating them. Such identities can be a tremendous enrichment of our humanity, but only when brought in as *inflections* of something else, something mysterious and indefinable that is already recognized as the Nothing (nothing nameable or definable) that is common to us all. Called for is not a politics of explicit identitarian revindications but rather an apophatic ethics, an ethics of unsaying (literally "away from" *apo*, "speech" *phasis*) that leaves differential, divisive identities out of the equation in attempting to negotiate fairly among all parties participating in society. All parties have a right to equal consideration as non-identically equal and as, in fact, incommensurable.

---

[183] As an example, Gordon MacLeod and Colin McFarlane, "Introduction: Grammars of Urban Injustice," Antipode 46/4(2014): 857-73, following the lead of David Harvey, *Social Justice and the City* (Baltimore: Johns Hopkins University Press, 1973) effectively unsettle certain abstract principles of the liberal paradigm of distributive justice in relation specifically to geographical relations among humans living in urban settings.

This, I submit, is the best way to quell present resentment along color, gender, and class lines, at least at the stage of reflection from which I now speak. I recognize that there are other moments and phases requiring class or gender militancy.

The laudable aim pursued by wokeism of giving recognition to all independent of race, class, and gender, is best fostered by *not* foregrounding these identitarian differentials. Justice without exclusions is indeed the goal, but for that to come about we need to start from recognition of the *non-identical* that all share in common. This means the indefinable, infinite mystery at the core of each individual rather than our differential identities defined and asserted over against one another. The latter, while seemingly concrete, immediate realities are actually shifting social constructions that are inevitably used for manipulation in the interests of brokering power and procuring privileges. The basis for true community is mutual recognition of common humanity beyond all the monolithic identity labels—and even beyond any definition of "humanity" that would make it other than, and exclusive of, the universal being that all existing beings are endowed with and share in common.[184] "Humanity" itself, like every identity, needs to be broken open to other species and to the All that indwells and envelops and "others" it.

What we observe with wokeism is exactly what we see with every historical religion. It has its grip on a transcendent truth shining with sacred splendor and beauty—the imperative of freedom and justice for all without exclusions. However, it takes this truth over in ways that make it serve as a means of consolidating power for those who control it. One establishes one's own power, then, by suppressing rivals who could contest the truth one defends or advocates. This includes heretics within one's own confession who undermine its positive doctrines by thinking them differently in the manner of free spirits and neglecting to toe the party line. This is what happens when wokeism becomes the establishment: it shifts from a prophetic posture calling out injustices abhorrent to the

---

[184] Such a metaphysical dimension of ethics was theorized also, earlier, for another time and in other terms, by Emmanuel Levinas in *Totalité et infini: Essai sur l'extériorité* (The Hague: Nijhoff, 1971). We need today to strive to think such an ethics beyond the frame of his humanism as articulated by Levinas in *Humanisme de l'autre homme* (Paris: Fata Morgana, 1972).

conscience of all and becomes entrenched in the highly fraught and rivalrous processes and mechanisms of conserving power and garnering privilege. This complicity in the rivalrous struggle for control involves also—with some heinous consequences—suppressing dissent and policing heterodoxy.

49.

Apophatic Universalism
and Religious Revelation

I have endeavored in this Part (V) to sketch the aftermath of decolonialist transformations of society and the broadly "woke" ideology revindicating rights of minorities and oppressed groups that has arisen out of it. All this follows with a certain historical necessity from the modern project of universal emancipation as it has developed since the Enlightenment. The impasses and contradictions that come out of this movement show why a postmodern turn breaking up universal concepts and consigning the universal, instead, to a dimension beyond any group's or any culture's conception of it has been and still is necessary to escape the historical cycles of repeated reciprocal vengeance and destructive rivalry (as modeled archetypally by Cain and Abel in the Bible or by Eteocles and Polyneices in classical Thebes). This dimension of the inconceivable and inarticulable that I call "apophatic" is the common horizon for all humans in their finitude and their ineluctable relationality to all others. It is the only common (un)ground on which we all will be able to pursue peace and social harmony or justice together.

I have suggested that this postmodern future should be specifically post-secular in the sense of recuperating essential insights of religious or spiritual and mystical traditions that look beyond the limits of the purely immanent material reality to which modern and now especially digital culture tends to reduce human existence and the cosmos. The traditions of Islam, Hinduism, and Buddhism, together with all sorts of pagan and animist religions, not to mention shamanistic practices, provide various registers of access to a spiritual universe that otherwise exceeds and escapes our ordinary conceptual logic and linguistic means. Many of these religious systems can point us beyond any system or language to a kind of nothingness (in material, definable terms) that we share in common as our foundation.

Christian revelation in particular insists on the infinite dignity and worth, but also on the creaturely nothingness, of all beings as created in God's image, yet *ex nihilo*. The ineffable God alone is true, self-subsistent and autonomous being—*ipsum esse per se subsistans* in the language of classical Christian Scholastic theology. Christian revelation has played a fundamental role in catalyzing the development of modern Western societies that have revolutionized the world. From the industrial revolution that made modernity possible in all its economic dynamism and terrifying military might through the democratic and social revolutions that continue to erupt in Western societies up to their woke and queer and trans expressions today, this Christian legacy is pervasively operative. [185] However, the dialectics of history teach us that every positive, self-identical expression of absolute value needs to be corrected and ultimately relinquished in a gesture of self-abandon. Only an unknowing embrace of all attains to true universality. A kenotic (self-emptying) ethics rather than identitarian revindications and self-affirmation are sorely needed in order to render possible a peaceful and productive mode of living together on our shrinking planet and in our irreversibly multicultural societies—both now and for the future.

---

[185] Tom Holland, *Dominion: How the Christian Revolution Remade the World* (New York: Basic Books, 2021).

Part VI.

Transcending Power Politics Negatively

50.

The Wokeist Challenge
to the Freedom to Speak the Truth[186]

Today, one of the most insidious challenges to our ability to tell the truth and reject the false can be found in "woke" ideology. From its seedbeds on the campuses of American universities, wokeism has spread throughout North American society with its liberal institutions and free markets. It has made considerable inroads in France and is increasingly appearing everywhere in Europe and even beyond the Western world.[187] This ideology is exerting coercive power within today's society, not only in academia but also in government agencies and even in the business sector. Private companies now operate under the imperative to conform to dictates deemed politically correct and imposed as mandatory regulations or codes of conduct. Protesting or calling into question the ways in which "diversity" or "inclusion" policies are applied can easily cost dissidents their positions. Statements made in a critical spirit and in the name of telling the truth can have disastrous consequences for the careers of those who dare to express themselves in a manner that does not at least pay lip service to woke codes and protocols. Numerous commentators are now sounding the alarm against an incipient form of "totalitarianism." They do

---

[186] An Italian version of this chapter of the book appeared as a contribution entitled "La sfida woke: Politiche identitarie e la libertà di dire il vero" invited for a volume on *Comunicare il vero e il falso*, eds. Giorgio Sandrini et al. (Milan: Mimesis, 2024), 138-150.

[187] See "Tracking Global Wokeism": Newsletter 4 | The Global Studies Center at Gulf University for Science and Technology (gust.edu.kw).

not shy away from making comparisons with Stalin's Soviet Union and Mao's communist China.[188]

The case of Jordan Peterson is representative of many such dissenters who have lost their jobs at universities or in government. They have become the object of campaigns to ruin their reputation and undermine their credibility because of their unwillingness to submit to the demands of public avowal of conformity to what they perceive as ideological positions. They balk at legislation compelling certain forms of expression and dictating behaviors that they deem to be infringements on their right to free speech and thought or expression. Peterson is an outspoken, scathing critic of Canadian prime minister Justin Trudeau and his liberal left-wing "woke" social agenda. He was a professor of psychology at the University of Toronto who refused to accept Canada's law Bill C-16 mandating use of preferred gender pronouns for students and faculty. He rues the myriad "micro-concessions" that academics have made to university administrations dominated by the "woke mob." This results in continual compromises and whitling away of the ability to speak one's mind and stand up for the truth as one honestly sees and believes it to be.

Peterson compares this gradual infringement to the erosion of civil liberties that led in the twentieth century to massively murderous totalitarian states such as Stalin's Soviet Union, Hitler's Nazi Germany, and Mao's Communist China. He equally denounces today's Iranian mullahs in their suppression of women and their right to free expression. He has studied and warns about how progressive capitulation to such coercion and its insidious encroachment on civil society's fundamental liberties of expression and self-manifestation allow societies to slip into a state of captivity to dictatorship.

There certainly has been a change in mentality at the universities and more generally throughout society in recent decades steered by hypersensitivity to woke-style demands and recriminations. One has to be very careful and monitor one's express views to keep them in line with

---

[188] Particularly widely circulating are the reflections of Jordan Peterson: You Must Stand Up Against Woke Ideologies - YouTube. A system of disinformation throughout American media and government is exposed also by Michael Shellenberger's Guide to Escaping the Woke Matrix (youtube.com). John O'Sullivan, *Sleepwalking into Wokeness* is well-documented and lively on this topic.

certain reigning orthodoxies. It seems that the incendiary power of speech in our now so densely wired mediatic lifeworld has become so great as to be no longer admissible without unprecedented controls. Truth and falsehood are manufactured by technological means of never-before-seen scope and power. In our now "post-truth" era, the very distinction between true and false seems to be threatened both in practice and in the public perception.[189] Any attempt at regulation of speech in the interests of truth is bound to be contested by some. All can claim to have their different sense of truth based on "alternative facts."

Some cases for such regulation have garnered enough consensus to be made into law. Hate speech and antisemitic or white supremacist discourse is outlawed with a wide consensus in European and other Western countries. Advocating to deny any ethnic or immigrant group the fundamental rights to exist and express themselves in the country is generally deemed intolerable in democratically constituted states. But these specifically targeted restrictions on free expression, too, can be felt as undemocratic by political factions that find themselves stigmatized and even banned from the public arena for holding what they consider to be alternative views of their national history and identity. On the extreme right, political parties such as Germany's AfD (Alternative für Deutschland) can find themselves stripped of statutory government funding or branded as illegal. Clamor for legal action against such movements mounts as their popularity increases. France's National Front appears increasingly capable of winning a future election and forming the government.

There is certainly an imperative against hate speech, but it is primarily a moral imperative. It can be most effectively enforced by moral conscience rather than by external coercion of law. No one can legislate the emotions that people feel. People have to be allowed to express what they think. Otherwise, rage and resentment will become rancorous. They will surreptitiously rankle until finally breaking out in violent acts or manifestations. Extremists need to be confronted with the equally honest reactions of others to the views they express. Individuals alone are responsible for their views in a free society. When we begin to officially

---

[189] Steve Fuller, *Post-Truth: Knowledge as a Power Game* (London: Anthem, 2018).

legislate against certain views as unacceptable, we implicitly dictate what views are acceptable, and this creates a shield against criticism. Instead, all need to be subject to the same standard of total responsibility for their own political opinions and their social expression.

Society can only educate the passions and their expression. This education, when it is open and free, can make us aware of a norm higher than the positive requirements of law in the state. By fostering critical insight into the limits of all our own formulations, we cultivate negative consciousness of this higher, moral law, whether it is conceived of as social (Durkheim) or natural (Hobbes) or divine (Aquinas). Each person is called on to acknowledge and to act on these higher ethical imperatives in their own way and according to the promptings of their own conscience, not by external compulsion or by inauthentic conformism. Forcing people's consciences eventually undermines loyalty and provokes resistance in kind to force. People need to be allowed, instead, to put themselves on the line for the opinions they hold and be judged by the public and their peers. Preventing them from doing so enables them to legitimize their protest in the name of freedom of speech and equal rights. They no longer have to stand up to judgment purely on the basis of the content of their view and its merits. We shift into a system of negative legitimization. On the international scene, this means that dictators like Putin or the Iranian mullahs are able to justify extreme measures of repression by the widely acknowledged evils (Western powers) they are fighting to resist.

It is not enough to be against something—whether Western imperialism or neo-Nazism—considered evil. The real challenge is to open a positive way for including all potentially in a common project. When we fall back on the more immediate and urgent objective of combatting our presumed enemies, we suspend the effort to construct a common world. This disorientation from the final and absolute good for all through focus on combatting what is perceived as evil from some partial perspective—whether that of the liberal West or the global South or radical Islam—leads us inevitably into war. We vie with one another in attempting to suppress the supposedly true culprit that we deem to be guilty of disturbing world peace (Russia or China, American imperialism or Islamic fundamentalism), but we are thus unconsciously participating in a war of all against all. In this underlying logic of conflict, the national political scene is a mirror image of international geopolitics.

Our governments are now legislating against this or that group as beyond the pale of "democracy" or "civil society," but we are not building a truly consensual ground for such judgments. Necessary is not discernment of this or that flaw or danger in a certain group so that it can be banned. All have their shortcomings and defects and dangers. First, we need to be oriented to self-critique and to understanding and love of "enemies." Only caring for the other rather than competing for power over one another can create the conditions for a collaborative society, one capable of compassion towards the less successful or less fortunate. Before trying to determine positively the controversial content of what is right and admissible, we need to refocus on how to encompass all individuals and parties, nations and cultures, without exclusions and then try to negotiate a consensual norm that no single constituent can dictate. The wisdom of the world religions and of the great moral systems of humanity converges on teaching and preaching such a lesson of love and hospitality towards others. Against it stands the selfish drive and covetousness characterizing a modernity focused on material and technological exploitation of all resources for always more material comfort and conspicuous consumption.

51.

Dealing with Evil Non-Dualistically and Letting Power Implode

Caring for and compensating disadvantaged groups is at the core of woke ethics. Wokeism, to this extent, is exemplary of an ethically inclusive approach to structuring and managing society. Still, the type of concern represented is often very material in nature—oriented to equality of wealth in monetary terms. Furthermore, wokeism is oriented to identity groups because they are the key to generating social traction and political power. But this sort of politics is bound to lead to factionalism rather than inclusiveness. With this splintering into rival camps, ethical imperatives of equality of access are likely to be turned into weapons for attacking and scapegoating others, particularly other social groups reprimanded as "dominant." Simply to protest against those governing or against those contesting the governing group does not solve the problem. Needed is affirmation of a more inclusive ideal. We have to deal with all as, firstly, people with legitimate concerns rather than trying to obliterate or inculpate those groups with whom we disagree. At least, we have to recognize all as having a right to express their concerns and submit them to public judgment.

We have to allow for a universal perspective which cannot be identical with our own. Only such an openness to this universal beyond our grasp can enable us and others—all others—to unite.[190] Religions figure this dimension in terms of a transcendent divinity. Humanisms can understand it as a dimension of infinity intrinsic to human being or existence in its inherent, existential openness. Such openness requires us to relate beyond

---

[190] I develop this logic in *On the Universality of What is Not: The Apophatic Turn in Critical Thinking* (2020).

ourselves and to recognize our own being as relative to this "beyond" (our common origin and destiny beyond anything anyone can define) in which all others share, and on which all depend. It exceeds us and grounds us and has a kind of authority over us all, although no one can interpret this authority definitively. Each individual or group is totally responsible for their manner of interpreting and applying the dictates they attribute to their god or unconditional value.

Ideologies like wokeism (or its opposite) pretend to be right in and of themselves, without anyone in particular assuming responsibility directly and personally for the positions propounded. If you resist the coercive power of the liberal woke orthodoxy that demands and extracts a certain confession of adherence from you, you are tarred as being unempathetic with oppressed minorities. Ironically, you are being forced to cave in and conform to superior force in the name of being caring and protective of the weak and defenseless. You are put in the position of being the oppressor by any attempt on your part to oppose bullying and oppression. There is here a contorted instrumentalization of victimhood for the seizing of power by those who profess to be proponents of the disempowered.

The extreme forms of wokeism offer a chilling illustration of how starting from morally right and irrefutable premises in defense of the defenseless can be taken up and twisted for purposes of exerting power. Such forms show how an entire society can enter into a collective delusion, an almost hallucinatory lie. This kind of fatal distortion has been the downfall of religions generally throughout history. This is one reason why so many analysts have observed that wokeism works like a religion. But any social credo can go this route. Recognized religions only manifest this syndrome most baldly through their explicitly declared "dogmas" and overt confessions of faith. Denis Diderot's landmark novel *The Nun* (*La religieuse*, 1792) is an enduringly significant exposé of the Christian religion's repression of individual rebellion even on the part of the sincerest believers in the underlying principles of its own faith. The novel's protagonist, Suzanne Simonin, is mercilessly persecuted. However, she embodies eminently the spiritual virtues that her persecutors pretend to model and claim to defend.

Those committed to religions and ideologies generally think that they are using power for the right reasons to oppose the forces of evil. This is presumably the case with sincere supporters of Putin's Russia and Xi's China every bit as much as of Western democracies or of the Catholic Church. The catch is that the drive for power itself gets the upper hand and becomes its own reason for being. This self-justifying reasoning posits or premises the need for power in order to do anything at all and especially for doing the good it intends. However, this is a sure recipe for brewing bad blood and concocting hypocrisy. The will to assert one's own power over others is the banal essence of evil more than the monstrous bogeys conjured up by our propaganda machines—whether in the guise of communism or capitalism or godlessness or fanaticism and radicalism.

When we pit "our" power against "theirs"—the "fanatics" or the "imperialists" or the "extremists" or the "reactionaries"—then it becomes a matter of good over evil and of resisting the supposed forces of darkness and destruction. We fail to see how we participate in evil by this very act of warring against what we perceive as evil—not in concrete, specific acts but in generalized stances against beliefs or identifiable groups that we hold to be evil. The stand-off between Republicans and Democrats in US politics can slide into such a mythic register. This happens whenever we fail to recognize the power beyond our own that gives us life and being beyond all ideological commitments—our own and those of our supposed enemies. We usurp for ourselves the power to judge what or who deserves to be or not to be, and this distorts our perception of our relation to others— *all* others—as equally gifted with life and being. I believe that recognition of an otherness beyond oneself and all tangible others is necessary to frame (or rather *un*frame) the arena within which we can relate to others and negotiate with other humans for the sake of collective benefits and establishing common purposes. This awareness opens a religious or spiritual dimension of life but remains critical of all positive religions and political ideologies.

From Noam Chomsky and Edward Herman's landmark *Manufacturing Consent: The Political Economy of the Mass Media* (1988) to Jordan Peterson's appeals to individuals to be true to their own convictions in defiance of the reigning social orthodoxy, which confronts us today in the form of wokeism, the appeal to break out of collective delusion rings out left and right. However, the named approaches to power are oppositional. They can be subjected to deconstruction à la Foucault.[191] To my mind, the way to undo power cannot be to frontally oppose it with counterforce but rather to recognize the power of affirming our own impotence in relation to a power beyond and above all the powers mustered by men and women—or by whatever kind of human being. This is a negative theological recognition of a power that we can participate and share in together with others but can never appropriate directly by our own will. It is a power that manifests itself concretely in giving up power: it is the power of love. This is the power—or rather the kenosis—of Christ, but equally of Krishna, Buddha, Milarepa, Hafez, Crazy Horse, Gandhi, Martin Luther King, etc. An object lesson in this type of love is provided by Roger McGowan, a falsely convicted black man on death row in Texas. He uses his suffering in an inhuman penitentiary to engender love and compassion even toward those whose job it is to punish him.[192]

This power of love issues in a non-violent form of resistance aligned with "kenosis" that undercuts all parties in their respective politics of domination. It requires us to recognize a power greater than our own at work between and among us in order effectively to resist the imposition of power by some on others.[193] Such imposition of power is always a compensation and a camouflage for weakness or fear of weakness: it only

---

[191] Michel Foucault, "Truth and Power," in *Power/Knowledge: Selected Interviews and Other Writings 1972-1977*, C. Gordon (ed.), trans. C. Gordon, L Marshall, J. Mepham, K Soper (New York: Pantheon, 1980), 109-33.

[192] See Roger W. McGowan *Messages de vie du couloir de la mort*, written with the collaboration of Pierre Pradervand (Switzerland: Jouvence, 2015).

[193] The paradoxical logic of resistance is lucidly parsed by Howard Caygill in *On Resistance: A Philosophy of Defiance* (London: Bloomsbury, 2015). In recognizing "the resistance of resistance to analysis," Caygill highlights the necessity of what is, in effect, an aporetic or apophatic approach that rhymes with kenosis. "A philosophy of resistance has itself to resist the pressure of concept-formation, of reducing the practices of resistance to a single concept amenable to legitimation and appropriation by the very state-form that it began by defying" (6). The unconceptualizability of resistance is the premise for its ability to avoid being appropriated into a system of power that will be used inevitably for domination. Resistance belongs, instead, to the universality that cannot be made present or be identified. See my *On the Universality of What Is Not*.

needs to be unmasked as such. We need to reflect back to the oppressor *not* recognition of their power by resisting it but, instead, the exposure of their manifest weakness and fear as what provokes their resort to force. Only so can we convert the human tragedy into a divine comedy of reciprocal support in a common project of building our world together. Of course, one side will not budge on its own. Only interaction based on the perception of reciprocal vulnerability and common interests can motivate collective action issuing in the embrace of an encompassing whole of which all are parts. The analyses of this book have aimed to critically break down and overcome polarization and alienation between political constituencies in entrenched camps by highlighting their common, universally shared non-identity. This (non)perspective alone renders all-encompassing, or rather non-exclusionary, vision possible.

By removal of resistance, we force upon aggressors the question: For what or whom are they fighting? What positive benefits do they envisage and for whom? No longer can the answer simply be to withstand the evil of others once the others have stopped fighting. A shift provoked by *un*defining objectives and opening to our infinite, indefinable common destiny can realign conflicts completely. A subtle change in tone can convert conflict into cooperation.

52.

Perpetuating Human Violence
versus Projecting Perpetual Peace

Tone and style have a lot to do with whether the discourse of wokeism (or anti-wokeism) will unite or divide humanity in facing the overwhelming challenges to its very existence, no less than to its well-being. These challenges are stubbornly material, as well as ethical and spiritual, in nature. The discourse of wokeism itself can be part of a cycle of aggression and counter-aggression, or it can catalyze attempts to shift from the register of conflict to a focus on common interests and goals. Discourse, through its negative capabilities of self-subversion, can be the key to opening a sphere beyond the discursive and its inherent oppositionalities.

This communication with an ultra-discursive dimension—the naked face-to-face of human encounter, as well as the ineffability of a religious absolute—is crucial, I believe, to what Jürgen Habermas calls "communicative action" ("kommunikatives Handeln"), in which reason rather than force is decisive in determining our relations and interventions within society. Such action requires a kind of common belief in and openness to one another as sharing stakes in a common life and society. It is manifest in an axis of thinking from Hegel and Ludwig Feuerbach to Walter Benjamin and Luce Irigaray ("Femmes divines"), in which alienation is overcome through projection of an idealized human essence in the form of God. The way in which this religious idea still underlies the very possibility of democracy has been thought through sociologically in our own times by Hartmut Rosa in *Demokratie braucht Religion* ("Democracy Needs Religion"). Rosa derives his claim for the religious basis of democratic culture from the traditions of Émile Durkheim, Marcel Maus, Max Weber, and others.[194]

Democracy of respect for all races and genders is the ideal projected by wokeism. This broadly Enlightenment tradition of thinking illuminates pragmatically how to achieve such an ideal by communication in negotiating differences rationally and non-violently among those identifying diversely. Reasoning tends to be contradictory and exclusive unless it is practiced with the kind of self-critical philosophical reflectiveness that Habermas has developed and championed. Habermas's own reflections led him to recognition that a certain openness to the religious and its unmatched force for fostering solidarity is necessary for the success of the democratic project. [195] I wish to pursue this understanding of the religious further in the same direction, emphasizing that a transcendent dimension of the unknown and open is the space to which we must open ourselves in order to be able to reconcile with others of different backgrounds and persuasions and find common cause with them in building a shared future.[196]

Wokeism, as a kind of religion making idols of identities, is more inclined to divide than to unify, which might make it qualify as a bad religion rather than a good one. However, things are not quite so simple. Christ himself said that he came not to bestow peace but to divide: "Do not think that I came to bring peace on earth. I did not come to bring peace but a sword" (Matthew 10: 34). Or even more joltingly: "Do you suppose that I came to give peace on earth? I tell you, not at all, but rather division" (Luke 12: 51). In Girard's terms, Christ's introducing division is necessary

---

[194] Hartmut Rosa, *Demokratie braucht Religion* (München: Kösel 2022).

[195] Jurgen Habermas, "Ein Bewusstsein von dem, was fehlt," in *Ein Bewusstsein von dem, was fehlt: Eine Diskussion mit Jurgen Habermas*, ed. Michael Reder and Josef Schmidt (Frankfurt am Main: Suhrkamp, 2008), trans. Ciaran Cronin as *An Awareness of What Is Missing: Faith and Reason in a Post-Secular Age* (Cambridge: Polity Press, 2010). Broadly relevant here is the Jewish Messianism backgrounding the Frankfurt School of Critical Theory. See Jürgen Habermas, *Religion and Rationality: Essays on Reason, God, and Modernity,* ed. Eduardo Mendieta (Cambridge: MIT Press, 2002).

[196] I develop my own reflection on why democracy depends on religion, specifically on negative theology in today's multicultural democracies, in "Why an Open or 'Public' Sphere is Necessary to Civil Society and its Entanglement with Religion," Epilogue to *Public Sphere and Religion: An Entangled Relationship in History, Education, and Society,* ed. Carl Antonius Lemke (Hildesheim: Olms, 2020), 230-49.

to break the unanimity of mimetic violence against the innocent victim, the *bouc émissaire*. [197] In Walter Benjamin's thought ("Theologisch-politisches Fragment"), rupture with previous history is necessary for its messianic redemption.

Considering that the beatitudes bless the peacemakers and prescribe an ethics of non-retaliation ("turning the other cheek"), and considering Jesus's preaching love of enemies in the Sermon on the Mount (Matthew 5: 43-48), we need to see that the division in question is not really against others as our enemies. It is rather a matter of a *self*-critical decision for love against hate. This can mean fierce battle with oneself and one's own: son against father, daughter against mother, daughter-in-law against mother-in-law, etc. (Luke 12: 53) but in the interest of the greater whole that unites all beyond unjust or invidious power hierarchies. Jesus's point is that this universal love is greater than that of any family or clan and must take precedence over it even at the price of division against some part of ourselves.

There is a moment of critique and crisis that is decisive and divisive: the word *krisis*, ἡ κρίσις in the Greek of the New Testament, says as much. There has to be the separation of the chaff from the wheat. This is the moment, above all, of self-critique, of the calling to conscience of each individual before a tribunal higher than that of worldly success, which so often does not weigh the means by which success is achieved. But beyond these crises of decision lies a still more all-encompassing unity without exclusions. We relate to this unitive dimension, letting it come over us, without being able to grasp or define it or even to choose it as such. We can open ourselves self-critically to it and respond to being chosen for witnessing to the unity beyond and nullifying all our own powers of articulation.

Let me admit and even insist that the apophatic or the kenotic gesture is not immediately the best nor even the right approach in all moments and in all circumstances. In conflict situations, defense especially of others (Levinas's third parties, "tiers," beyond the bipolar self–other relation) is pragmatically necessary and morally imperative. The apophatic attitude of infinite openness to others is recommended for preparing peace when it is

---

[197] René Girard, *Je vois Satan tomber comme l'éclair*, 235-36.

still possible positively to promote it, constructing future cooperation proactively long before tensions harden into immoveable impasses such as those between Israelis and Palestinians, or between Turks and Kurds. These, like numberless other conflicts, prove to be practically irresolvable, having reached a point of no return. Ukrainians and Russians are in the process of creating such an unbridgeable abyss. Apophatic thinking is not immediately the solution to such problems but rather the way of creating the sort of mutual respect among humans that is our only defense against degeneration into desperate conflict aimed at destruction or elimination of others without repeal. Apophatic thinking is about fostering positive premises for peace far in advance of the irremediable situations that develop into wars in which there are no alternatives that are not catastrophic.

The apophatic attitude of openness to what lies beyond our knowing and saying and beyond humanity altogether, demands openness to all one's fellows, to all humans, and even to the non-human or the divine.[198] It can work powerfully to foster the conditions of peace in which people are free to abandon themselves to their infinite inter-relatedness rather than being constrained to fight doggedly tooth and nail to resist violence and their own perishing. There is a time for constructing community, including international community, but it is no longer possible to operate on this basis once irreconcilable, irresolvable conflict has entrenched itself. This is the point at which it is necessary to act with courage to defend and preserve what Levinas calls the "third party," *le tiers*, beyond the dyad of self and other that defines the basic ethical relationship—however, always with a view to preserving the whole triad of which it is a part.

---

[198] A detailed argument for something resembling a pragmatic application of this approach is advanced by Pope Francis in his encyclical *Fratelli tutti. Lettera Enciclica sulla fraternità e l'amicizia sociale* (Rome: Libreria Editrice Vaticana, 2020), English online version: Fratelli tutti (3 October 2020) | Francis (vatican.va).

53.

Personal Responsibility and Aftermath of the Incalculable

To return to where we started, I do not think that I can judge wokeism. It has its necessity and reason for being. I can only react to it in a way that makes visible aspects of reality that it may blend out or occult. The political edge of wokeist activism has sometimes been necessary to bring fully to consciousness the unconscionable horrors of slavery and sexism and genocide. A tremendous labor of revisionary historiography and a campaign of public awareness-building driven largely by wokeist discourse and sensibility has brought about a social revolution and a conversion of conscience and consciousness in our time that are monumental achievements for humanity and justice.

But the focus on assigning to specific identity groups generic merits and demerits, identity-based entitlements and stigmas, often proves to be noxious in the extreme and engenders forms of collective blindness and indignation. Facing up to injustices and taking to heart the wrongs done throughout history is all to the good. However, that certain identity groups are made out to be innocent because they are not directly implicated in the identities of those presently designated wholesale as perpetrators is delusive and serves as a ground preparing for invidious labelings perpetuating resentments and further injustice.

We are presently enslaving and exploiting other species in no less outrageous ways than those decried by wokes with reference to specific races and genders of humans. However, these systematic abuses have not yet become universally recognized largely because we can still do it with impunity. People are not yet ready to renounce the enjoyment of eating meat, and other species have remained powerless against human technological means of instrumentalizing them. Even just as humans, we are all perpetrators or belong to guilty groups, if woke standards are to be applied consistently. Predation of various sorts, of course, runs all through nature and from long before the Anthropocene age. However, the industrial scale of our massive and merciless slaughter of other animal species is mind-boggling and heart-rending even in this long, ultra-historical perspective. We have created death camps of chillingly rational efficaciousness predicated on absolute disrespect for fellow creatures regarded as nothing but things, or living matter, at our disposal and serving our pleasure.

We are all also victims in countless ways, be it only of the technologies through which we dominate the world—and by which we are dominated in turn. There is hardly anyone who does not feel insulted and offended, if by nothing else, then, at least by all sorts of seemingly arbitrary, technical regulations and restrictions encountered anywhere and everywhere in public and private life today—not to mention all the bureaucratic blockades and administrative frustrations to which we are all constantly subjected, according to our belonging to various groups or categories. This is especially so now that each individual "user" can be held independently responsible for administrative processes. All are automatically presumed to have digital access to the system, although its satisfactory functioning lies far beyond the control of each.

Still, to make this personal and collective sense of umbrage our lens for viewing the world and taking offense is, in many cases, to sink into narcissistic obliviousness and delusion. We focus on how someone else is responsible for our woes and therefore owes us apologies and reparations instead of on what we can do to improve our lot and that of others.[199] For our sense of being injured and disrespected, moreover, we can always find easy explanations in terms of one identity or the other. We easily convince ourselves that it is because we are women or men, black or white, trans-gendered, or cis-gendered, that we are victimized, or at least not favored.

On another level, by the very same logic, the entire world is plummeting into war because of our attachment to generic identity terms of nation-states such as Russian, Chinese, or American, not to mention

---

[199] For a revealing discussion of this issue, see: Douglas Murray Thoroughly EMBARASSES Woke Lawyer, Leaving Her Speechless! (youtube.com)

Israeli or Palestinian. World war is brewing, and is already in part being waged, over these identities and their contradictory claims to defend the innocent and the upright against the wicked and the aggressors. If we remain in this logic, we are likely to destroy humanity and the planet, too.[200] Americans once felt themselves called on by their sacred duty to prevent communism from taking over the world. The Russian and Chinese governments, together with other heavy weights among the great powers such as India, Brazil, and South Africa joined in the Brics alliance, are on a sacred crusade (or counter-crusade) to bring down American domination with its, to them, unfair subjugation and Satanic (to use the terms of their Iranian ally) exploitation of the rest of the world. So long as these identities wield their enormous ideological power, we remain unable to dialogue with one another as human beings all doggedly self-interested yet also commonly in dire need of shared peace and mutual cooperation. Apophatic thinking can be practiced concretely in human interactions only upstream from irremediable, irreconcilable conflict. At least this holds for common mortals.

This same logic, which is manifest in international relations, applies equally to the internecine conflicts within our societies that are tearing them asunder. The histories of oppression are multiple, often two-edged, and innumerable, but every one of them becomes a world unto itself that self-encloses and is thereby liable to do injustice to others. Poverty and prejudice are not combatted just because more women or more blacks or more gays or queers or trans persons are in positions of power and prestige. Shifting the identity lines of privilege does not change the fact of misery for multitudes.[201] The real difficulty for Justice is that people are judged and punished, or promoted, on the basis of appearance rather than of real deserts, which lie deeper than any identity labels and are much more difficult to discern. Wokeism does not address this problem but tends rather to accentuate it by focusing so exclusively on outwardly identifiable characteristics.

---

[200] Noam Chomsky's innumerable analyses in print and in podcasts lucidly expose these dangers and delusions.

[201] This point is developed incisively by McWhorter in *Woke Racism: How a New Religion Has Betrayed Black America*.

One of the worst aspects of the whole controversy, for example, around race-conscious college admissions is that it deprives individuals of being the makers of their own destiny. All that we are individually is seen as (and to that extent actually becomes) determined by the favor or disfavor accorded our race or ethnic group by institutional authorities. Advancement in our careers, or in any other endeavors, depends not on what we do and produce but on qualifying for advantages by some specific criteria of diversity. In the background generally is some claim for compensation for past wrong done to a race or gender.

That individuals feel recognized and respected by their communities and the state is crucial for motivating them to give the best of themselves in their undertakings, professional or otherwise. Individuals of all types need to feel this respect. But the sense of individual responsibility is undermined when political reasons based on group identities overwhelm performance of individuals in determining their opportunities and their success.

Gender is a key factor in determining the fortunes of individuals. However, it always operates together with other factors. It is wrong to take a generic identifier like "woman" as per se prejudicial. It has to be considered "intersectionally"—and not just for the sake of compounding grievances. In many contexts and circumstances—like avoiding conscription for war—being female can comport distinct advantages. Furthermore, being female can be an advantage for some but not for other individuals depending on how they present and ply this particular attribute in specific situations and circumstances—in hiring processes or in divorce suits, to take a couple of examples, or in innumerable kinds of persuasion or seduction in which gender can count a great deal.

One moves into a dimension of abstraction by identifying with a cause in the name of a generic identity label like Woman. There is power in such abstractions, a kind of Platonic truth of eternal Forms that gives the impression of allowing us to see reality whole and to penetrate the power structures of its systemic discriminations. But this kind of exalted vision from a superior perspective also has some illusory propensities built into its visionary, revelatory impetus. We cannot remain statically attached to a transcendent truth such as animated some of the most inspired civil rights and feminist writings of the past century. We must also move flexibly into other registers, recognizing the limits of every discourse, including those inspired by whatever polemics.

Only the discourse that can recursively critique itself and reflect on its own limits can escape the fate, however noble its original intentions, of turning unjust toward untold others. Our discourse must turn, instead, to the infinity surrounding it and open itself also to the infinity of others that co-interpret this unfathomable origin or goal that grounds and bounds all that we are and think. After the dissolution of our own individual, finite form of existence, which on a physical plane happens definitively with our death, we are reabsorbed into this circumambient infinity. Only in this ultimate relation can our finite form remain eternally *as* a form of the infinite and not be *just* its own finite and perishing self.

The "apophatic" discourse offered between the covers of this book endeavors to perform this dissolution and transfiguration of self. By relating every distinction to the indistinction of the infinite, I mean to open my mind and myself beyond all my identity markers. What is called for here is a rational critique that surpasses even reason itself and relates reason and humanity to what encompasses and enables them, without ever being susceptible itself to being apprehended as an object of knowledge. Necessary is an orientation beyond oneself and one's own conceptions to the infinity of others around us and to the infinite richness that is our own intimate core and ungraspable being.[202]

This critical consciousness of one's own limitations together with a belief in the unlimited potency of what one does not grasp constitutes the gist of the negative theology traced out here. It combines unlimited rational critique with a longing beyond the scope of all rational faculties for the completeness that cannot be humanly grasped but can be granted only from beyond us. No positive knowledge of divinity is postulated here but rather an orientation to the infinite and inexhaustible that, at the same time, requires an openness towards all others around one because they too stand in relation to this ungraspable absolute that grounds or bounds all

---

[202] We can be helped to think this profound paradox, with particular accents on "glory" and "joy" in the endeavor, by the thought of the contemporary Italian philosopher Emanuele Severino, *Oltrepassare* (Milan: Adelphi, 2007).

relative forms of existence. Any fundamental challenge to our contingent being and our fundamental relationality as human beings opens this dimension of existence in relation to the infinite and unknown that can be approached through negative theology as articulated in this book. The ethical challenges posed by wokeism, with their irrecusable demand for justice for all without exclusions, together with the ineradicable paradoxes and equivocations of any finite being's imposing such demands, force us, or at least invite us, to respect and even to reverence a justice other to and higher than our own. The dilemmas and exigencies posed by wokeism should awaken us to this—must we not say—metaphysical dimension in which our life as humans in relation to others transpires.

To close this meditation, I return to the epigraph from Paul's Letter to the Ephesians: "For we wrestle not against flesh and blood, but against principalities, against powers, against the rulers of the darkness of this world, against spiritual wickedness in high places" (6: 12). Paul's vision or revelation places evil not in any other social group intrinsically but rather in "spiritual" powers and in the structure building into the world a "height" and dominion that are not God's but belong rather to the "rulers" of this world's darkness. True moral height and authority has to stand above us all, transcending our world, in order to norm and regulate our conflicts. Only recognizing this higher norm, but at the same time relinquishing our own definitions and symbolizations of it, can we save ourselves from reciprocal hostility and mutual destruction. Only respecting the equal validity of others' approaches to the absolute can concretely enact respect for the absolute beyond our own relative conceptions and apprehensions of it. Therein lies the lesson of apophatic thinking and its implicit critique of wokeism. This critique can and should be an internal critique whereby wokeism also becomes a type of self-reflective revelation to us all of our calling to serve social justice in truth and sincerity of heart all the days of our life.

54.

Blessing *and* Curse:
The Woke Revolution
and its Totalitarian Turn

The woke *revolution* is a continuation of Christian *revelation*, its last or latest configuration in our own postmodern times. The core idea, at its origin, is that of the infinite and inviolable value of every person in the eyes of God. Each person has an incommensurable dignity which confers equal worth independent of one's status or grade in society. This teaching can be hailed as a triumph of liberation, as in the Enlightenment narrative of progress. But it might also be abominated as a triumph of resentment against the aristocratic order of the ancient world, particularly the Greco-Roman world, as it was by Nietzsche. That women and slaves and socially emarginated groups should have equal dignity with their lords and masters was a radical undermining of time-honored values and hierarchy: it could mean placing the underlings on top and making the last first, as explicitly proclaimed by the Christian Gospel (Matthew 20: 16; Mark 10: 31; Luke 13: 30).

This upending of values was inscribed in the triumph and glorification of God as victim dying on the Cross. It was utter foolishness or even madness in terms of the wisdom of the world as previously known and established. Paul of Tarsus realized this full well and stated as much in his first Letter to the Corinthians: "Because the foolishness of God is wiser than men; and the weakness of God is stronger than men. . . . God hath chosen the foolish things of the world to confound the wise; and God hath chosen the weak things of the world to confound the things which are mighty" (I: 25, 27).

Both assessments and attitudes, that of liberation and that of resentment, are manifest in Christian history and quite clearly in wokeism, too. Wokeism, in theory, liberates from dominion (of the white male heteronormative) but then heightens the bid for hegemony with its own, new, moralizing world order. This new order is imposed, in turn, with all the attendant oppressions of dissidents and suppressions of heretics.[203] The woke revolution in our society aims to subjugate everything and everyone to its own idea of social justice based on social identities. Wokeism repeats both the Christian revolution, the revolution of the victims, *and* its betrayal once it is overtaken by all the usual powers of worldly domination that turn it into an engine of repression in its own right.

Wokeism is both the extension into our times of Christianity and the betrayal of this Christian inspiration. Wokeism incarnates a radicalization of Christianity's valorization of the victim as holy and saving *and* its reversal by appropriating this revaluation of values into the old system of the previous way of the world and its power politics (*Realpolitik*). Nietzsche conflates these two moments of Christian history and reads Christianity's inaugural moment only in the light of its corruption. He sees Christianity as *only* an attempt to exert the will to power by underhanded means of morality—calling the strong and dominant "evil" while lauding the powerless and weak *ipso facto* as "good." He elides the authentic moment, at the inception of Christianity, of renunciation of force. He simply ignores the resolve to conquer only by love and even at the cost of accepting death as modelled by Christ on the Cross. Evidently, Nietzsche does not hold any such self-sacrifice for the sake of love to be possible (although his own tragic life might tell a different story). Indeed, this incarnation of love is where the human becomes divine. Recognizing and entering into this experience requires a kind of faith.

Christianity projects and propounds this revolutionary ideal of self-immolation in the flame of love, which has somewhat miraculously conquered our world in word and as an ideal. Those recognized as victims are treated as holy and inviolable. No force with the power to crush them is accepted as right because of its might—at least not in theory. But even

---

[203] Burchill, *Welcome to the Woke Trials*, is one strident witness. Another is Downey, This politically-correct witch-hunt is killing free speech (substack.com).

this radically revolutionary levin, the original Christian reliance on the power of love alone as subversive of all worldly power, is appropriated for purposes of furthering worldly agendas and using force to stifle opposition. This becomes the case repeatedly in the history of the Christian Church with its relentless persecutions. The Church, in its turn, became a perpetrator of atrocity and oppression, although the narratives of this straying are widely divergent and contradictory.

The dilemmas and debacles of wokeism are those constantly encountered by Christian love throughout its two millennia of history in the world and still today. We encounter them, as disturbingly as ever, in the ecclesiastical scandals of priests who pervert Christian love into an instrument of power to prevail over those who genuinely and innocently believe in love as preached in the Gospel. The perpetrators then use their worldly power again to cover over their nefarious actions. Such are the paradoxes of power that riddle the history of Christian morality. The revolutionary power of love, as discovered in the world-shattering revelation of God on the Cross, becomes a power like any other that is folded back into the logic of domination for worldly ends and purposes of self-aggrandizement and for making others serve one's selfish desires.

I do not oppose the woke revolution. I wish to challenge it to be consistent with and true to its own founding insights and inspiration. If we think through completely its ethical principle of unconditional respect for others, for racial, gender, class alterity or diversity, we have to affirm the otherness of the real beyond all our definitions and classifications and control. We have to acknowledge radical alterity even beyond all the terms and categories that we apply to others and to ourselves. This realization takes us to the brink of acknowledging the to-us-indefinable alterity that is interpreted by theology as God, or in a more neutral register as "the Transcendent." This further move beyond what we can grasp is necessary to prevent us from identifying justice simply with a system of our own making and its positive distinctions.

We can never be completely just in and by ourselves. Justice is relational; ultimately, it is a gift from beyond us. To live justly, we have to live in openness to the Other beyond ourselves and beyond our own determinations of justice. This *can* mean living in openness to God. In any case, it is a necessary part of remaining open to love that exceeds and evades all the reappropriations of power. The machinations of power inevitably reassert their force in our existence as human beings with concrete interests and biases and finite perspectives that will set us into conflict with others unless we cultivate and educate our capacity for self-negation through love. This is what Jesus Christ revealed on the Cross in a world-historically significant and world-shattering manner. I am very willing to find a similar sort of revelation in Siddhartha Gautama Buddha or Martin Luther King or Crazy Horse or Simone Weil, or you name her, if it breaks us open to the revelation of the love without limit which is God. The core of ethics, in any case, is self-denial in openness toward and service of the Other.

Self-identifying conservative liberals like Jordan Peterson think of ethics as based on affirmation of the "sovereignty" of the self, the "individual." They do not generally go the full length of embracing an alterity-based ethic of radical, infinite obligation to the Other such as Emanuel Levinas articulates with unparalleled philosophical penetration. They often express their contempt for "postmodern" thought or "deconstruction." [204] The latter developed out of Jacques Derrida's appropriation of Levinas's thinking of alterity, rigorously reflecting on the paradoxes produced by "difference" as the condition of meaning in language. Douglas Murray, like Peterson, expresses disdain for the postmodern with the full force of his eloquence of vituperation. Yet he also feels a necessity to remain open to dialogue with Christian faith and its theological heritage, even while confessing himself not able personally to identify as Christian. [205] Tom Holland does so identify, though without embracing some of the more self-certain versions of Christian belief. [206]

I am inclined to think that Holland's confessedly Christian attitude is a possible expression of what, with St. Anselm, we could recognize as "faith seeking understanding." Beyond ethics as centered on the sovereign individual, the ethics of infinite obligation to the Other is the more radical

---

[204] What Postmodernism Got Right & How It Fails | Jordan B Peterson (youtube.com) Accessed 8-30-2024.

[205] Truth as Glorious Adventure | Douglas Murray | EP 376 (youtube.com) Accessed 4-29-2024.

[206] Tom Holland on his bestseller Dominion (youtube.com) Accessed 4-29-2024.

and revolutionary child of Christian revelation. Both ethics issue from Christianity, with its infinite valorization of all, women equally with men, slaves equally with masters, Gentiles and Jews alike. The emancipation of individuals in Western democratic society has been possible largely because of the revolutionary impact of Christian revelation and ethics. The more radical ethical exigency lies in unconditionally serving the Other—and only thereby affirming one's own inviolable worth and dignity. This is the radical exigency displayed and demanded by the Cross—by Christ's self-sacrifice out of love for every individual human being. This is the deeper ground for the liberationist social revolution that Christianity sparked and that extends its irresistible influence all the way to wokeism today.

55.

Conclusion: Revolution of the Victims as Revelation of the Divine

Acknowledging that one does not possess the truth is the only way of remaining faithful to truth. The truth is ultimately God—or the unsayable, if you prefer. The infinite is indescribable for us, incomprehensible in its essence. On this point, Christian apophatic doctrines (expounded by Dionysius the Areopagite, Meister Eckhart, Theresa of Avila, etc.) accord with those of Judaism, Islam, Buddhism, Hinduism, Taoism, the Sioux Great Spirit or Mystery *Wakan Tanka*, Navajo *Hózhǫ́*, and countless other cultures. Concerning "God"— and this goes equally for Justice—all our human conceptions are inadequate, all our speech is insufficient.

Recognizing the limits of our understanding and concepts, not to mention of our own language and the cultural assumptions embedded within it, forces us to acknowledge alterity, even absolute alterity. It teaches us specifically not to elevate ourselves, our identity, our culture, or our own truth above those of others, triggering mimetic rivalry. Instead, venturing out before others in the respectful attitude of listening and learning from them emerges as the royal road to offering hospitality also to the divine.

The revolution of the victims is the ultimate working out of the Christian revelation of God on the Cross. The victim of the most terrible tortures and humiliations is revealed as God in person! This revelation transformed and revolutionized the world. [207] The core of the woke

---

[207] Tom Holland, *Dominion: How the Christian Revolution Remade the World* (New York: Basic Books, 2021) persuasively recasts virtually everything in our contemporary world as the result of Christianity and its revolutionary exaltation of the

revolution, the revolution of the victims, is yet another iteration of this world-historical reversal and upheaval. And yet, as always in the history of Christianity, this revelation of the revolutionary power of love is recuperated by worldly power, by the play of powers against one another, in which everyone tries to dominate over everyone else. The Church's pedophile scandals are a glaring, festering wound that demonstrates how the revolutionary and divine power of love can be corrupted and converted into a worldly and unjust power. The power of love is betrayed and overwhelmed by the dynamic of domination over others, which leads almost ineluctably to abuse of power. This is just as true of other human institutions as of the Church. However, the Church has been called on currently and publicly to bear this cross.

The ethical question today is generally reduced to demanding justice for victims conceived in terms of social identities. This reduction bogs us down in injustices and wars because we lack a metaphysical or religious—or, better, an "apophatic"—perspective, by which I mean a perspective beyond positive, divisive, sectorial identifications. We are lacking a vision that can unite us in an orientation towards a common good, which might be nothing other than this very aspiration itself—an aspiration necessarily shared by all who aim to live together in one world. I do not propose any dogma or concept in which everyone must believe. Kenotic ethics is empty of positive precepts. It presupposes, instead, a negative theology—which entails the admission that we know neither God nor any truth or ideal in its absoluteness yet must seek precisely such an indefinable norm together, yielding to one another's insufficient attempts and contributing our own. We all struggle to be true to the absolute truth or Justice that binds us as sharers of one world yet escapes the exclusive grasp of any of us. Admitting this, we then willingly accept and welcome correction by others and comparison with their approaches.

Everything changes if we accept being oriented towards an absolute truth or reality that we do not know—even just to the absolute otherness of the other person standing before us, facing us. Such is the common condition of our existence together on earth until death. Group identities,

---

victim. See further: Tom Holland On How Christianity Has Shaped Western Morality - YouTube.

when politicized, are formulas that divide society into oppressors and oppressed beyond all possibility of uniting and concerting our efforts and loves. We will never agree on who is the oppressor and who the oppressed, or on which group started or continues to cause a given war—any war: the Russian Federation or NATO, Israel or Hamas or Hezbollah or Iran, China or the USA. We must overcome this way of reasoning blindly on the basis of finite, mutually exclusive entities identified by our concepts and our linguistic categories. We must open them towards their infinite truth rooted in our unlimited interconnectedness. Doing so, we open our ideas beyond their finite content and open ourselves in order to begin to build a history and a world together.

Bibliography

Adorno, Theodor (1966) *Negative Dialektik*. Frankfurt a.M.: Suhrkamp.

Adorno, Theodor and Max Horkheimer (1947) *Dialektik der Aufklärung*. Amsterdam: Querido. Trans. Edmund Jephcott as *Dialectic of Enlightenment*. Stanford: Stanford University Press, 2002.

Agamben, Giorgio (2000) *Il tempo che resta: Un commento alla lettera ai Romani*. Turin: Bollati Boringhieri. Trans. Patricia Dailey as *The Time That Remains: A Commentary on the Letter to the Romans*. Stanford, CA: Stanford University Press, 2005.

al-Gharbi, Musa (2024) *We Have Never Been Woke: The Cultural Contradictions of a New Elite*. Princeton: Princeton University Press.

Arendt, Hannah (1973) *The Origins of Totalitarianism*. New York: Harcourt Brace Jovanovich.

Badiou, Alain (1997) *Saint Paul: La fondation de l'universalisme*. Paris: Presses Universitaires de France. Trans. Ray Brassier as *Saint Paul: The Foundation of Universalism*. Stanford, CA: Stanford University Press, 2003.

Baldwin, James (1998) *Collected Essays*. New York: Library of America.

Baldwin, James (1972) *If Beale Street Could Talk*. New York: Dial.

Balibar, Étienne (1995) "The Infinite Contradiction." *Yale French Studies* 88: 142–64.

Barzun, Jacques (1965) *Race: A Study in Superstition*. New York: Harper & Row.

Bawer, Bruce (2012) *The Victims' Revolution: The Rise of Identity Studies and the Closing of the Liberal Mind*. New York: HarperCollins. Tenth Anniversary Edition: *The Victims' Revolution: The Rise of Identity Studies and the Birth of Woke Ideology*. New York: Post Hill Press, 2022.

Benjamin, Walter (1977 [1940]) "Geschichtsphilosophische Thesen." In *Illuminationen. Ausgewählte Schriften*. vol. I. Ed. Siegfried Unseld. Frankfurt am

Main: Suhrkamp. 268-281. Translated as "Theses on the Philosophy of History," *Illuminations: Essays and Reflections*. Ed. Hannah Arendt. New York: Harcourt Brace Jovanovich, 1968.

Benjamin, Walter (1977 [1937-38]) "Theologisch-politisches Fragment." In *Illuminationen. Ausgewählte Schriften*. vol. I. Ed. Siegfried Unseld. Frankfurt am Main: Suhrkamp. 282-83. Translated as "Theological-Political Fragment." *Illuminations: Essays and Reflections*. Ed. Hannah Arendt. New York: Harcourt Brace Jovanovich, 1968.

Bible, Holy (1611) The Authorized King James Version. Modified in light of the Greek New Testament.

Biggar, Nigel (2023) *Colonialism: A Moral Reckoning*. London: HarperCollins. Birbalsingh, Katharine. Decolonising Shakespeare: 'White guilt will destroy the West' – Katharine Birbalsingh - YouTube. Accessed 3-20-2025.

Blanco, Eric (2019) *Les Gueules Rouges*. ARDECHE IMAGES - Les Gueules rouges (lussasdoc.org).

Bloom, Alan (1987) *The Closing of the American Mind: How Higher Education Has Failed Democracy and Impoverished the Souls of Today's Students*. New York: Simon and Schuster.

Bloom, Harold (1994) *The Western Canon: The Books and School of the Ages*. New York: Harcourt Brace.

Bock-Côté, Mathieu (2021) *La Révolution racialiste: et autres virus idéologiques*. Paris: Presses de la Cité.

Botz-Bornstein, Thorsten (2006) *Re-Ethnicizing the Minds? Tendencies of Cultural Revival in Contemporary Philosophy*. Amsterdam: Rodopi.

Botz-Bornstein, Thorsten. Ed. (2025) *Tracking Global Wokeism*. Amsterdam: Brill.

Bouhdiba, Abdelwahab, Muḥammad Maʿrūf Dawālībī. Eds. (1998) *The Individual and Society in Islam*. Paris: UNESCO.

Brague, Rémi (1992) *Europe, la voie romaine*. Paris: Critérion.

Braunstein, Jean-François (2022) *La religion woke*. Paris: Gasset.

Braunstein, Jean-François. Les dangers du wokisme - Jean-François Braunstein - Conférence - YouTube.

Braunstein, Jean-François. "La religion Woke": Jean-François Braunstein est l'invité de Culture médias (youtube.com)

Bruckner, Pascal (2006) *La tyrannie de la pénitence: Essai sur le masochisme occidental.* Paris: Grasset.

Burchill, Julie (2021) *Welcome to the Woke Trials: How #Identity Killed Progressive Politics.* Washington: Academica Press.

Caldwell, Christopher (2020) *The Age of Entitlement: America Since the Sixties.* New York: Simon & Schuster.

Caputo, John (1993) *Against Ethics: Contributions to a Poetics of Obligation with Constant Reference to Deconstruction,* Bloomington: University of Indiana Press.

Carlson, Tucker. https://www.youtube.com/watch?v=1t9Cr88sAbk. Accessed 7-16-2023.

Caygill, Howard (2015) *On Resistance: A Philosophy of Defiance.* London: Bloomsbury.

Cervantes Saavedra, Miguel de (1918 [1616]) *El Ingenioso Hidalgo Don Quijote de la Mancha.* Eds. Salvador Fajardo and James A. Parr. Asheville, North Carolina: Pegasus Press. Trans. Edith Grossman as *Don Quixote.* New York: HarperCollins, 2003.

Chazaud, Anne-Sophie (2019) *Liberté d'inexpression: nouvelles formes de la censure contemporaine.* Paris: L'Artilleur.

Cicero, Tullius (1913) *De Officiis.* Trans. Walter Miller. Cambridge, Mass.: Harvard University Press.

Coates, Ta-Nehisi (2015) *Between the World and Me.* New York: One World.

Crenshaw, Kimberle (1989) "Demarginalizing the Intersection of Race and Sex: A Black Feminist Critique of Antidiscrimination Doctrine, Feminist Theory and Antiracist Politics," *University of Chicago Legal Forum.* No. 1, art. 8, 139–67

Dark, David (2009) *The Sacredness of Questioning Everything.* Grand Rapids: Zondervan.

Das, Saitya Brata (2023) *Political Theology of Life.* Eugene, Oregon: Pickwick.

Daub, Adrian (2024) *The Cancel Culture Panic: How an American Obsession Went Global.* Stanford: Stanford University Press. Originally *Cancel Culture*

Transfer: Wie eine moralische Panik die Welt erfasst. Frankfurt a.M.: Suhrkamp, 2022.

DiAngelo, Robin (2018) *White Fragility: Why It's So Hard for White People to Talk About Racism.* Boston: Beacon Press, 2018.

Downey, Sarah A. This politically-correct witch-hunt is killing free speech (substack.com)

Dreher, Rod. The Exact Formula That Helped Hungary Beat 'Wokeness' | Rod Dreher | INTERNATIONAL | Rubin Report - YouTube. Accessed 7-14-2023.

Durkheim, Émile (2013 [1893]) *De la division du travail social.* Paris: Presses Universitaires de France.

Eagleton, Terry (2014) *Culture and the Death of God.* New Haven: Yale University Press.

Eder, Klaus (2011) "Europe as a Narrative Network: Taking the Social Embeddedness of Identity Constructions Seriously." In: S. Lucarelli, F. Cerutti and V. A. Schmidt (eds), *Debating Political Identity and Legitimacy in the European Union: Interdisciplinary Views.* London: Routledge. 38–54.

Emerson, Ralph Waldo (1841) Self-Reliance.pages (emersoncentral.com)

Fanon, Frantz (1961) *Les damnés de la terre.* Paris: Maspero. Trans. Richard Philcox as *The Wretched of the Earth.* With a foreword by Homi K. Bhabha and a preface by Jean-Paul Sartre. New York: Grove Press, 2004.

Fields, Karen E. and Barbara J. Fields (2012) *Racecraft: The Soul of Inequality in American Life.* London: Verso.

Flaig, Egon (2009) *Weltgeschichte der Sklaverei.* München: Beck.

Foucault, Michel (1980) "Truth and Power," in *Power/Knowledge: Selected Interviews and Other Writings 1972-1977.* C. Gordon (ed.). Trans. C. Gordon, L Marshall, J. Mepham, K Soper. New York: Pantheon. 109-33.

Francis, Pope (2020) *Fratelli tutti. Lettera Enciclica sulla fraternità e l'amicizia sociale.* Rome: Libreria Editrice Vaticana. English online version: Fratelli tutti (3 October 2020) | Francis (vatican.va)

Franke, William (2007) *On What Cannot Be Said: Apophatic Discourses in Philosophy, Religion, Literature, and the Arts.* 2 vols. Edited with Theoretical and Critical Essays by William Franke. Notre Dame, Indiana: University of Notre

Dame Press. Vol. I: Classic Formulations; Vol. II: Modern and Contemporary Transformations.

Franke, William (2009) *Poetry and Apocalypse: Theological Disclosures of Poetic Language*. Stanford: Stanford University Press.

Franke, William (2014) *A Philosophy of the Unsayable*. Notre Dame: University of Notre Dame Press.

Franke, William (2015) *The Revelation of Imagination: From Homer and the Bible through Virgil and Augustine to Dante*. Evanston: Northwestern University Press.

Franke, William (2016) *Secular Scriptures: Modern Theological Poetics in the Wake of Dante*. Columbus: Ohio State University Press.

Franke, William (2018) *Apophatic Paths from Europe to China: Regions Without Borders*. Albany: State University of New York Press, 2018.

Franke, William (2019) "A Negative Theological Critique of Postmodern Identity Politics." *Religions* 10/488: 1-15.

Franke, William (2020) "Why an Open or 'Public' Sphere is Necessary to Civil Society and its Entanglement with Religion." Epilogue to *Public Sphere and Religion: An Entangled Relationship in History, Education, and Society*. Ed. Carl Antonius Lemke. Hildesheim: Olms. 230-49.

Franke, William (2020) *On the Universality of What Is Not: The Apophatic Turn in Critical Thinking*. Notre Dame: University of Notre Dame Press, 2020.

Franke, William (2021a) "Amphibolies of the Postmodern: Hyper-Secularity or the Return of the Religious?"]. In Morgan (2021), 9-33.

Franke, William (2021b) *Dante's* Paradiso *and the Theological Origins of Modern Thought: Toward a Speculative Philosophy of Self-Reflection*. New York: Routledge.

Franke, William (2021c) *The Divine Vision of Dante's* Paradiso*: The Metaphysics of Representation*. Cambridge, UK: Cambridge University Press.

Franke, William (2021d) *Dante's* Vita Nuova *and the New Testament: Hermeneutics and the Poetics of Revelation* (Cambridge, UK: Cambridge University Press.

Franke, William (2023) "Not War, nor Peace. Are War and Peace Mutually Exclusive Alternatives?" *War: Thinking the Unthinkable.* Special Issue of *Continental Thought and Theory: A Journal of Intellectual Freedom* 4/1: 25-35. Eds. Cindy Zeiher and Mike Grimshaw.

Franke, William (2024) *Don Quixote's Impossible Quest for the Absolute in Literature: Fiction, Reflection, and Negative Theology.* New York: Routledge.

Franke, William (2024) "Plato's Apophatic Legacy," *Archives of the History of Philosophy* 69, special issue for Professor Seweryn Blandzi, ed. Dariusz Piętka. 1-21.

Franke, William (2025) *Pandemics and Apocalypse in World Literature: The Hope for Planetary Salvation.* New York: Routledge.

Frazer, James (1890) *The Golden Bough: A Study in Comparative Religion.*

Furedi, Frank (2024) *The War Against the Past: Why the West Must Fight for its History.* Cambridge: Polity.

Fuller, Steve (2018) *Post-Truth: Knowledge as a Power Game.* London: Anthem.

Funk, Max. Wokeism—The New Religion of The West - Converge Media. Accessed 1-22-2023.

Girard, René (1972) *La violence et le sacré.* Paris: Grasset.

Girard, René (1982) *Le bouc émissaire.* Paris: Grasset. Trans. Yvonne Freccero as *The Scapegoat.* Baltimore: The Johns Hopkins University Press, 1989.

Girard, René (1999) *Je vois Satan tomber comme l'éclair.* Paris: Grasset. Trans. James G. Wilson as *I See Satan Fall Like Lightning* (Maryknoll: Orbis Books, 2001).

Girard, René (2001) with J.-M. Oughourlian and Guy Lefort, *Des choses cachées depuis le commencement du monde.* Paris: Grasset. Translation available by Stephen Bann and Michael Metteer as *Things Hidden Since the Foundation of the World* (Stanford: Stanford University Press, 1987).

Glaude, Jr., Eddie S. (2021) *Begin Again: James Baldwin's America and its Urgent Lessons for Our Own.* New York: Penguin Random House.

Gordon, Joseph K. (2022 [2019]) *Divine Scripture in Human Understanding: A Systematic Theology of the Christian Bible.* Notre Dame: University of Notre Dame Press.

Gary, Romain (1970) *Chien blanc*. Paris: Gallimard.

Graziani, Romain (2019) *L'usage du vide: essai sur l'intelligence de l'action, de l'Europe à la Chine*. Paris: Gallimard.

Guttiérez, Gustavo (1971) *Teología de la liberación. Perspectivas*. Lima: CEP. Trans. Caridad Inda and John Eagleson as *A Theology of Liberation: History, Politics, and Salvation*. Maryknoll: Orbis, 1988; 1st ed., Maryknoll: Orbis, 1973.

Habermas, Jürgen (2002) *Religion and Rationality: Essays on Reason, God, and Modernity*. Ed. Eduardo Mendieta. Cambridge: MIT Press.

Habermas, Jurgen (2008) "Ein Bewusstsein von dem, was fehlt." In *Ein Bewusstsein von dem, was fehlt: Eine Diskussion mit Jurgen Habermas*. Ed. Michael Reder and Josef Schmidt. Frankfurt am Main: Suhrkamp. Trans. Ciaran Cronin as *An Awareness of What Is Missing: Faith and Reason in a Post-Secular Age*. Cambridge: Polity Press, 2010.

Han, Byung-Cul (2013) *Digitale Rationalität und das Ende des kommunikativen Handelns*. Berlin: Matthes und Seitz.

Han, Byung-Cul (2017) *In the Swarm: Digital Prospects*. Trans. Erik Butler. Cambridge: MIT Press.

Harrison, Peter. "Enlightened Racism?" Enlightened racism? - ABC Religion & Ethics

David Harvey (1973) *Social Justice and the City*. Baltimore: Johns Hopkins University Press.

Hegel, Georg Wilhelm Friedrich (2005) *Die Philosophie des Rechts. Vorlesung von 1821/22*. Frankfurt a.M.: Suhrkamp Verlag.

Heinich, Nathalie (2023) *Le wokisme serait-il un totalitarisme?* Paris: Albin Michel.

Herrero, Montserrat (2024) *Filosofía política. De la antigüedad al mundo contemporáneo*. Madrid: Rialp, S.A.

Holland, Tom (2021) *Dominion: How the Christian Revolution Remade the World*. New York: Basic Books.

Holland, Tom Tom Holland on his bestseller Dominion (youtube.com)

Irigaray, Luce (1985) "Femmes divines," *Critique* 41/454: 294-308.

Khan, Rachel (2021) *Racée*. Paris: Humensis.

La Fontaine, Jean de (1842) *Fables*, 1678-1679. Paris: Aubert.
Lefort, Claude (2020) "La modernité de Dante," introduction to Dante, *La Monarchie*, translated from Latin to French by Michèle Gally (Paris: Belin, D.L., 1993). English trans. Jennifer Rushworth as "Dante's Modernity: An Introduction to the *Monarchia*." Berlin: ICI Berlin Press.

Levet, Bérénice (2018) *Libérons-nous du féminisme*. Paris: Editions de l'observatoire.

Levet, Bérénice (2022) *Le Courage de la dissidence: L'esprit français contre le wokisme*. Paris: L'Observatoire.

Levinas, Emmanuel (1971) *Totalité et infini: Essai sur l'extériorité*. The Hague: Nijhoff.

Levinas, Emmanuel (1972) *Humanisme de l'autre homme*. Paris: Fata Morgana. Trans. Nidra Poller. Urbana, IL: University of Illinois Press, 2003.

Levinas, Emmanuel (1974) *Autrement qu'être ou au-delà de l'essence* (The Hague: Martinus Nijhoff. Trans. Alphonso Lingis as *Otherwise than Being and Beyond Essence*. Dordrecht: Kluwer, 1991.

Lilla, Mark (2007) *The Stillborn God: Religion, Politics, and the Modern West*. New York: Knopf.

Lilla, Mark "Coping with Political Theology." Coping with Political Theology | Cato Unbound (cato-unbound.org) Accessed 2-12-2023.

Lloyd, Vincent (2017) "The Negative Political Theology of James Baldwin." In *A Political Companion to James Baldwin*. Ed. Susan J. McWilliams. Lexington, KY: The University Press of Kentucky, 171–94.

MacDonald, Heather (2018) *The Diversity Delusion: How Race and Gender Pandering Corrupt the University and Undermine Our Culture*. New York: St. Martin's Press.

Malik, Kenan (2023) *Not So Black and White: A History of Race from White Supremacy to Identity Politics*. London: Hurst.

McGowan, Roger W. (2015) *Messages de vie du couloir de la mort*. Written with the collaboration of Pierre Pradervand. Switzerland: Jouvence.

McGowan, Todd (2020) *Universalism and Identity Politics*. New York: Columbia University Press.

McKenna, Tony (2024) *Has Political Correctness Gone Mad? Interrogating a Right-wing Conspiracy Theory*. London: Bloomsbury Academic.

MacLeod, Gordon and Colin McFarlane (2024) "Introduction: Grammars of Urban Injustice," *Antipode* 46/4: 857-73.

McLuhan, T. C. Ed. (1971) *Touch the Earth: A Self-Portrait of Indian Existence*. New York: Outerbridge & Lazaard. Trans. as *Pieds nus sur la terre sacrée*. Paris: Denoël. 2021.

McWhorter, John (2021) *Woke Racism: How a New Religion Has Betrayed Black America*. New York: Portfolio/Penguin.

Madsen, Deborah L. Ed. (2010) *Native Authenticity: Transnational Perspectives on Native American Literary Studies*. New York: SUNY Press.

Miéville, China (2018) "Silence in Debris: Towards an Apophatic Marxism," *Salvage* 6: 115–44.

Miéville, China (2022) *A Spectre, Haunting: On the Communist Manifesto*. Chicago: Haymarket Books.

Miéville, China (2004) *Between Equal Rights: A Marxist Theory of International Law*. Amsterdam: Brill Academic Publications.

Mitchell, Joshua (2020) *American Awakening: Identity Politics and Other Afflictions of our Time*. New York: Encounter Books.

Möller, Hans-Georg (2022) Wokeism—the leftwing of neoliberalism—Redline (wordpress.com)

Möller, Hans-Georg (2023) Media Philosophy: A Critical Wrap-Up (youtube.com)

Möller, Hans-Georg (2023) Reply to Jordan Peterson: Individualism, Wokeism, and Civil Religion - YouTube.

Möller, Hans-Georg. Wokeism - YouTube. Accessed 7-4-2023.

Moore, Sean D. (2019) "'Whatever Is, Is Right': The Redwood Library and the Reception of Pope's Poetry in Colonial Rhode Island." *Slavery and the Making of Early American Libraries: British Literature, Political Thought, and the*

Transatlantic Book Trade, 1731-1814. Oxford; online edn, Oxford Academic, 17 Apr.

Morgan, Stephen. Ed (2021) *Sacred and the Everyday: Comparative Approaches to Literature, Religious and Sacred.* Macau: University of Saint Joseph Academic Press.

Murray, Douglas (2022) *The War on the West: How to Prevail in the Age of Unreason.* London: HarperCollins.

Murray, Douglas (2024) Douglas Murray: Why conservatives will win the war on the West (youtube.com). Accessed 4-15-2024.

Murray, Douglas (2024) Douglas Murray Thoroughly EMBARASSES Woke Lawyer, Leaving Her Speechless! (youtube.com)

N'Diaye, Tidiane (2010) *Der verschleierte Völkermord. Die Geschichte des muslimischen Sklavenhandels.* Reinbek bei Hamburg: Rowohlt.

Neiman, Susan (2023) *Left is not Woke.* Cambridge: Polity.

Niebuhr, Reinhold (1940) *Christianity and Power Politics.* New York: Scribner.

Nietzsche, Friedrich (1882) *Die fröliche Wissenschaft.* Trans. Walter Kaufmann as *The Gay Science.* New York: Vintage, 1974.

Nietzsche, Friedrich (1886) *Jenseits von Gut und Böse.* Leipzig: C. G. Naumann. Translated as *Beyond Good and Evil.* Projekt Gutenberg.

Nietzsche, Friedrich (1887) *Zur Genealogie der Moral: Eine Streitschrift.* Trans. Walter Kaufman as *On the Genealogy of Morality: A Polemic.* New York: Vintage, 1967.

O'Brien, Ani. Wokies are the establishment—Redline (wordpress.com). Accessed 7/6/2023.

O'Sullivan, John (2024) *Sleepwalking into Wokeness: How We Got Here.* Washington: Academica Press.

Ogien, Albert (2023) *Émancipations. Luttes minoritaires, luttes universelles.* Paris: Textuel.

Patterson, James M. (2023) Wokeness and the New Religious Establishment | National Affairs

Peterson, Jordan: You Must Stand Up Against Woke Ideologies - YouTube.

Pelluchon, Corine (2017) *Manifeste animaliste: Politiser la cause animale.* Paris: Alma.

Ramaswamy, Vivek (2021) *Woke, Inc.: Inside Corporate America's Social Justice Scam.* New York: Hachette Books.

Rhodes, Carl (2022) *Woke Capitalism: How Corporate Morality Is Sabotaging Democracy.* Bristol: Bristol University Press.

Rosa, Hartmut (2022) *Demokratie braucht Religion.* München: Kösel. Trans. Valentine A. Pakis as *Democracy Needs Religion.* New York: Polity, 2024.

Rosa, Hartmut (2018) *Unverfügbarkeit.* Frankfurt a.M.: Suhrkamp. Trans. James Wagner as *The Uncontrollability of the World.* New York: Polity, 2020.

Rufo, Christopher F. (2023) *America's Cultural Revolution: How the Radical Left Conquered Everything.* New York: Broadside.

Sandrini, Giorgio, Gianpiero Gamaleri, Walter Minella, Diego Centonze, Paolo Mazzarello, eds. (2024) *Comunicare il vero e il falso: La comunicazione oggi tra mondo digitale, etica e neuroscienze.* Milan: Mimesis.

Saussure, Ferdinand de (1916) *Cours de linguistique générale.* Eds. Charles Bally and Albert Sechehaye. Paris: Payot, 1955.

Schröter, Susanne (2024) *Der neue Kulturkampf: Wie eine woke Linke Wissenschaft, Kultur und Gesellschaft bedroht.* Freiburg: Herder.

Shellenberger, Michael. Michael Shellenberger's Guide to Escaping the Woke Matrix (youtube.com).

Severino, Emanuele (1972) *Essenza del nichilismo.* Brescia, Paideia, 1972. Second edition enlarged. Milano, Adelphi, 1982. Trans. Giacomo Donis as *The Essence of Nihilism.* Ed. Ines Testoni and Alessandro Carrera. London-New York, Verso Books, 2016.

Severino, Emanuele (1992) *Oltre il linguaggio.* Milan: Adelphi. Trans. Damiano Sacco as *Beyond Language.* London: Bloomsbury, 2024.

Severino, Emanuele (2007) *Oltrepassare.* Milan: Adelphi.

Sowell, Thomas (2023) *Social Justice Fallacies.* New York: Basic Books.

Stoll, Mark (2015) *Inherit the Holy Mountain: Religion and the Rise of American Environmentalism.* Oxford: Oxford University Press.

Taylor, Charles (1994) *Multiculturalism: Examining the Politics of Recognition.* Ed. Amy Gutmann. Princeton: Princeton University Press.

13TH | FULL FEATURE | Netflix (youtube.com)

Thurman, Howard (1975) "The Negro Spiritual Speaks of Life and Death." In *"Deep River" and "The Negro Spiritual Speaks of Life and Death."* Richmond, IN: Friends United Press.

"Tracking Global Wokeism": Newsletter 4 | The Global Studies Center at Gulf University for Science and Technology (gust.edu.kw).

Vattimo, Gianni and Pier Aldo Rovatti, eds. (2010) *Il pensiero debole.* Milan: Feltrinelli.

Vizenor, Gerald (1998) *Fugitive Poses: Native American Indian Scenes of Absence and Presence.* Lincoln: University of Nebraska Press.

Vizenor, Gerald (2003) *Hiroshima Bugi: Atomu 57.* Lincoln: University of Nebraska Press.

Walker, Corey D. B. (2012) "The Race for Theology: Toward a Critical Political Theology of Freedom." In *Race and Political Theology.* Ed. Vincent W. Lloyd. Stanford: Stanford University Press, 2012. 146-49.

Weiss, Bari (2021) We Got Here Because of Cowardice. We Get Out With Courage – Commentary Magazine

Weiss, Elizabeth (2024) *On the Warpath: My Battles With Indians, Pretendians, and Woke Warriors.* Washington: Academica Press.

Williams, Joanna (2022) *How Woke Won: The Elitist Movement that Threatens Democracy, Tolerance and Reason.* Wanstead, UK: John Wilkes Publishing.

Williams, Thomas Chatterton (2022) "Saving Classics from Identity Politics," *The Atlantic* https://www.theatlantic.com/ideas/archive/2022/01/ideas-vs-identity-liberal-arts-montas-padilla/621241/

Williams, Thomas Chatterton (2025) *Nothing Was the Same: The Pandemic Summer of George Floyd and the Shift in Western Consciousness.* New York: Knopf.

Wittgenstein, Ludwig (1953) *Philosophische Untersuchungen*, trans. G.E.M. Anscombe as *Philosophical Investigations*. London: Blackwell.

Žižek, Slavoj (2000) *The Fragile Absolute—or, Why Is the Christian Legacy Worth Fighting For?* London: Verso.

www.ingramcontent.com/pod-product-compliance
Lightning Source LLC
Chambersburg PA
CBHW071640280326
41928CB00068B/1993